Juliane House

A Model for Translation Quality Assessment

Tübinger Beiträge zur Linguistik

herausgegeben von Gunter Narr

88

JULIANE HOUSE

A Model for Translation Quality Assessment

gnv Gunter Narr Verlag Tübingen

CIP-Kurztitelaufnahme der Deutschen Bibliothek

House, Juliane

A model for translation quality assessment. – 2. Aufl. –
Tübingen: Narr, 1981.

(Tübinger Beiträge zur Linguistik; 88)
ISBN 3-87808-088-3

2. Auflage

Druck: Zeeb-Druck, Tübingen
Printed in Germany

ISBN 3–87808–088–3

Preface

This book is essentially the text of my Ph.D. dissertation which was submitted to the University of Toronto in February 1976.

I would like to thank H.H. Stern, H. Schogt, and M. Swain for their helpful comments, suggestions, and criticisms during the preparation of this work.

Assistantships from the University of Toronto and a Canada Council Doctoral Fellowship are also gratefully acknowledged.

The study deals with problems of interest to both linguists and language teachers concerned with the nature of translation and its uses in the foreign language classroom. As the study contains an illustrative corpus of German-English translation texts, it was not felt necessary that the manuscript be used as its own test case. I have therefore left the text in English as it was originally written.

Bochum, May 1977 J. H.

Preface to the Second Edition

Since the publication of the first edition the ideas developed in this book have been presented to audiences of linguists, applied linguists, teachers, and students at a number of congresses and workshops. Feedback from these sources as well as from several reviews which have appeared has, of course, contained both positive and negative points: the model's unwieldiness as a working tool for the practising translator and translation evaluator and its relatively technical complexity for use in teaching have been mooted while it has also been recommended as useful to the teacher of translation, and as not totally lacking in theoretical insight.

Given this balanced reception, I have not changed the text from that published in the first edition. The current state of the art concerning translation quality assessment does not seem to me to warrant an updating of the book either. (This is not, of course, to deny that some highly valuable studies on translation have appeared since the first edition, see, e.g., W. Koller's *Einführung in die Übersetzungswissenschaft,* Heidelberg 1979, to give but one example). However, I might mention that the totally theoretical notion of a "cultural filter" posited in my work (cf. Chapter VI) as of possible relevance to a *covert translation* has been given some substance in work on pragmatic contrastive analysis – see here, e.g., my "Interaktionsnormen in deutschen und englischen Alltagsdialogen" *Linguistische Berichte* 59 (1979), pp. 76–90, or the article by G. Kasper and myself "Politeness Markers in English and German" in F. Coulmas (ed.) *Conversational Routine,* The Hague: Mouton, 1980.

Hamburg, December 1980 J. H.

TABLE OF CONTENTS

ABSTRACT

The study attempts to develop a model for assessing translation quality and to explore some of the model's theoretical and practical implications for the teaching of foreign languages.

The model is set up on the basis of pragmatic theories of language use. It provides for the analysis of the linguistic-situational peculiarities of a given source text (ST) and its translation text (TT), a comparison of the two texts, and the resultant judgement of their relative match or mismatch.

The basic requirement for equivalence of ST and TT posited in the model is that a TT, in order to be equivalent to its ST, should have a function--consisting of an ideational and an interpersonal functional component--which is equivalent to ST's function. Moreover, TT should employ equivalent pragmatic means for achieving that function. The method of operation of the model involves initially an analysis of ST according to a set of eight <u>situational dimensions</u>, for which linguistic correlates are established. ST's resultant <u>textual profile</u> which characterizes its function, is then taken as the norm against which TT is measured, and the degree to which TT's textual profile and function, derived from an analogous analysis of TT, match or do not match ST's profile and function, is the degree to which TT is more or less adequate in quality.

In evaluating the relative match between ST and TT, a distinction is made between dimensional mismatches or covertly erroneous errors and non-dimensional mismatches or overtly erroneous errors, the latter comprising both mismatches of the denotative meanings of ST and TT elements and breaches of the target language system. The final qualitative judgement of TT consists of a listing of both covertly erroneous and overtly erroneous errors, and of a statement of the relative match of the two functional components.

In order to demonstrate its practicability, the model is tried out with a corpus of eight English and German textual pairs. On the basis of the results of these test cases, a distinction between two types of translation is suggested: overt translation and covert translation. An overt translation is (normally) called for whenever ST is source-culture linked and has independent status in the source language community; a covert translation is (normally) required whenever neither condition holds.

The discovery of these two types of translation leads to a modification of the initially proposed principle of functional equivalence: only in cases of covert translation is it possible to achieve an equivalent function. In cases of overt translation, a similar, second-level function must be posited as a criterion for adequate translation. Covert translation presents more subtle cultural transference and evaluation problems, since differences in cultural presuppositions may necessitate the application of a cultural filter. The unjustified application of such a filter leads to the production of a covert version, which is to be differentiated from an overt version resulting from the addition of a special, secondary function to TT. In the absence of completed linguistic-cultural contrastive studies, the evaluation of these two types of translations and versions inevitably contains a subjective, hermeneutic element.

It is hoped that the proposed model, the distinction between two types of translations and versions, and the resultant consequences for translation quality assessment will bring some clarification into a problematical area of translation theory.

An important by-product of the study is the demonstration of the usefulness of both the model and the theoretical conclusions for foreign language teaching. Several suggestions for using translation activities in the development of students' communicative competence are put forward, and further studies on translation and on pedagogical uses of translation are proposed.

CHAPTER I

INTRODUCTION

A. Purpose of the Study

In seeking to describe and explain the process of translation, Kade (1968) and Nida and Taber (1969) have developed models in which the translator is represented as a bilingual mediating agent between monolingual communication participants in two different language communities. As an interlingual act of communication which involves code switching, translation is described as having a more complicated communication structure than a "normal" intralingual act of communication: the mediating agent who is to reproduce a source language message in the receptor language is both receptor (of the original message) and source (of the new message). These models of translation represent a considerable progress over earlier traditional, largely anecdotal and aphoristic-impressionistic treatments of the subject by philologists, poets, philosophers, professional translators, or anyone else who happened to be fascinated by the phenomenon of translation. While these more recent communication models of translation have advanced our theoretical understanding of the process of translation, they have hitherto not proved to be of immediate usefulness in solving the practical problems of describing and assessing translations as finished products. In this area, therefore, the same impressionistic, vague and general treatment of the subject from aesthetic, philosophical or stylistic viewpoints, which has been typical of traditional discussions of the requirements of a "perfect" translation, is still the norm rather than the exception. The two paradoxical requirements for a translation which were probably first formulated by Cicero: "ut orator--ut interpres", ("a translation should be free--a translation should be literal"), have --with varying degrees of modification--dominated the debate about translation quality through the past two centuries. These two requirements are, of course, far too general and elusive to be of any use as criteria in the concrete evaluation of a translation.

As yet, no explicit practical guidelines for a coherent analysis and evaluation of a translation have been given. It is the purpose of this study to bring some clarification into the field of translation quality assessment by developing an eclectic model for characterizing the linguistic-situational peculiarities of the source text, comparing source and translation texts, and making objective statements about the relative match of the two texts. The model to be developed in this study is to be tried out for its practicability with a corpus of textual pairs (source texts and translation texts), and on the basis of the results of these "test cases" we aim to make some generalizations about translation and translation quality assessment. It is the additional aim of our study to investigate the implications of both the suggested model and the theoretical conclusions for the teaching of foreign languages. Translation has been a controversial subject in discussions of foreign language teaching methodology for a long time. As Nida (1975) has recently pointed out, the main reason for the continued debate about translation, and for the peculiar phenomenon that many foreign language teachers use translation and, at the same time, repudiate it, seems to be the incompetent use of translation in the classroom. In this study, we aim to outline some alternative ways of using "translation activities" such that translation may begin to play a truly useful role in developing students' communicative competence.

B. Organization of the Study

We shall first describe earlier treatments of translation quality assessment, and review their merits and defects. Having established the insufficiency of previous attempts at setting up guidelines for the assessment of translation quality, we shall then proceed to develop an eclectic model of translation quality assessment on the basis of pragmatic theories of language use. We shall draw on speech act theory, and on functional and contextual views of language as well as on textlinguistic considerations.

In order to exemplify and demonstrate the suggested model in use, we shall go on to investigate its practicability by applying it to a corpus of pairs of German and English source and translation texts. A short description of the methods of selection, analysis, comparison, and evaluation of the textual pairs precedes the actual work on the texts. The results of applying the model to the corpus of texts will then be discussed, and several theoretical implications about types of translation and about translation quality assessment will be presented.

Finally, we shall give a short description of some trends in the role of translation in foreign language teaching, and we shall use the findings of the study to make several concrete suggestions for alternative uses of translation in foreign language teaching.

CHAPTER II

REVIEW OF THE LITERATURE ON TRANSLATION QUALITY ASSESSMENT

In this chapter, we shall first discuss a number of pre-linguistic studies in which translation quality assessment has been dealt with in an anecdotal and largely subjective manner; secondly, we shall review a series of theoretical and experimental studies in which an attempt to objectify translation quality assessment has been made by linking translation quality to the observable response a translation is supposed to elicit in its receptor(s). Since the review of these studies will reveal that a comparison of responses which ignores the need for a basic model of source and target text analysis and comparison is both arbitrary and inadequate, we shall finally deal with a few recent suggestions which emphasize the necessity of source text analysis as the basis for the evaluation of any translation text.

A. Pre-linguistic Studies

There is a long tradition of anecdotal reflections undertaken by professional translators, philologists, and poets on the subject of translation and translation quality (for an overview see, e.g., Amos, 1920; Postgate, 1922; Störig, 1963). In these treatments of translation quality, the relative importance of criteria such as the faithfulness to the original, the retention of the original's specific flavour, local colour or spirit as opposed to a natural flow of the translation, and the pleasure and delight of the reader were discussed at great length. At the Third Congress of the International Federation of Translators which was held at Bad Godesberg in 1959, and whose topic was "Quality in Translation", the same type of discussion was the norm rather than the exception. The volume of its proceedings (ed. by E. Cary and R. W. Jumpelt, 1963) is full of divergent, and--as Bausch (1970) has pointed out--altogether vague and subjective statements of what quality in translation is supposed to mean. Thus, Savory attempts to link the quality of a translated text to the personalities of the translator, the author, and the audience:

> The most satisfying translations are made by those whose personalities are in tune with those of the writers and also those of the readers. (Savory, 1963:154)

Elsen maintains that a good translation is one which is not identified as a translation:

> Une traduction... de qualité est une traduction dont la forme fait oublier au lecteur qu'il s'agit précisément d'une traduction. (Elsen, 1963:74)

Friederich (1963:350) makes the valid, but vague and commonplace statement that quality in translation rests largely on the translator's precise understanding of whatever it is that the original writer wants to convey.

Govaert's (1971) study also exemplifies the subjectivity of the argumentation used in most pre-linguistic, philological discussions of translation quality assessment:

> C'est le modèle qui compte et le rôle du traducteur ou du photographe est d'être l'instrument sensible par lequel une personalité se révèle. Ils n'ont pas à créer des formes, mais à les reproduire. (Govaert, 1971:425)

Gold's article (1972) is representative of the type of anecdotal treatment of translation quality assessment which persists up to the present time: he starts out with a pronouncement that any attempt at deriving general principles for translation quality is futile, and then proceeds to discuss a number of concrete and random examples of translation problems and their optimal solutions.

Examples of the bewildering profusion of alternative (and vague) principles that a translation of optimal value should fulfill according to the studies mentioned above are listed by Savory:

1. A translation must give the words of the original.
2. A translation must give the ideas of the original.
3. A translation should read like an original work.
4. A translation should read like a translation.
5. A translation should reflect the style of the original.
6. A translation should possess the style of the translator.
7. A translation should read as a contemporary of the original.

8. A translation should read as a contemporary of the translator... (etc.). (Savory, 1968:50).

B. Response-Based, Psycholinguistic Studies

Theoretical Studies

Even those more communicatively oriented studies that attempt to link translation quality to the effect a translation is supposed to have, have not progressed beyond the pronouncement of broad and non-verified principles of the following kind: a good translation is "one which fulfills the same purpose in the new language as the original did" (Forster, 1958:6), or "a translation is considered good when it arouses in us the same effect as did the original" (Zilahy, 1963:285). Nida's three criteria for judging translations seem to be equally programmatic and general: "1. general efficiency of the communication process, 2. comprehension of intent, 3. equivalence of response" (Nida, 1964:182). By "efficiency of the communication process", Nida means "the maximal reception for the minimal effort of decoding" (1964:182). The second criterion comprises the accuracy with which the meaning of the source language message is represented in the translation, judged in terms of its comprehensibility in the receptor culture. Equivalence of response, the third criterion for judging translations, is not really separable from the second criterion, the nature of the response being closely linked to the (presumed or actual) intent of the message. The equivalence of response criterion is, of course, closely related to Nida's well-known basic principle of "Dynamic Equivalence of a Translation" (1964:159): the manner in which receptors of the translation text respond to the translation text must be equivalent to the manner in which the receptors of the source text respond to the source text. "Equivalent" does not mean identical: the response can never be identical because of different cultural, historical, and situational settings.

It is, of course, undeniably true that a translation should produce equivalent responses. The question is, however, whether the degree to which this requirement is met can be empirically tested. If it cannot be tested, it seems fruitless to postulate the requirement, and the appeal to "equivalence of response" is really of no more value than the philologists' criterion of "capturing the spirit of the original".

Nida and Taber suggest three similar criteria for the ultimate test of a translation, worded and ordered slightly differently:

> 1. the correctness with which the receptors understand the message of the original...,
> 2. the ease of comprehension,
> 3. the involvement a person experiences as the result of the adequacy of the form of the translation.
>
> (Nida and Taber, 1969:173)

Item 1 is further explained as the translation's faithfulness to the original as determined by the degree to which receptors comprehend the meaning; in item 2, the authors refer to something like the "readability" of the text (cf. Flesch, 1948; Klare, 1963), i.e., the degree of "difficulty of style", but this may well vary for the source text and the translation text, as has been proven by Dye (1971). Item 3 is not further explained.

The above statements that a translation should be understood as correctly and easily as the original, and that it should elicit an equivalent response of involvement in the receptors have, as Koller (1972: 114) has pointed out, lately been generally recognized as superordinate to the principles of primacy of form or of content in both theory and practice of translation. However, these behavioural criteria--in the form presented above--do need to be further explained and put to the practical test. Newmark rightly maintains that the equivalent response principle especially "is mentalistic and needs further definition" (1974: 65). As stated above, it is intuitively correct that a translation should produce equivalent responses to the responses which the source text produced. However, the crucial question is whether the responses can be measured. Experimental studies which attempt to operationalize the response-based criteria of translation quality assessment suggested above will be described in the following section.

Experimental Studies

Under this rubric, we shall review both suggestions for experiments, and experiments that have actually been undertaken. We shall start with the former.

Nida and Taber (1969:168-173) give some concrete recommendations for translation quality assessment in their chapter "Testing the Translation". They suggest the following practical tests.

1. The Cloze technique, in which the degree of comprehensibility of a text is related to its "degree of predictability", i. e., it is assumed that the easier it is for the reader to guess the next word in a sentence of a translation text, the easier it is to comprehend that word in the given context. The reader is provided with a translation text in which, for example, every fifth word is deleted, and asked to fill in whatever words seem to fit the context best. The greater the number of correct guesses, the easier the text is to comprehend because its predictability is greater.

The limitations of this test are obvious:

a. it may be extremely difficult to analyze the results of such a test, i. e., to find out exactly why incorrect guesses were being made. For any true statement of translation quality, this question of the reason of a deviance should be answered;

b. for a detailed qualitative judgement of a translation's benefits and deficiencies, the Cloze technique seems to be too rough an instrument; it only attempts to measure intelligibility or ease of comprehension--criteria which cannot necessarily be equated with overall quality of translation.

c. The test cannot be used to make judgements about the intelligibility of a translation vis à vis its source text, but can only be used for comparative judgements. The Cloze test provides only a relative yardstick because there is no such thing as a "norm of comprehension". If the Cloze procedure establishes that one translation has a higher rate of predictability than another translation, it may still be possible that this "better" translation has a much lower intelligibility profile than is to be expected from an optimal translation of the particular source text.

Given the total lack of reference to the source text, the assumption that higher predictability rate and relative ease of comprehension equals higher quality in a translation is not necessarily valid, because the source text itself may have a relatively low predictability rate. What we need to establish in translation is a match in relative ease of comprehension between source and translation text.

2. As a second practical test, Nida and Taber (1969:171) suggest the elicitation of respondents' reactions to several translation alternatives. The investigator presents sentences in two or more different "versions", and asks questions such as: "Which way sounds the sweetest?", "Which is plainer?", "What words will be easiest... to understand?" (Nida and Taber, 1969:171).

As with the Cloze test, such a test merely compares several

translations, but fails to undertake the more basic task of judging a translation against its source text. Thus, for instance, one may present respondents with several "inadequate" translations and never establish true criteria for their quality because of the non-inclusion of the original as a yardstick for quality.

Also, test questions of such a generality can, of course, not possibly reveal any subtle qualitative differences between different translations. Moreover, the great variation in personal tastes and preferences--variables which it is extremely difficult to control--make the reliability of such a test questionable for uses other than a rough indication of people's general, undifferentiated impression of a translation. As Bullock points out, relying exclusively on the responses of judges "is of very limited value... because of the vast number of imponderables involved" (1963:151).

3. As a third test for translation quality, it is suggested that the translation text be read out to some other person who will then be asked to explain the contents to several other individuals who were not present at the first reading of the text. With this test, one hopes to find out "how well the meaning comes across, both in terms of the total content and in terms of the correctness of understanding" (Nida and Taber, 1969:172).

This test seems altogether too global and general: finer stylistic shades of a translation will not be tapped by this method which boils down to giving a précis of the translation. Further, this test relies entirely on the individual, who is asked to report on the translation text, rather than on the translation.

4. The last and, according to Nida and Taber, "one of the best tests of a translation" (1969: 172), is the reading aloud of a translation by several individuals before an audience, such that the reading will (presumably) be equivalent to communicating the message of the text. In the reading aloud, any places in the text at which the readers clearly have difficulty in reading the text fluently (i. e., stumble, hesitate, or make substitutions of any kind) will indicate those points at which the translation presents problems.

A major limitation of this test seems to be the fact that too many variables other than the mentioned "problems of translation" may also be responsible for failure in the public presentation of the translation text. Thus, the test may, for instance, measure the readers' different knowledge of the subject matter or their general knowledge and competence in oral presentation rather than point to an inadequacy of the translation. One would also need to know how well the source text would be read <u>orally</u> in order to make a comparison.

The same limitations that characterized the other tests suggested by Nida and Taber appear to be also applicable here. We may summarize them as follows:

a. the tests have the limited goal of establishing ease of comprehension and degree of intelligibility. They are unfruitful and non-diagnostic unless these two aspects of the translation which the test purports to measure can be strictly defined, and the linguistic means by which they are given expression can be clearly identified;

b. the tests completely lack reference to the source text. It is an unwarranted assumption that greater ease of comprehension equals "better translation". The source text's degree of comprehensibility must be taken into account because a translation should match it; in other words, the tests suffer from the relativity of any judgement that lacks a norm (which could be provided by the source text).

Several other experimental methods in which an observable, verifiable response is taken to be the ultimate criterion of translation quality have been suggested and illustrated by Miller and Beebe-Center (1958): 1. asking the opinion of several competent judges; 2. testing translations against a "criterion translation", i.e., a translation of "granted excellence" using a variety of statistical indices; 3. having respondents answer questions about a passage when the respondents had seen either its source text, or its translation text. If the answers are equivalent across the respondents, then source text and translation text are to be considered equivalent. This suggestion has also been put forward by Macnamara (1967).

As concerns 1, the procedure appears to be of obvious relevance--provided that the source text is first analyzed in detail such that those features which constitute its unique communicative value, and which should be kept invariant can be clearly identified. Questions posed to the judges should be "informed" ones, based on this analysis, i. e., they should not merely be designed to elicit inexplicit general-evaluative statements from the judges. Also, we should stress the point that it is not really the judges who give judgements of translation quality, since they do not judge independently of the questions put to them, i. e., it is really the questions which contain the basic criteria for the judgement. In other words, the most important step seems to be to know which questions to ask. The role of the judges is rather a secondary one.

Since no model for the analysis and comparison of source text and translation text in which criteria for judgement are made explicit exists to date, it seems to be appropriate to first concentrate one's efforts on the development of such a model which may provide experimenters with the right type of questions to ask, and only secondly consider the involvement of judges.

With regard to 2, the main problem seems to be the assumption underlying the suggested test that a translation of "granted excellence" exists. However, even if one assumes that such a translation exists, the problem of establishing reliable "criteria of excellence" for the criterion translation still remains. Such criteria cannot be simply "taken for granted", rather their development constitutes the crux of the problem of translation quality assessment.

Number 3 can only be regarded as useful as a very rough test of the intelligibility of a translation and of correspondence of referential meaning of original and translation. As mentioned under 1 above, the basis for the construction of questions to be asked must always be a detailed analysis of the source text.

Miller and Beebe-Center (1958) further suggest that if people can perform bodily responses or movements after having been exposed to either source or target language instructions, and if the results of the bodily movement criterion are similar across all respondents, then the original and its translation must be equivalent. This test is, of course, obviously limited to material that can be examined through bodily movements.

Carroll (1966a) conducted an experiment in which discrete, randomly ordered sentences taken from three human and three mechanical translations into English of four passages from a Russian work on cybernetics, were rated first by a number of native English speakers with no knowledge of Russian selected for their high verbal intelligence and scientific knowledge and interests, who compared the test translations with a criterion translation, and second by a number of native English speakers, with an expert reading knowledge of Russian, who compared the English translations with the Russian original. Carroll used two rating scales: one for intelligibility, i. e., that a translation should read like normal, readily understandable prose, and one for fidelity, i. e., that a translation should distort the meaning intended by the original writer as little as possible. Fidelity was rated in terms of the "informativeness" of the original relative to the translation: the translation sentences were evaluated on the basis of judgements of how "informative" the original sentences were perceived to be <u>after</u> the translation sentences had been examined. (For example, when a translation sentence already conveyed much information, the original sentence was considered to be low in "informativeness" relative to the translation sentence being evaluated.) It was expected that intelligibility and "informativeness" would be inversely related, i. e., that an original sentence would be informative to the degree that the translation sentence was lacking in intelligibility.

The two rating scales contained nine and ten values respectively with descriptions ranging for the intelligibility scale from "hopelessly unintelligible" to "perfectly clear and intelligible", and for the informativeness scale from "not informative at all" to "extremely informative". Not surprisingly, the three human translations were all deemed much better than the three mechanical translations in terms of intelligibility. Results from the two scales also indicated that there is a high negative correlation between average intelligibility rating and average informativeness rating, and the monolingual judges were found to produce more reliable and more differentiated ratings than the bilingual judges.

The limitations of Carroll's study seem to be the following:

a. as Carroll himself stresses, his procedure is applicable for scientific translations only, in which straightforward terminology plays a major role.

b. Carroll used isolated sentences for the rating. These sentences were presented in random order to the judges, so as to seriously reduce the possibility that a judge could take context into account. By disregarding the importance of both contextual and co-textual aspects of meaning, Carroll removes his experiment from the reality of translation practice in which one most frequently deals with texts.

c. Carroll's procedure may be valuable and refined enough for determining differences between such broad classes of translations as human and machine translations, and for evaluating the adequacy of a translation in terms of such general categories as intelligibility and informativeness. However, with such scales alone, it seems impossible to determine the reasons for the degree of intelligibility or informativeness, let alone reveal the more subtle stylistic-textual differences between original and translation which play such an important role in non-scientific texts. Equating overall translation quality with degrees of intelligibility and fidelity/informativeness seems to be somewhat reductionistic.

A weakness underlying most of the theoretical and experimental studies discussed above has been the lack of a norm against which the results of any response test may be measured. This norm should--following the _equivalent_ response requirement for translation quality--obviously be established by the source text. The source text is, however, rarely taken into consideration in the response-based studies. This bias may arise from a confusion as to the notion of translation quality assessment: the quality of a translation may be measured _absolutely_ only by reference to the text which is translated; to compare two or more translations of the same text is merely to establish their _relative_ value. A pre-requisite for establishing the (absolute) quality of a specific translation is some yardstick whereby the nature of the source text may itself be measured as a basis for its comparison with the translation text. It appears imperative to develop an objective method of determining the particular semantic, stylistic, functional, and pragmatic qualities of the source text, and then try to determine whether and to what extent the translation matches these characteristics. Suggestions of translation quality assessment along these lines will be discussed in the following section.

C. Source Text-based Studies

In his general survey of the state of the art in "translation criticism", Wilss (1974) points out that, in order to overcome the inadequacies of previous attempts to assess translation quality, it is necessary to build a consistent model featuring criteria both for the detailed description and explanation of the source text and for the evaluation of the "dependent" translation text. Wilss suggests that for the objectivization of translation criticism, the area of the "Gebrauchsnorm",[1] i.e., the norm of usage in a given language community with reference to a given situation should be taken as a yardstick. It is the norm of usage which--being part of the competence of the speaker-hearer in a language community--accounts for the speaker-hearer's metalinguistic judgements. Therefore, a translation may be judged according to whether or not it is adequate vis à vis the "normal" standard usage of native speakers in a given situational context.

However, it has to be kept in mind that there will always be several variants which are legitimately possible within the "Gebrauchsnorm" and which depend on the individual's choice. Like any linguistic activity, translation is a creative process which always leaves the translator a freedom of choice between several approximately equivalent possibilities of realizing situational meaning (cf. Lĕvy, 1967:1171). Moreover, the given situation in which the source text was written is, by definition, unique, and therefore the notion of a "norm" existing in the source culture for a particular unique text is a somewhat optimistic

---

[1] For a discussion of the problems of norms of usage, see, e.g., Polenz (1972), Lerchner (1972).

one. Even more optimistic is the idea that there should exist a "norm" for this unique text inside the target culture. In addition to the theoretical unsoundness of Wilss' suggestions, one should not underestimate the immense difficulty of empirically establishing what _any_ "Gebrauchsnorm" is.

Koller (1974) points to the necessity of developing a comprehensive, linguistic model of translation quality assessment. Such a model should consist of three main stages: 1. source text criticism with a view to transferability into the target language; 2. translation comparison in which the particular methods of translation used in the production of the given translation text are described; and 3. evaluation of the translation, _not_ according to vague, general criteria such as "good" or "highly intelligible", etc., but according to "adequate" or "not adequate" given the text-specific features derived in 1, and measured against the native speaker's faculty for meta-linguistic judgements. Although presenting stimulating ideas, Koller does not go beyond a very general outline with no suggestions for operationalization.

Reiss' (1968, 1971a, b, 1973) approach to the problem of translation quality assessment is also a useful general outline of a model without any demonstration of its practicability. Reiss suggests that for determining the quality of a translation, it is first necessary to determine the function and the textual type of the source text. Following an earlier classification by Juan Luis Vives (quoted in Reiss, 1971a:

140), she claims that different types of texts can be differentiated on the basis of Bühler's (1965) three functions of language (for a detailed description, see below, p.35): "inhaltsbetonte" (content-oriented) texts, i.e., news, scientific-technical texts; "formbetonte" (form-oriented) texts, i.e., poems and many other types of literary works; and "appellbetonte" (conative) texts, i.e., advertisements and texts of a rhetorical, polemic, and apologetic bent. To cover translations of texts involving other media than print, Reiss suggests a fourth, additional type of text: "subsidiäre" (subsidiary) or audio-medial texts, e.g., operas, songs, radio plays, for which different rules of translation apply if translation adequacy is to be reached. According to Reiss, it is these textual types which have to be kept equivalent in an adequate translation: in the case of the content-oriented texts, invariance on the content plane is the primary consideration; in the case of the form-oriented texts, invariance on the content plane as well as on the expression plane, is to be established to the greatest possible extent; and in the case of the conative texts, the "effect" of the source text is to be upheld in the translation text above all other features. An adequate translation of subsidiary texts must keep the adaptation of the "text" proper to such extralinguistic components as musical rhythm etc., invariant. The determination of the textual type presupposes a careful analysis of the source text. It is here that the weakness of Reiss' suggestions become apparent: her model of translation quality assessment is programmatic only, she gives no indication as to the precise method of establishing textual function and textual type.

Both Koller's and Reiss' ideas, which we consider to be potentially useful for solving the problems of translation quality assessment, need to be further developed and made more concrete in order to form a workable model of translation quality assessment. It is the aim of the following chapter to do this.

CHAPTER III

TOWARDS A MODEL OF TRANSLATION QUALITY ASSESSMENT BASED ON PRAGMATIC THEORIES OF LANGUAGE USE

A. Towards a Definition of Translation

Before attempting to develop a model for translation quality assessment, we first have to be more precise about what we mean by translation. The essence of translation lies in the preservation of "meaning" across two different languages. There are three basic aspects to this "meaning": a semantic aspect, a pragmatic aspect, and a textual aspect of meaning. We shall deal with each in turn:

1. The semantic aspect of meaning consists of the relationship of reference or denotation, i. e., the relationship of linguistic units or symbols to their referents in some possible world. By "possible world", we mean any world that the human mind is capable of constructing. This definition takes account of the fact that semantically meaningful utterances occur even though the terms of that utterance have no referents in the real world, as is, for instance, the case in science fiction.

To a very large extent, the nature of the universe (i. e., the subjective interpretation of possible worlds) is common to most language communities; thus the referential aspect of meaning is the one which (a) is most readily accessible, and for which (b) equivalence in translation can most easily be seen to be present or absent, e. g, the distinction betweel stool and chair in English is more easily ascertained than the (superficially similar) difference between residence and abode, which may have the same denotation, namely a particular building, but different "pragmatic uses" (see below). This relative ease of accessibility of semantic meaning is one of the reasons why it has been given preference in many earlier treatments of translation. Vinay and Darbelnet's statement is typical of this focus on semantic meaning in many translation studies:

> Le traducteur... part du sens et effectue toutes ses opérations de transfert à l'intérieur du domaine sémantique. (Vinay and Darbelnet, 1967:37)

2. The importance of the pragmatic aspect of meaning for translation has been given attention in more recent studies (cf. Neubert, 1973; Rülker, 1971, 1973; Jäger, 1973a,b, 1975). In order to define the pragmatic aspect of meaning, we may first compare semantics and pragmatics. The difference between the two has been formulated by Stalnaker in the following way:

> Semantics studies the relationships between signs and designata whereby the elements of sentences which are theoretical constructs are construed into propositions. Pragmatics is the study of the purposes for which sentences are used, of the real world conditions under which a sentence may be appropriately used as an utterance. (Stalnaker, 1973:380)

Pragmatics thus relates to the correlation between linguistic units and the user(s) of these units in a given communicative situation. The study of pragmatics corresponds to what Widdowson has referred to as the study of "discourse", i. e., "the communicative use of sentences in the performing of social actions" (1973:69). So-called "connotative meaning", i. e., the "communicative value an expression has... over and above its purely conceptual content" (Leech, 1974: 14) also forms part of pragmatic meaning.

The distinction between semantic meaning and pragmatic meaning underlies the theory of speech acts developed initially by Austin (1962) and Searle (1969). Pragmatic meaning is here referred to as the illocutionary force that an utterance is said to have, i. e., the particular use of an expression on a specific occasion. The illocutionary force of an utterance is to be differentiated from its propositional content, i. e., the semantic information that an utterance contains. The illocutionary force of an utterance may often be predicted from grammatical features, e.g., word order, mood of the verb, stress, intonation, or the presence of performative verbs.[1] In actual speech situations, it is, however, the context which makes unambiguously clear what the illocutionary force of an utterance is. For example, the utterance: The water is boiling can have various pragmatic meanings or

---

[1]For a definition, see Austin (1962: 12-13).

illocutionary forces given different contexts. It may be (a) an invitation (context: 'come, join me for a swim!'), (b) a reprimand (context: 'you'll kill the baby bathing it in water of that temperature!'), or (c) an order (context: 'go and make the tea now!'). Only the context will make the pragmatic meaning of this simple statement clear. As opposed to its pragmatic meaning, the sentence <u>The water is boiling</u> signifies semantically that a specific volume of a certain fluid is currently at a temperature at which that fluid begins to turn into a gas.

Since translation--which handles language in use, i. e., <u>parole</u> (cf. Kade, 1968: 1)--is concerned with instances of <u>acts of speech</u> (including writing), considerations of illocutionary force or pragmatic meaning are of great importance for translation. In effect, translation operates not with sentences but with <u>utterances</u>, i. e., units of discourse characterized by their use-value in communication. In translation, it is always necessary to aim at equivalence of pragmatic meaning, if necessary at the expense of semantic equivalence. Pragmatic meaning thus overrides semantic meaning. We may therefore consider a translation to be primarily a pragmatic reconstruction of its source text.

3. The <u>textual</u> aspect of meaning which is to be kept equivalent in translation has been stressed by Catford (1965, 1966) and also by Gleason (1968). Translation is a textual phenomenon. In order to explain this statement, we have to define what we mean by "text". In our

view, a text is any stretch of language in which the individual components all relate to one another and form a cohesive whole (cf. Dressler, 1972). A text is thus a linkage of sentences into a larger unit. Various relations of co-textual reference take place in the process of text constitution, e.g., occurrences of pro-forms, substitutions, co-references, ellipses, anaphora. It is these different ways of text constitution which account for the textual meaning that should be kept equivalent in translation. For example, in the sequence of sentences

1. It is the team leaders that'll get the results first
2. They, in turn, will inform the individual team members

the use of cleaving as a device for giving thematic prominence to the noun phrase the team leaders (sentence 1), the use of the anaphoric pronoun they as well as the anaphoric adjunct in turn (sentence 2), is part of the textual aspect of meaning which must be taken into account in translation.

The importance of the textual aspect of meaning has often been neglected in the practice and theory of translation, although, as Gleason points out, "many of the most crucial problems [of translation] lie in attaining connectivity between successive sentences while conveying the message" (1968:40).

Given these three aspects of meaning which we consider relevant for translation, we can now proceed to give a (tentative) definition of translation: translation is the replacement of a text in the source language by a semantically and pragmatically equivalent text in the target language. In our view of translation, these texts are available in written form. Translation of oral texts is called interpretation.

In this definition, the term "equivalent" is the key term. The concept of "equivalence" may also be taken as the fundamental criterion of translation quality (cf. Zenner, 1971). Thus, an adequate translation text is a semantically and pragmatically equivalent one. The notion of semantic-pragmatic equivalence needs, of course, to be made further explicit: as the first requirement for semantic-pragmatic equivalence we posit that the translation text have a function equivalent to that of its source text. Such a use of the concept of function presupposes that there are elements in any text which--given appropriate analytical tools--can reveal that text's function. As we have seen above (pp. 9-20), the notion of measuring equivalent responses to source and translation texts presents severe problems. Similarly, the notion that texts should have equivalent author intentions is impractical because it is self-evident that the source text writer's intention cannot be empirically established. What links a writer's intention to a reader's response is, however, immediately open to empirical investigation, i.e., the text itself. It may be arguedthat--given sincerity conditions and competence on the part of the original text producer--the function of a text may be seen as corresponding to the text producer's intention in producing the text. However, our concern with textual function rather than original author's intention appears reasonable as the original author's intention in producing the text is of interest only insofar as that intention is realized, and can be seen to have been realized in the actual text.

Our use of the term function is open to misinterpretation, first because different <u>language functions</u> can co-exist inside what we shall describe as an individual text's function, and second because language functions have often--and in our opinion incorrectly--been directly correlated with textual types. We propose to discuss briefly various investigations of language functions and their application to textual types in order to sharpen our own notion of the function of a text.

B. Functions of Language Versus Functions of Texts

Many different views of the functions of language have been put forward. We shall review only a few influential ones in order to gain some clarity about the way the concept "function of language" has been used in the literature.

1. Ogden and Richards, in their classic work, <u>The Meaning of Meaning,</u> differentiate five functions of language:

> (1) symbolization of reference,
> (2) expression of attitude to listener,
> (3) expression of attitude to referent,
> (4) promotion of effects intended,
> (5) support of reference. (Ogden and Richards, 1946:227).

Having grouped together functions (2), (3), (4), and (5), which form a complex of "emotive" functions, Ogden and Richards (1946:229) go on to differentiate between two basic uses of language: the symbolic use of language and the emotive or evocative use of language. In the symbolic use of language, the essential considerations are the correctness of the symbolization and the truth of the references; in the emotive-evocative use of language, the character of the attitude aroused in the addressees is of prime importance.

2. Karl Bühler (1965:28-33) distinguishes three basic functions of language in his "organon model of language", each linked to one of the three variables of his model: (1) the "Darstellungsfunktion" (representational or referential function) is linked to objects and relations in the real world; this function serves to describe extralinguistic reality; (2) the "Ausdrucksfunktion" (emotive-expressive function) is linked to the speaker/writer of the message; (3) the "Appellfunktion" (conative function) is centered on the receiver of the message. According to Bühler, the representational function is the central or unmarked function which is present in any message (except in a few interjections like ouch or yippie); the other two functions are marked functions. As with Ogden and Richards' model, we can thus again recognize a fundamental division into the absolutely necessary symbolic function and additional functions.

3. One of the most intuitively plausible as well as best argued models of the functions of language is the one developed by Jakobson (1960:353-57). Jakobson starts out from Bühler's model taking over Bühler's three basic functions: the referential, the emotive-expressive, and the conative functions, but he adds three more functions and fits all of the resulting six functions into the following schema of verbal communication: The _addresser_ sends a _message_ to the _addressee_; the message requires a _context_ (extralinguistic world) referred to by the addresser, a _code_ at least partially in common to addresser and addressee, and a _contact_, a physical channel or psychological connection between the addresser and addressee. From orientations towards _addresser_, _addressee_, or _context_, Jakobson derives the three functions already mentioned in Bühler (see above, p. 32). From an orientation towards _contact_, Jakobson derives a _phatic_ function--this function is predominant if a message has the predominant purpose of establishing, prolonging, or discontinuing communication. When speech is focussed on the _code_, it has a _metalingual_ function. Strictly speaking, another level of language--metalanguage, i.e., communication about language, is being employed whenever the metalingual function is being employed. The _poetic_ function in Jakobson's model consists of a focussing on the _message_ for its own sake.

But even in Jakobson's elaborate six-function model,[1] the basic dichotomy between the primary referential function, and all the other "non-referential", secondary functions still holds. Jakobson himself states:

> Obviously, we must agree with Sapir that, on the whole, 'ideation reigns supreme in language', but this supremacy does not authorize linguistics to disregard the 'secondary factors'. (Jakobson, 1960:353)

4. Halliday (1970a, b, 1971, 1973) distinguishes three "macro-functions": the ideational, the interpersonal, and the textual functions of language. Through its ideational function, language expresses content: the speaker's vision of the external world as well as the experience of the internal world of his own consciousness. In its interpersonal function, language serves as a means for conveying the speaker's relationship with his interlocutor(s), and for expressing social roles including communication roles such as questioner and respondent. Through the textual function, language makes links with itself and with the situation: the construction of texts becomes possible because of this linkage.

Halliday's functional theory differs from the other approaches mentioned above in that only his first two functions, i. e., the ideational and the interpersonal functions, are comparable to the notion of function

---

[1]A model very similar to Jakobson's has been suggested by Hymes (1968). Hymes adds, however, a seventh function: a contextual or situational function.

used in the other approaches as a basic mode of language in use. Halliday's textual function relates to a different intra-language level, to a level of internal organization of linguistic items. Viewed in this way, Halliday's model also seems to confirm the basic split of language use into a referential or content-oriented function and a non-referential (interpersonal) function.

This basic division into cognitive and emotive-expressive functions, is, of course, paralleled by the customary division of meaning[1] into cognitive (or denotative) meaning including concepts which people have with regard to the content of verbal communication, and emotive meaning covering the emotional reactions which people have with regard to various linguistic forms.

Having reviewed some ways of characterizing language functions, we can now proceed to examine how language functions have been related to textual functions. On the assumption that a text is a stretch of language, the simple equation of textual function with one of the above-mentioned language functions (the dominant one), has frequently been undertaken and, as a further step, textual function has been taken to be the basis for textual type. Thus, Reiss (1968, 1971a, b, 1973) (see above, p. 23) and Kern (1969) take Bühler's three language functions as determining three different textual types: the referential, the

---

[1]See, for instance, Nida (1974:33).

emotive-expressive, and the conative-persuasive textual types. Similarly, Oomen (1971) differentiates two basic textual functions and two textual types on the basis of the "two uses of language": the referential and the non-referential one. However, we believe that such an equation of language function and textual function and type, is overly simplistic: given that language has functions a to n, and that any text is a self-contained instance of language, it should follow that a text will also exhibit functions a to n, and not, as is presupposed by those who set up functional text typologies, that any text will exhibit one of the functions a to n. We believe that if the notion of functionally based text typology can have any empirical validity, it can only be a probabilistic one as the ground for placing any text inside text type A can only be that this particular text exhibits language function A to a greater extent than it exhibits other language functions. In other words, while some extremes, i. e., text A is clearly predominantly of type Y, may be readily characterized, there is a cline between such extremes. This simplistic probabilistic text typology based on a predominant language function exhibited in the text is of no use in terms of determining precisely an individual text's function, let alone of establishing functional equivalence.[1] However, such a typology may be useful as a basis for

---

[1]Other attempts at setting up text typologies on linguistic grounds, notably the recent one by Gülich and Raible (1975) who try to delimit text types according to different systems of linkage between parts of the text ("Gliederungsmerkmale") have proved equally inconclusive for our purposes.

selecting and classifying texts for analysis as well as for providing convenient labels for the two <u>components</u> of a text's function which must, of course, be specified more precisely for each individual text (see below, part C). We shall therefore use the traditional dichotomy of the two broad (pre-analytical) functions, which we established to be prevalent in all the functional models reviewed above, for choosing and grouping our sample of texts and for labelling the two components of the textual function discovered in the individual texts. We shall adopt Halliday's terms <u>ideational</u> and <u>interpersonal</u> as labels for the referential and the non-referential functional components, because we shall also use a Neo-Firthian model for the linguistic description (see below, p. 52).

C. A Model for Establishing Functional Equivalence

In order to characterize the function of an individual text specimen, we have to define function differently: the function of a text is the application (cf. Lyons, 1969:434) or use which the text has in the particular context of a situation. We have to stress the fact that any text is embedded in a unique situation. From this, it follows that, in order to characterize the function of a text precisely, we must analyze the text in detail. For our purpose of establishing functional equivalence between a source and a translation text, we posit that the source text be analyzed first, such that the equivalence which is sought for source text and translation text can be stated precisely. Since we defined textual function as the use of the text in a particular situation, we will have to refer each individual text to the particular situation in which it is embedded. We shall have to develop a model for the determination of the source text's function and the ensuing comparison of the source text and the translation text's function.

If the function of a text is to be characterized through referring the text to the situation in which it is embedded, we will have to look for ways of breaking down the notion of situation into more specific situational dimensions. The most elaborate and refined system of situational dimensions to date is the one suggested by Crystal and Davy (1969).[1] Their system of "situational constraints" by which the notion of situation is broken down into manageable parts shall serve as the basis for our eclectic model of multi-dimensional analysis of the source text and of comparison of source and translation texts. We shall first briefly describe the original model and then show how we adapt it for our special purpose of incorporating it into a tool for translation quality assessment. Crystal and Davy's scheme is as follows:

---

[1]Other attempts by Neo-Firthian linguistics to set up various situational-contextual dimensions include the work by Reid (1956), Hill (1958), Strang (1962), Enkvist, Spencer and Gregory (1964), Halliday, McIntosh and Strevens (1964), Dixon (1964), and Ellis and Ure (1969).

A

INDIVIDUALITY

DIALECT

TIME

B

DISCOURSE

(a) [SIMPLE/COMPLEX] MEDIUM (Speech, Writing)
(b) [SIMPLE/COMPLEX] PARTICIPATION (Monologue, Dialogue)

C

PROVINCE

STATUS

MODALITY

SINGULARITY

(Crystal and Davy, 1969:66)

Under A, Individuality refers to the idiosyncratic features of language as used by an individual in unselfconscious utterance, features which identify someone as a specific person, e.g., a person's handwriting, voice quality or certain pet words or phrases which are over-represented in his speech. Dialect refers to features which mark a text producer's geographical origin (regional dialect), where the unmarked case is either Standard American English or Standard British English (cf. Quirk and Greenbaum, 1973:4), or his position on a social scale (social class dialect), where the unmarked case is the educated middle class speaker of the standard language. Time refers to those features which provide clues to a text's temporal provenance. The three dimensions listed under A constitute relatively permanent and stable features pertaining to the language user.

The features under B are self-explanatory. It is only the simple/complex option that needs explanation: the category Medium may function in a "removed" or "explanatory" way whenever Medium is being used as a means to an end rather than as an end in itself, i. e., the category is conceived as a temporary device meant to facilitate a later switch to the alternative category. This phenomenon is called Complex Medium (e. g., language which is "written to be spoken", with possible further sub-classification) as opposed to the Simple Medium where language stays within one category, i. e., spoken to be heard or written to be read (in the sense of "not read aloud").

The category Participation may also be complex, i. e., when a text produced by only one person (a "monologue") nonetheless contains features which would normally be assumed to characterize a dialogue, e. g., imperative forms or question tags.

Under C, Province reflects occupational or professional activity. Examples of Province would be "the language of advertising", "the language of public worship", "the language of science", etc. Crystal and Davy point out that

> province features should not be identified with the subject matter of an utterance, as has sometimes been suggested in connection with the notion of

> "register". Subject matter insofar as this is a question of the use of distinctive vocabulary, is but one factor among many which contribute to a province's definition. (Crystal and Davy, 1969:73)

Status is the term used for the relative social standing of the speaker/writer and listener/reader in terms of formality, respect, politeness, intimacy, etc. Modality refers to differences in the form and medium of communication such as the differences between a report, an essay, or a letter. Modality thus corresponds roughly to the traditional term "genre", a term which is deliberately avoided by Crystal and Davy because it has often been employed simultaneously to such broad categories as poetry or prose, and the finer distinctions between, e. g., an essay and a short story. It is the latter kind of a more delicate distinction which is being envisaged under Modality. Singularity is a term for occasional personal idiosyncracies which are said to differ from features of Individuality in that they are usually deliberately introduced into a person's speech in order to achieve a specific linguistic effect (e. g., the introduction of linguistic originality into a poem).

For our purposes of constructing a model for situational-functional source text analysis and assessment of translation match, we shall eclectically adapt Crystal and Davy's model in the following manner:

We collapse the three sections A, B, and C into two sections: dimensions of language user and dimensions of language use, featuring the following subcategories:

A. Dimensions of Language User:
1. GEOGRAPHICAL ORIGIN
2. SOCIAL CLASS
3. TIME

B. Dimensions of Language Use:
1. MEDIUM [SIMPLE / COMPLEX]
2. PARTICIPATION [SIMPLE / COMPLEX]
3. SOCIAL ROLE RELATIONSHIP
4. SOCIAL ATTITUDE
5. PROVINCE

In the section dimensions of language user (A), we list Crystal and Davy's two factors under Dialect, i. e., regional dialect and social class dialect, separately as Geographical Origin and Social Class respectively. These two dimensions as well as the dimension Time are defined in the sense of Crystal and Davy (see above, pp. 39-40). The dimension of Individuality will be omitted in our scheme for the following reasons: (1) the dimension may very likely not be relevant given the small sample of texts which we shall investigate, and more importantly (2) those idiosyncratic features of the text producer's language use that are recognizable in the text will be captured in the other dimensions, i. e., Social Role Relationship, Social Attitude, and Province. The introduction of a separate dimension of Individuality would unnecessarily duplicate entries on those dimensions.

In the section dimensions of language use (B), the following modifications of Crystal and Davy's model will be made:

1. Medium / simple \ complex. We shall refine the category of Complex Medium by using some of the delicate distinctions suggested by Gregory (1967) with respect to writing only due to the nature of our task of translation quality assessment which involves written texts only (cf. the above definition of translation, p. 29-30).

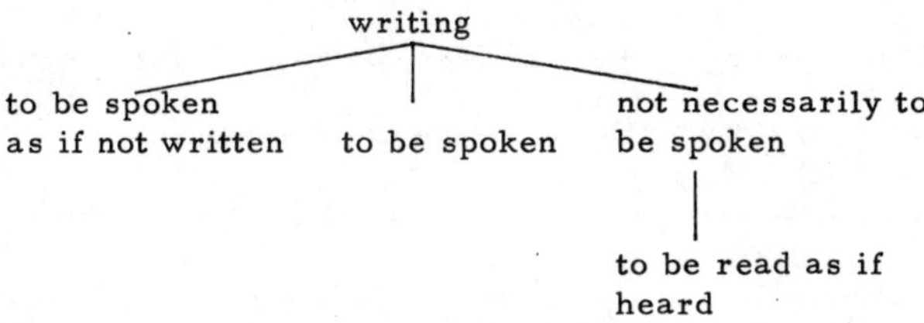

(adapted from Gregory, 1967:189)

These distinctions between different combinations of spoken and written modes are necessary because, even if a text is meant to be spoken and is, in fact, at some stage spoken, there is still--as has been aptly pointed out by Abercrombie (1967)--a difference between genuine spoken language (e.g., in a conversation) and the above mentioned "spoken" subcategories of the written mode. However, our analysis will, in fact, reveal that even Gregory's classification is a relatively unsophisticated analytical tool for our purposes. Therefore, we shall introduce appropriate refinements in the course of the textual analyses conducted in Chapter V.

In determining features of the spoken mode in the various manifestations of a Complex Medium, we shall mainly build on a recent research report by Söll (1974). On the basis of earlier empirical studies (e.g., Blankenship, 1962; Feider, 1969), Söll sets up several general characteristics of spoken language before examining the particular features of spoken and written French, i.e., structural simplicity and incompleteness of sentences, specific manner of text constitution, particular theme-rheme sequence (see below, p.54), subjectivity (marked for instance, through the presence of "Abtönungspartikel", i.e., qualifying modal adverbals, or interjections), higher redundancy, etc. We shall examine in our analyses of texts how far these features are applicable to the Complex Medium categories found in the texts.

2. Participation (simple / complex). We shall refine this parameter by examining under Complex Participation various ways of "participation elicitation" and "indirect addressee participation" which are manifest linguistically, for instance, in the specific use of pronouns, switches between imperatives, interrogatives, exclamations, presence of contact parentheses, etc.

3. Social Role Relationship. We shall subdivide Crystal and Davy's

dimension Status into two categories: Social Role Relationship and Social Attitude (see below 4.).[1] Under Social Role Relationship, we analyze the role relationships between addresser and addressees. We differentiate between two basic constellations: symmetrical and asymmetrical role relationships. The former is characterized by solidarity and equality between addresser and addressees; the latter is marked by some kind of an authority relationship between addresser and addressees. With respect to the addresser's social role vis à vis the addressees, we further distinguish between the relatively permanent position role (e.g., of teacher, priest, etc.) and the more transient situational role (e.g., of guest, visitor in a prison, etc.). In making this distinction, we simplify the standard sociological division of roles undertaken within the framework of interactionist role theory (cf., e.g., Dreitzel, 1972; Coburn-Staege, 1973) into position role, situational role, and personal or status role, by collapsing position role and personal/status role.

4. Under the dimension Social Attitude, we describe the degrees of social distance or proximity. We shall adopt Joos' (1959, 1961) distinction of five different styles or degrees of formality: frozen,

---

[1] Chiu (1973) makes a similar subdivision of a dimension referred to as Manner of Discourse.

formal, consultative, casual, and intimate providing, of course, for the possibility of transitional styles such as consultative-casual, etc. The most neutral, "normal", style level is the consultative one. It is the norm for conversations or letters between strangers; it is mostly marked negatively, i.e., through the absence of both formal and informal style markers. In using consultative style, the addresser does not assume that he can leave out certain parts of his message--which he may do in a socially close relationship where much of the message is "understood". In consultative style, the addresser has to be fairly elaborate in supplying background information. A further characteristic of consultative style is the participation of the addressee(s)--hence the term "consultative"--either directly or implied (as in the case of Complex Participation where the addressee(s)' involvement is elicited through various linguistic means).

Casual style is especially marked by various degrees of inexplicitness in which the addresser may indulge because of the level of intimacy between himself and the addressee(s). Background information is not necessary: casual style is used with friends or "insiders" of all kinds with whom the addresser has something to share--or desires or imagines that there is something to share. Ellipses, contractions, and the use of lexical items and collocations marked [-formal] are characteristic linguistic markers of casual style.

Intimate style is the language used between people who are personally very close to each other. Its major feature is referred to as "extraction" by Joos: "the speaker extracts a minimum pattern from some conceivable _casual_ sentence" (1961:30). Extraction is thus an extreme type of ellipsis. The interlocutors are so close to each other that they can presuppose a maximum of shared background information. We may hypothesize that this style level will rarely, if ever, occur in the kinds of written texts we shall examine in this study. The _consultative_ and the _casual_ style levels, which Joos (1961:29) also refers to as _colloquial_ styles, are used to deal with public information. By contrast, _intimate_ style excludes public information.

Formal style deviates from _consultative_ style in that addressee participation is to a large extent omitted. Formal texts are well-structured, elaborate, logically sequenced, and strongly cohesive. They clearly demonstrate advance planning.

Frozen style, like _intimate_ style an extreme style, is the most formal, pre-meditated, often "literary" style level. Frozen texts may be consummate products of art meant for the education and edification of the readers, but frozen style may also be used in business letters, in which the social distance between addresser and addressee is thus given expression.

To illustrate the differences between the five styles, we may quote Strevens' illustration of how the same message may be conveyed in five different ways:

Frozen: Visitors should make their way at once to the upper floor by way of the staircase.

Formal: Visitors should go upstairs at once.

Consultative: Would you mind going upstairs right away, please.

Casual: Time you all went upstairs now!

Intimate: Up you go, chaps!
(Strevens, 1965:74)

5. The dimension Province is more comprehensive in our scheme than in Crystal and Davy's model (see above, p.40). We subsume both Province and Modality in Crystal and Davy's sense under our term Province. In our model of translation quality assessment, Modality clearly does not warrant a separate dimension because Modality will always remain equivalent for source and translation texts, e. g. , a letter will be translated as a letter unless the translation text is a completely different version (cf. below, p. 59) which will not be considered in our model. Further, Province does not only reflect occupational and professional activity, as was suggested by Crystal and Davy, but also the field or topic of the text in its widest sense of "area of operation" of the language activity, as well as details of the text production as far as these can be deduced from the text itself.

We omit Crystal and Davy's dimension of Singularity just as we omitted Individuality, and for the same reasons (see above, p. 42).

We posit in our model that the function of a text which should be kept equivalent if a translation is to be adequate, can be determined by "opening up" the linguistic material in terms of the above set of extra-linguistic, situational constraints. The evidence in the text which characterizes it on any one particular constraint or dimension, is, of course, itself linguistic evidence. In our model, we propose to break this linguistic evidence down into three types: syntactic, lexical, and textual. This tripartite division will later be expanded upon (see Chapter IV) when the linguistic realization of the theoretical model will be developed.

The situational dimensions and their linguistic correlates are considered to be the means by which the text's function is realized, i. e., the function of a text is established as a result of an analysis of the text along the situational dimensions outlined above. The basic criterion of functional match for translation equivalence can now be refined: a translation text should not only match its source text in function, but employ equivalent situational-dimensional means to achieve that function, i. e., for a translation of optimal quality it is desirable to have a match between source and translation text along the dimensions which are found--in the course of the analysis--to contribute in a particular way to the two components of the text's function.

By using situational dimensions for opening up the source text, we obtain for the source text a particular <u>textual profile</u>. This profile, which characterizes the function of that text, is, in our theory, the norm against which the quality of the translation text is to be measured. i. e., a given translation text is analyzed using the same dimensional scheme, and in the same detail, and the degree to which its textual profile does not match the source text's profile is the degree to which that translation text is inadequate in quality. This is our provisional theoretical model, which will later be refined (see Chapter VI) in the light of the results of its implementation.

CHAPTER IV

DEVELOPMENT OF THE MODEL: LINGUISTIC REALIZATION

In order to demonstrate the practicability of the theoretical model of translation quality assessment outlined above, we shall, in this chapter, investigate its operation with cohesive stretches of language, i. e., texts. In the first part of the chapter, we shall outline the method of operation of the model. In doing so, we shall first describe the method of analyzing and comparing texts by indicating how the various situational dimensions of the model are realized syntactically, lexically, and textually, using a number of concepts deemed useful for the establishment of linguistic correlates to the dimensions; secondly, we shall develop an evaluation scheme for the measurement of mismatches between source and translation texts. In the second part of the chapter, we shall attempt to justify the suggested method of operation of the model.

A. Description of Method

1. Method of Analysis and Comparison of Texts

Starting from the assumption that in order to make qualitative statements about a translation text (TT), TT must be compared with the source text's (ST's) textual profile which determines a norm against which the appropriateness of TT is judged, our first task will be the detailed analysis of ST. Using the set of situational dimensions as outlined above, we shall establish text-specific linguistic correlates to the situational dimensions.

The grammatical model used for the analysis is a Neo-Firthian one, specifically Quirk and Greenbaum's (1973) approach to grammar.[1] For convenience, we shall also make use of the convention of expressing the components of meaning by means of feature symbols such as [$\pm$ human], [$\pm$ abstract] etc. Further, we shall use rhetorical-stylistic concepts such as alliteration and anacoluthon. In addition, use will be made of the concept of illocutionary force (see above, p. 27) and the two concepts of foregrounding and automatization. The concepts of foregrounding and automatization have been developed by Prague school linguists (for a detailed explanation see especially Havránek, 1964, who coined the terms). Foregrounding is a linguistic device for making the reader conscious of a particular linguistic form such that the linguistic form itself attracts attention, and is felt to be unusual or "de-automatized" (as is the case, for instance, in alliteration, assonance, onomatopoeia, puns, and wordplays). Automatization is the

---

[1]This approach was chosen because it seemed to us to be most compatible with the kind of "stylistic" textual analysis conducted in this study.

opposite of foregrounding, i. e., a conventional, "normal" use of the devices of language such that linguistic forms themselves do not attract attention. In analyzing the Hiberno-English text (Comedy Dialogue) we have referred to Metscher (1968). In analyzing the German texts we have referred to Wunderlich (1970) and Admoni (1973).

On each of the situational dimensions, we differentiate syntactic, lexical, and textual means, although it may not always be the case that all three categories are found to be operative on a particular dimension. As all our texts are written texts, phonology plays no part in the textual profile. However, if a text to be analyzed according to our scheme was to attempt, in its graphic form, to reflect phonological distinctiveness (e. g., cum 'ere for come here), then such features of the text would be discussed under graphical means. Important for our model is the inclusion of textual means which are neglected by Crystal and Davy. In fact, one of the more serious objections to their method of textual analysis, made, for instance, by Widdowson (1973), is that their approach is too atomistic in that it only involves a breaking down of stretches of language into their constituent linguistic elements without seeking to establish ways of sentence connection, thematic movement, etc. This objection is not valid for our approach, which does take account of textual devices, thus transcending Crystal and Davy's atomicism.

Since Quirk and Greenbaum (1973) deal with textual aspects only marginally in their grammar, we will base our treatment of textual means of realizing a particular situational feature eclectically on Enkvist (1973), on work done in the Prague school on theme-rheme distribution, and on Söll (1974).

In adapting Enkvist's (1973: 115-26) ideas, we distinguish three main textual aspects: theme-dynamics, clausal linkage, and iconic linkage.

(1) Theme-dynamics charts the various patterns of semantic relationships by which "themes" recur in a text (e. g., repetition, anaphoric and cataphoric references, pro-forms, ellipsis, synonymy) and takes account of "functional sentence perspective", a concept first used by Mathesius (1971). For our purposes, the notion of functional sentence perspective will, rather simplistically, be interpreted as follows: any utterance consists of two basic parts which differ in the function they have in carrying information: (a) the theme which refers to facts either taken to be universally known, taken for granted, or given from the context, and which therefore do not, or only marginally, contribute to the new information conveyed by the total utterance; (b) the rheme containing the main "new" information to be transmitted by the utterance. Word order is the primary formal means of realizing the theme-rheme distribution: in "normal", unmarked speech, the theme precedes the rheme (Mathesius' "objective position"); in emotive speech, how-

ever, the rheme precedes the theme ("subjective position").[1]

(2) Clausal linkage is described by a system of basically logical relations between clauses and sentences in a text, e.g., additive, adversative, alternative, causal, explanatory, or illative relations.

(3) Iconic linkage occurs when two or more sentences in a text cohere because they are, at the surface level, isomorphic, e.g., Chomsky's famous pair John is easy to please and John is eager to please are cases of iconic linkage or "structural parallelism".

Furthermore, following Söll (1974:51), we distinguish between two basic types of text constitution which in analogy to a distinction introduced by Pike (1967) are referred to as emic texts and etic texts. An emic text is one which is solely determined by text-immanent criteria, and an etic text is one which is determined through text-transcending means, i.e., temporal, personal, or local deictics pointing to the various features of the situation enveloping the text, the addresser, and the addressees.

We shall also consider textual features such as overall logical structure, presence of narrative formulae, and presence (or lack) of

---

[1]Mathesius' original dyadic conception of "dynamic communication" has been relativized by other Prague school linguists especially by Firbas (1964, 1966) who considered the possibility that elements belonging to the theme or rheme of a sentence may be linked by a transitional element, which is neither theme nor rheme.

redundancy.

While stressing the importance of a textual approach to the assessment of translation quality, we are, of course, aware of the fact that both the actual translation process and the analysis and comparison of an ST and a TT are conducted <u>not</u> on the level of the text as a whole, but on the level of what Neubert has called the "textual utterance" (1972a:486). It is these textual utterances which will constitute the basic units of analysis and comparison.

Following the analysis of ST, TT will be analyzed in the same manner, and the two resulting textual profiles will be compared for their relative matching. In the presentation of the results of the analysis of TT, we shall, however, restrict ourselves to listing the mismatches on the various dimensions. Thus, if no mismatches are mentioned on any one dimension, it is to be assumed that TT is satisfactory on that dimension.

2. Evaluation Scheme

If a TT, in order to be adequate, has to fulfill the requirement of a dimensional and, as a result of this, a functional match, then any mismatch along the situational dimensions constitutes an error. Such dimensional errors, which we will term <u>covertly erroneous errors</u> (cf. Corder, 1973:272), must be clearly differentiated from those <u>overtly erroneous errors</u> which result either from a mismatch of the denotative meanings of ST and TT elements, or from a breach of the target language system, and which do not involve dimensional mismatching. However, overtly erroneous errors will have a certain specifiable impact on the relative match of the functional components in ST and TT, i.e., we may hypothesize that mismatches of the denotative meaning of ST and TT elements detract from a match of the ideational functional components of the two texts. Cases where the denotative meaning of elements in ST have been changed by the translator will be further subdivided into: (a) omissions, (b) additions, (c) substitutions consisting of either wrong selections or wrong combinations of elements. Cases of overtly erroneous breaches of the target language system will be further subdivided into: (a) cases of ungrammaticality, i.e., clear breaches of the language system, and (b) cases of dubious acceptability, i.e., breaches of the "norm of usage" which we define as the bundle of linguistic rules which underlies the actual use of language as opposed to the language system which is concerned with the possibilities of the language.

Both these groups of overtly erroneous errors have traditionally been given most attention, whereas the kind of covertly erroneous errors vis à vis a particular textual profile or dimensional constellation which this study sets out to reveal have been frequently neglected since they demand a much more subtle, qualitative-descriptive assessment. The relative weighting of individual errors both within the categories of overtly erroneous errors and covertly erroneous errors, and across the two categories, is a problem whose solution will vary from individual text to individual text. We shall therefore deal with this problem after the textual analyses (cf. below p. 207-09).

The notion that a mismatch on a particular dimension constitutes a covertly erroneous error, presupposes:

(1) that the socio-cultural norms, or, more specifically, the norm-conditioned expectations generated by the text, are essentially comparable in the case of the Anglo- and Germanophone language communities. The cultural distance between the respective source and target language communities is not substantial. Obvious differences in the unique cultural heritage of the two communities must, of course, be considered in translation and translation quality assessment, e.g., references in a German text to a specific national holiday or a national custom will have to be made explicit;

(2) that the differences between the two languages, English and German, are such that they can largely be overcome in translation. We hypothesize a fundamental similarity of the two languages in their deep structure, i.e., the existence of language universals,[1] which provides

---

[1]For proposals of language universals within a transformational-generative framework, see, for instance, Bach (1968) or Bierwisch (1970).

strong support for the intertranslatability of two languages. In our view, the languages with which we are concerned in this study differ mostly in the selection and low-level physical realization of elements taken from a deep universal stock. Languages are creative systems, and these low-level differences can always be overcome in translation. Both languages are equally well equipped to express any aspect of human life (cf. Jakobson, 1966:234). Exceptional cases in which differences in the language systems render direct equivalence impossible, (e.g., the obligatory _du_ versus _Sie_ choice is not available in English except for limited registers, for example, biblical _thou_) will be stated explicitly. Such cases have to be discussed individually and _in situ_; (3) that no special secondary function is added to TT, i.e., translations for special addressees (e.g., classical works "translated" for children) and translations for special purposes (e.g., "interlinear translations" which are designed for a clarification of the structural differences between the two languages) are excluded from our scheme. Such translations are no longer translations, but will be defined as different _versions_ of an ST.

We thus assume that TT's addressees form a basically similar sub-group in the target language community to the sub-group formed by the addressees of ST in the source language community, both being defined as contemporary _standard language_ speakers. We define standard language as that supra-regional variety which is used by the educated middle-class speaker and which is, as an "ideal norm", at the same time accepted by the majority of the whole language community. We assume that there are two national standards of English (cf. Quirk and Greenbaum, 1973:4): Standard British English and Standard American English, both of which we shall take as unmarked norms.

The degree to which the above three rather global assumptions are shown to be valid by our textual analyses and suggestions as to how these assumptions should be modified will be pursued in chapter VI below.

To give a brief summary of the method of operation of the model: we shall first analyze a given ST according to a set of situational dimensions for which we shall establish linguistic (syntactic, lexical, textual) correlates. ST's resulting textual profile, which characterizes its function such that each situational dimension contributes in a particular way to the two functional components, the ideational and the interpersonal, is then taken as the norm against which the corresponding TT is measured. TT will thus be analyzed according to the same set of dimensions as realized by linguistic means, and its resultant textual profile and function will be compared with ST's.

Given the three assumptions of basic comparability of the sociocultural norms in the source and target communities, basic intertranslatability between the two languages investigated in this study, and the absence of an added, secondary function in TT, we postulate that any dimensional mismatch is a covertly erroneous error. Exceptional cases in which the above three assumptions no longer hold will be discussed in the course of the individual textual analyses. Non-dimensional mismatches, i.e., mismatches of the denotative meanings of ST and TT elements, and breaches of the target language system, will be regarded as overtly erroneous errors. It is hypothesized that overtly erroneous errors have a certain specifiable impact on the relative match of the functional components in ST and TT.

The final qualitative judgement of TT consists of a statement of the mismatches on the individual dimensions, i.e., covertly erroneous errors, and the number and type of overtly erroneous errors, as well as a statement of the resulting (mis)match of each of the two functional components.

B. Justification of Method

Apart from using the objectively fixed set of situational dimensions, our suggested method of determining the appropriateness of a TT relies, of course, on the analyst's native (German) and near-native (English) speaker intuition. In the course of the analyses of the texts, recourse to the judgements of other native speakers of English, German, and Hiberno-English has been made whenever necessary. (In the case of the two technical texts, two experts in the fields--a mathematician and an economist--have been asked for advice concerning technical terminology.)

This approach of relying on native speaker intuition in combination with a corpus of texts and the objective grid of situational dimensions seems to us the only feasible method of putting our model of translation quality assessment into practice. The reliance on the analyst's (and occasionally, a few other native speakers') intuition does not lead us back to pre-scientific methods like Spitzer's famous "Zirkel im Verstehen" (cf. Spitzer, 1948), because all the intuitive judgements presented in our investigation are <u>argued</u>, i.e., the analyst's judgements are taken as hypotheses which are being objectively validated by the reasons given for them. The use of the fixed set of situational dimensions and the use of authentic texts rather than pre-fabricated linguistic examples (which are, for instance, used in transformational-generative works) makes our investigation more objective. Unfortunately, scientifically exact and completed contrastive analyses of the German and English languages--and, indeed, of any other language pair--detailing the system of potential equivalence relations, do not yet exist. Thus, the decision about the appropriateness of linguistic elements in a TT must necessarily contain a subjective and hermeneutic element. Further, we may consider the equivalence relationships between two languages as non-absolute ones falling on a scale or cline of more or less equivalent with a range of equivalents in both directions running from more to less probable (cf. Halliday, McIntosh, and Strevens, 1964:124). The degree of this probability can only be judged by native speaker intuition.

To give priority to native speaker intuition and evidence gained partially through introspection is, in our view, a legitimate procedure if it yields useful insights. To be concerned with "objectivity" as a goal in itself, i. e., to aim at a strictly objective and exclusively empirical procedure at the cost of gaining useful insights into a phenomenon seems a futile undertaking. In view of the strictly experimental suggestions and studies on translation quality assessment reviewed in Chapter II above, we fully endorse Chomsky's statement:

> The social and behavioural sciences provide ample evidence that objectivity can be pursued with little consequent gain in insight and understanding. (Chomsky, 1965:20)

A reduction of the problems of assessing the quality of a translation to features which can be objectively measured seems less desirable than an intensive analysis of the kind we suggest in this study.

Since we adopt a textual approach to the problem of translation quality assessment, an elicitation experiment using selected informants and designed to study textual acceptability and appropriateness would also be "forbiddingly complex" (Enkvist, 1973:113). The possibility of involving a whole range of other native speakers on a systematic basis to supplement the analyst's judgements (i. e., not only using them, as has been done in the present study, for validating or revising the analyst's judgement), as has, for instance, been suggested by Riffaterre (1959,1961), has not been undertaken in this study, whose main aim is the development of a model for translation quality assessment. However, later studies may be conducted eliciting informants' judgements on the basis of the model suggested here. It should be pointed out, though, that the results of asking the opinions of a whole range of judges are unlikely to vary significantly from those achieved through our method: variation in intuitive judgements is not as marked as is generally assumed:

> Intuitions are consistent enough...to form the basis of satisfactory argumentation. Differences of intuition amongst speakers of a language...may indicate a certain difference of "dialect" between one speaker or another, but are not likely to affect crucially the argument for or against a...descriptive account. (Leech, 1974:83)

Translation is a complex, hermeneutic process. Translation assessment is consequently also characterized by what Reiss has called "die subjektive Bedingtheit des hermeneutischen Prozesses" (1971b: 106), which is due to the fact that human beings are important variables. It seems to be unlikely that translation quality assessment can ever be completely objectified in the manner of the results of natural science subjects. Within the social sciences, our method may be placed among one of the major modes of the social science analysis, the case study approach[1] in which an intensive in-depth examination of the many characteristics of one unit is conducted. Case studies have been used with benefit to supplement traditional experiments involving the extensive observation of large samples. The case study method which rests on the recognition of the crucial importance of specifying the complex contextual embeddedness of the phenomenon under study, has also been used with relation to language by adherents of the school of "general semantics" (cf. e. g., Hayakawa (1972) who points to the importance of interpreting meanings in situational contexts). Case studies, such as ours, have two general purposes: (1) to arrive at a comprehensive understanding of the phenomenon on hand; (2) to develop more general theoretical statements. Our study has the added purpose of verifying a scheme of concepts with which to analyze and evaluate a set of texts and their translations.

---

[1] For an overview of the case study approach, see Pigors and Pigors (1961) and Davidson and Costello (1969).

CHAPTER V

IMPLEMENTATION OF THE MODEL: TEST CASES

A. Selection of Texts

Starting from the two broad functional categories, the ideational and the interpersonal (see above, p. 37), four pairs of texts (ST and TT) were selected for each category. The texts were selected so as to cover a varied range of Provinces, i.e., in the ideational category, a scientific and a commercial text, an excerpt from a journalistic article and a tourist information booklet were chosen; and in the interpersonal category, excerpts were selected from a religious sermon, a political speech, a moral anecdote, and a comedy dialogue (see diagram, below). The texts within the ideational category have been further subdivided into technical (i.e., those using technical terminology) and non-technical ones; texts within the interpersonal category have been further subdivided into fictional[1] and non-fictional ones. The texts are all published texts, thus the TTs all fall into the category of "finalized translations" corresponding to what Kade (1964) has called druckreife Übersetzungen

---

[1]A fictional text may be defined for our purposes as a text in which a world is created which the text producer intends the reader to recognize as a possible world other than the real world (cf. Schmidt, 1972:69).

as opposed to Rohübersetzungen ("rough translations") and Arbeitsübersetzungen ("working translations"). Texts are matched in respect of the two languages, i. e., in each functional category two STs are German (G) and two are English (E). Texts are varied in length ranging from a minimum of 550 running words to a maximum of 1, 200.[1] The following schema results:

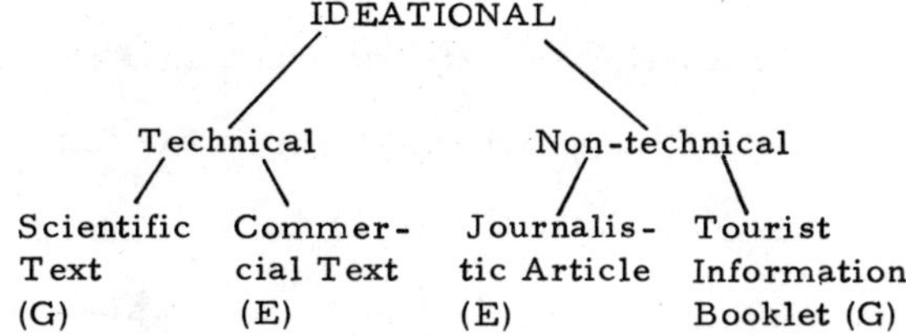

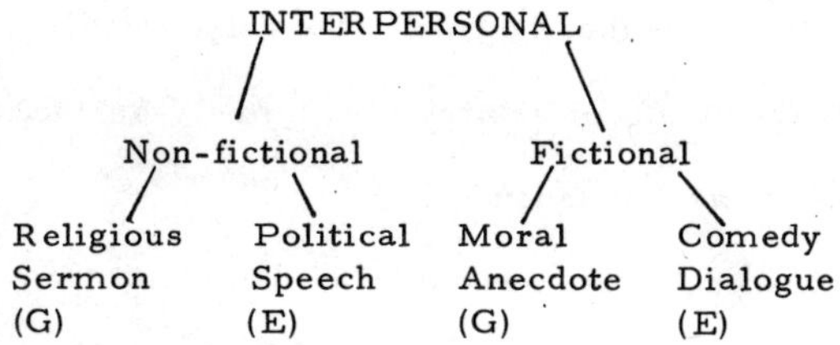

It has been necessary to exclude from the interpersonal category texts which may be considered to be predominantly poetic-aesthetic or "form-oriented", i. e., in which the form of their linguistic units has

---

[1]The respective lengths of the individual texts analyzed in this study were decided upon as a result of an analysis of the entire texts. On the basis of this analysis of the whole text, an extract which typified the function of the whole text was chosen, when to include the analysis of the full text would have been unwieldy.

taken on a special, autonomous value, e.g., poems. As Wellek (1969: 20) has pointed out, in a poetic-aesthetic work of art, the usual distinction between form and content (or meaning) no longer holds. In poetry, the form of linguistic units cannot be changed without a corresponding change in (semantic, pragmatic, textual) meaning. Since the form cannot be detached from its meaning, this meaning cannot be expressed in other ways: paraphrases, explanations, borrowing of new words are not possible in a translation of a poetic-aesthetic work of art. As Politzer (1956:321) has pointed out, in poetry the signifiers have an autonomous value and can therefore not be exchanged for the signifiers of another language, <u>although</u> they may express the same signified concept (or referent): since the physical nature of signifiers in one language can never be duplicated in another language, the relations of signifiers to signified, which are no longer arbitrary in a poetic-aesthetic work, cannot be expressed in another language.

Poetic-aesthetic texts are characterized by a maximum of <u>foregrounding:</u> in fact, foregrounding is here used for its own sake such that language is then not being used

> in the service of communication but in order to place in the foreground the act of expression, the act of speech itself. (Mukarovsky, 1964:19)

True, in many other texts, indeed in some of the texts included in our corpus (e.g., the religious sermon, the political speech, and the tourist information booklet), foregrounding also occurs, i.e., there are cases of alliteration, wordplays, etc., which are difficult or impossible to translate. However, in these cases foregrounding is always subordinate to communication. The basic purpose of these non-poetic texts which use foregrounding occasionally is always to draw the addressees' attention more intensely to the subject matter expressed by the foregrounded linguistic item but not to the expression itself. This is the reason for the possibility of translation in the case of non-poetic texts. In predominantly poetic-aesthetic texts, however, the limits of translatability[1] are reached: a TT is no longer a translation but a kind of creative transposition.

B. Analysis and Comparison of Source Texts and Translation Texts[2]

We shall start with the analysis and comparison of the ideational texts (I-IV) followed by the analysis and comparison of the interpersonal texts (V-VIII).

---

[1]For a good description of cases of untranslatability, see Söll (1971). See also Jakobson (1966:238) who states that poetry is by definition untranslatable. Similarly, Nida and Taber maintain that "anything that can be said in one language can be said in another, unless the form is an essential element of the message" (1969:4).

[2]The texts are appended to the thesis(pp.273-344). The paragraphs of each text have been numbered sequentially using Roman numerals, and the sentences inside a paragraph are sequentially numbered in Arabic numerals. In those cases in which a sentence in ST differs numerically from the equivalent sentence in TT, the bracketed Arabic numeral refers to the sentence in TT. The sign ≠ is used to indicate both covertly and overtly erroneous errors.

I. SCIENTIFIC TEXT (ST German; TT English, see Appendix, pp. 273-82.

1. Analysis of ST and Statement of Function

Dimensions of language user:

(1) Geographical Origin: non-marked, Standard High German

(2) Social Class: non-marked, Educated Middle Class

(3) Time: non-marked, contemporary German

Dimensions of language use:

(1) Medium: simple: written to be read, as realized by the following linguistic means:

syntactic means:

a. absence of elliptical clauses, contractions, contact parentheses and comment parentheses, and specific spoken language signals such as *also*, *wissen Sie*, *Sehen Sie*, etc.

lexical means:

a. presence of mathematical formulae which require the written mode for reasons of performance constraints: such formulae are too high in information load to be held in short-term memory,

b. absence of qualifying modal adverbials, interjections, vulgarisms, and other subjectivity markers of the spoken mode.

textual means:

a. the text is totally emic, i.e., the text producer never relies on the situation of production or reception in organizing the message. A result of this is the text's high degree of explicitness.

b. lack of redundancy (no repetitions).

(2) Participation: simple: monologue, witness the following linguistic means:

syntactic means:

a. exclusive use of declarative sentences; the lack of interrogative and imperative sentences suggests that the presence of addressees is never assumed, and addressees' responses are never directly or indirectly elicited,

b. lack of direct address (no second person personal or possessive pronouns).

(3) Social Role Relationship:

Asymmetrical role relationship: addresser has professional authority over addressees.

Position role of addresser: professor of mathematics, expert in a particular field of science.

Situational role of addresser: writer of textbook.

At first glance, one might regard the social role relationship in this text as virtually non-existent; in the text in which the addresser tries to instruct the addressees--students of science--particular stress is laid on the imparting of precise, factual information. The addresser himself as well as the addressees recede into the background: the social relationship between addresser and addressees is considered unimportant and is made subservient to the cognitive content of the text.

Thus, the social relationship may be described as being highly impersonal.

However, upon closer analysis, we recognize that the roles of teacher and textbook writer are also noticeable, i. e., we recognize that this is a text taken from a course book and not an article in a scholarly journal aimed to inform equals in terms of level and nature of knowledge of subject matter. The following linguistic means have been found to support the impersonality of the role relationship:

syntactic means:

a. use of impersonal pronoun man: I_1, $II_{3,5}$, V_8

b. absence of personal pronouns. The pronoun wir is used here as an impersonal one corresponding to man. It collapses the first and second person thus facilitating the dismissal of both addresser and addressees as distinct elements from the communication process and achieving a heightened concentration on the text's subject matter, i. e., the truth of what is stated is never dependent on who is addressing whom. The pronoun wir may also be seen as conforming with the scientific convention of hiding the addresser's identity and making the text impersonal, detached, and neutral.

c. frequency and complexity of [-human] noun phrases, e. g., $I_{1,2,3}$; $II_{1,2,3}$; $III_{1,2,3}$; $IV_{1,2}$; V_{1-4}, etc.

d. use of verbs which merely signal logical connection and thus mainly point to other semantically more significant textual content, i. e., they shift the attention to the noun phrases and therefore give an impression of abstractness and impersonality, e.g., I_3, $II_{1,6}$; $III_{1,2}$; $IV_{1,2}$; $V_{1,7,13}$.

However, the relationship of teacher to student is also manifest in certain textual means:

a. detailed nature of description; deliberate explicitness, i.e., descriptions are designed to have high explanatory value for novices in the field. See especially the detailed account of the derivation of formulae, e.g., II_4,

b. use of explanatory brackets: II_8 and V_8, and of explanatory phrases, III_1, to safeguard against possible misunderstanding by students and rule out alternative, undesirable interpretations,

c. reference to "Übungsaufgaben": III_3

(4) Social Attitude: formal, i.e., marked social distance and impersonality.

syntactic means:

a. frequency and complexity of noun phrases using both heavy premodification and post-modification, e.g., $I_{1,2,3}$; $II_{1,2,8}$; $III_{1,2,3}$; $IV_{1,2}$; $V_{1-4,15}$ coupled with the use of verbs whose main function is the signalling of logical connections (cf. Social Role Relationship). The result of this combination of devices is an impression of impersonality.

b. presence of "overcorrectness", i.e., strict, conversationally unnatural grammaticality, e.g., use of future tense for (the more common) present tense: III_3 and of subjunctive: V_1,

c. absence of contractions and elliptical clauses (cf. Medium).

lexical means:

a. absence of qualifying modal adverbials, interjections, vulgarisms, etc., all of which would render the text more personal (cf. Medium),

b. presence of lexical items and collocations marked [+formal] due to the fact that they most typically occur in impersonal settings, e.g., I_3 - zum Fortfall gebracht; $II_{4,7}$ - Indem; III_2 - entsprechend; IV_2 - vornehmsten; sogleich; V_{11} - tritt in Kraft; V_{12} - besagt.

(5) Province: science text dealing with the use of partial differential equations in physics. The text forms part of a course book for science students.

lexical means:

a. frequency of complex technical terminology in the form of compound nouns, i.e., noun phrases using nominal pre-modifiers: I_1 - Feldwirkungsstandpunkt; III_1 - Transversalschwingungen, IV_1 - Gleichgewichtszustände, etc.

b. frequency of foreign and loan words derived from Greek and Latin roots, e.g.,: I_1 - Gravitationstheorie; II_1 - Hydrodynamik; inkompressibel, etc.

c. presence of scientific formulae, and particular conventional scientific phrases: e.g., V_1 - es sei; V_8 - Bezeichnen wir... so gilt,

d. frequency of lexical items marked [+abstract],

e. all lexical items lack, to a large extent, connotative meanings in the sense of "feeling tones" (cf. Sapir, 1921:40),

f. complete lack of emotive-expressive words like qualifying modal adverbials, interjections, etc. (cf. Medium, Social Role Relationship), and of figurative language.

textual means:

presence of strong textual cohesion due to the employment of various mechanisms of theme dynamics and clausal linkage:

theme dynamics:

a. factual coherence of the material through the logical procession of the content as reflected in the formulae. The formulae are numbered sequentially, and anaphoric and cataphoric referencing using both the numbers and individual terms inside the formulae as pro-forms is conducted freely, weaving the text together tightly. The formulae constitute the informational skeleton around which the text is constructed,

b. other use of pro-forms (for noun phrases, adverbials, clauses or sentences): e.g., II_7 - in letzterem Falle; II_8 - ihre Konstante... ihrer Dichte; III_2 - entsprechend, etc.,

c. use of explicit phrases to mark the theme, e.g., I_1/II_3 - man kennt; I_2 - bekanntlich; II_2 - wir erwähnen auch,

d. use of foregrounded word order (thematic fronting) in order to preserve theme-rheme sequence: I_3, II_6, IV_2, $V_{2,4,15}$.

clausal linkage:

Use of logical clause connectors, e.g., II_4 - indem; II_7 - schreiben wir...indem; III_1 - (nicht)... sondern; $V_{3,5,6}$ - dann...dann...dann ...dann = a non-temporal, logical connector, to be glossed as 'if this holds, then...', V_9 - daher, dass.

The province feature "textbook" is further characterized by the detailed and explicit nature of the descriptions, specially geared at novices in the field, the use of "fool-proof" explanatory phrases, and the references to exercises to be done by the addressees (cf. Social Role Relationship). The general overlap between the dimensions Province and Social Role Relationship in this text is an inevitable consequence of the fact that while a tightly knit logical textual structure may be said to characterize a scientific text, the degree to which this structure is present is also the degree to which the non-specialist reader is enabled to follow the logic of the text's arguments. Hence, the marked logical cohesion in this text contributes indirectly towards the instructional nature of the text as outlined under Social Role Relationship.

Statement of Function

The function of the text consisting of an ideational and an interpersonal functional component (see above, p.37) may be summed up in the following way: the addresser's main purpose is to inform, to pass on factual information as precisely and efficiently as possible. However, he also wants to make sure that the information is understood properly by the addressees--novices in his special field--therefore, he adjusts the texts to the particular needs of the addressees.

This summary statement of the text's function has been derived by examining the particular way in which the dimensions are marked in this text and in which they contribute to the two functional components.

On the dimension Medium, the written to be read mode operates in support of the ideational component of the text's function: it facilitates an economical flow of information which is unhampered by social implications that would arise through the (assumed or real) presence of interlocutors in any type of spoken language. The text is fully premeditated; no addressee interruptions or potential changes in the information flow had to be taken into account. In the same vein, the fact that there is an absolute lack of addressee participation which makes for a high degree of condensedness, and an uninterrupted, non-alternating passing on of information also supports the ideational component of the textual function.

On the dimension Social Role Relationship, the addresser's roles of instructor and textbook writer seem to support the interpersonal component of the text's function in that the text reveals, on this dimension, the addresser's concern about the addressees' understanding the information he is passing on to them. On the same dimension, however, we found that the social relationship between addresser and addressee is characterized as being highly impersonal, completely suppressing the respective identities. This impersonality clearly supports the ideational component of the text's function, i. e., its purpose of passing on information as efficiently as possible, undisturbed by social considerations.

The dimension Social Attitude defined as formal operates in support of the ideational component. The formality which is marked by an absence of subjectivity markers, elliptical clauses, as well as by a frequency of complex noun phrases facilitates a condensed, explicit, non-subjective flow of information.

The dimension of Province operates first of all in support of the ideational component of the textual function: the frequency of well-defined, totally automatized scientific terms and formulae, the fact that the lexical items lack connotative meanings (and therefore indeterminacy), and the creation of textual cohesion--all of these province-features add to the text's purpose of efficiently passing on information. However, the text's instructive-didactic nature--Province feature: textbook--supports the interpersonal part of the text's function, i. e., the addresser's attempt to make sure that the way the information conveyed is appropriate for the addressees in terms of unambiguity and logical-cohesive presentation.

2. ST and TT Comparison and Statement of Quality

Mismatches on the following dimensions have been discovered following the analysis of TT and the comparison of ST and TT:

Social Role Relationship: TT is, in a few instances, of a less markedly didactic-instructional nature, i.e., TT makes less allowance for the needs of the particular addressees of this text by being less unambiguously explicit in using certain terms: $II_{8(9)}$ - pro Flächen-bzw. Längeneinheit ≠ per unit of area or of length. TT omits bzw. (respectively). In doing so, TT is no longer as unambiguously clear (and this unambiguity is necessary for novices in the field) as is ST. $II_{8(9)}$ - Eigenelastizität ≠ a proper elasticity, which is too ambiguous for a learner (elasticity of its own would have been less ambiguous). $V_{2(1)}$ - den ins Auge gefassten Aufpunkt P umgeben wir mit einem infinitesimalen Raumelement ≠ let the initial point P be surrounded by an element of volume. Despite the omission in TT of equivalent expressions for ins Auge gefasst and infinitesimal, the referential meaning of the clause in TT is not invalidated (therefore these two omissions are not classified as overtly erroneous errors). The information conveyed in ins Auge gefasst is implicitly understood by experts in the field; so is the notion infinitesimal which is expressed in the sign ∂T

which ensues. However, on this parameter these two omissions do constitute a mismatch as they clearly detract from the explicitly instructional nature of the text. $V_{6(5)}$ - von Ausdehnung und Arbeitsleistung abstrahieren ≠ neglect expansion. The omission in TT of an equivalent term for Arbeitsleistung is again not an overtly erroneous error as it does not detract from the denotative meaning of the clause: expansion always involves work and mentioning it explicitly may be considered unnecessary for the expert mathematician. However, this omission must be considered a mismatch on this parameter as the addresser's concern for the addressees' reception of the text is clearly deficient in this instance.

Province:

a. the above mismatches on Social Role Relationship may also be considered to be mismatches on Province because of the overlap of the two dimensions in this text (see above, p.76),

b. in certain instances, TT lacks ST's textual cohesion as established above in our analysis of ST: $II_{5(6)}$ - the Indem-clause in ST leads up to the equation. In TT, the equation precedes the giving of reasons for, and methods of, deriving it. The natural theme-rheme sequence is thus disrupted in TT, which makes TT less clear and understandable. $II_{6(7)}$ - foregrounded word order in ST to preserve theme-rheme sequence is not matched in TT. The "given-new" scheme is thus destroyed in TT and this clearly detracts from TT's textual clarity. $II_{7(8)}$ - Indem ≠ setting: TT lacks the force of logical linkage. The dependent -ing-clause does not provide as strong a logical link as would, for instance, the structure by + V-ing, e.g., by setting. $II_{8(9)}$ - ihre Konstante... aus der ihnen... ihrer Dichte TT omits the anaphoric pronominal reference provided in ihre, ihnen, ihrer thus making existent relationships less unambiguously clear. $V_{8(7)}$ - Bezeichen wir... so gilt: The relation of condition is explicitly stated in ST. In TT, this conditional relation is less clearly expressed as TT uses a dependent -ing-clause: Denoting: Factual cohesion is weaker in TT in this instance. $V_{15(13)}$ - Mit (12) entsteht aus (11), The logical relationship expressed in ST is weakened in TT through the use of a dependent-ing clause: Introducing.

There are no overtly erroneous errors.

Statement of Quality

The comparison of ST and TT along the eight dimensions shows that there are a number of mismatches on the two (overlapping) dimensions of Social Role Relationship and Province. The mismatches on Social Role Relationship which detract from the text's didactic-instructional nature clearly weaken the interpersonal component of the text's function. The mismatches on Province which render TT less textually cohesive also weaken the interpersonal component by making the text potentially less easily digestible for novices in the field.

Taken together, the ideational component of the text's function which consists of passing on factual information has been preserved on all contributing dimensions, and also due to the fact that there are no mismatches of the denotative meaning of items in ST and TT. However, the interpersonal component of the textual function, i.e., the adjustment of the material to the needs of the text's addressees, has been violated in the specified instances on both the dimensions which were found to contribute to that component.

II. COMMERCIAL TEXT (ST English; TT German), see Appendix, pp. 283-90.

1. Analysis of ST and Statement of Function

Dimensions of language user:

(1) Geographical Origin: non-marked, Standard American English

(2) Social Class: non-marked, Educated Middle Class

(3) Time: non-marked, contemporary American English

Dimensions of language use:

(1) Medium: simple: written to be read, as realized by the following linguistic means:

syntactic means:

a. absence of elliptical clauses, contractions, contact parentheses and comment parentheses, and any kind of spoken language signals such as <u>well</u>, <u>you see</u>, <u>you know</u>, etc.,

b. placing of expanded subordinate clauses of purpose before the main clause: this is a focussing device typical of the written mode as its use in spoken language is restricted by performance constraints, e. g., V_3,

c. presence of expanded postnominal modification resulting in the separation of the head of the subject noun phrase and the corresponding finite verb. This construction is typical of the written mode as there are performance constraints in spoken language: IX_1.

<u>lexical means</u>:

a. absence of qualifying modal adverbials, interjections, and other subjectivity markers typical of the spoken mode.

<u>textual means:</u>

a. the text is predominantly emic. There are a few pronominal references to the addresser and the addressees; however, the immediate circumstances of the production and reception of the text are clearly irrelevant for the organization of the message. As a result of this, the text is largely determined through text-immanent criteria and is marked by an explicitness and elaborateness typical of the written mode,

b. lack of repetititions resulting in a lack of redundancy,

c. frequent use of passivization as a typically "written" means of complex syntactic linkage for text-constitutive purposes, i. e., especially for the preservation of the theme-rheme sequence, e. g., II_2, IV_2,

$V_{2,4}$, X_1, XI_2.

(2) Participation: complex: monologue with addressees being directly addressed and given instructions. However, the addressees' potential reactions are not being taken into account by the addresser. The addressee-oriented nature of the text is thus limited to the direct address and the request for action. This characterization is manifest in the following linguistic means:

syntactic means:

a. presence of second person personal and possessive pronouns for direct address: I_1, $V_{1,3,4}$, $VI_{1,2}$, VII_1,

b. presence of requests put to the addressees through the use of the verb require in the passive, modal auxiliaries of obligation, and the mandative subjunctive in a that-clause: $V_{3,4}$, $VI_{1,2}$,

c. absence of interrogative sentences. This is indicative of the predominantly monologous character of the text which--with the exception of the participatory devices listed above in a and b--allows for no direct (even imaginary) participation of the addressees.

(3) Social Role Relationship:

Asymmetrical role relationship: addresser has de facto economic authority over the addressees.

Position role of addresser: president of an international financing company, of which the addressees are shareholders.

Situational role of addresser: representative of the interests of the company informing the shareholders about recent developments in the company.

The role relationship as manifest in the text may be detailed in the following way: in the interests of his company (I. O. S.), the president is diplomatically indirect, non-committal, and evasive, avoiding any statement of an assumption of direct responsibility for the new VCL-company on the part of I. O. S. The relationship is an impersonal, distant one: the shareholder is not being approached as an individual but as a _type_, as a member of the class of shareholders. The text's role relationship is further characterized by a deliberate attempt on the part of the addresser to downplay his own and the company's power status and give the addressees the illusion of possessing more influence than they really have. The addresser flatters the addressees and tries to create a feeling of security, loyalty, and trust in the well-being of the company. This characterization of the text's role relationship has been derived through an examination of the following linguistic means:

syntactic means:

a. use of second person singular personal pronoun _you_ and possesive pronoun _your_ in a specific way, i. e., for addressing corporate members not "persons" as such (witness the substitution of _each shareholder_ for _you_, e. g., in II_3): $V_{1,3,4}$, $VI_{1,2}$, VII_1. Notable is the use of these personal and possessive pronouns in "flattering contexts" only, i. e., in connection with possible rights, actions, etc., on the part of the addressees,

b. use of the first person plural personal pronoun we to refer to the addresser or the company (I. O. S.) or the Board of Directors, i.e., the addresser avoids referring to himself as an individual (although the letter is personally signed): V_4, VI_1,

c. frequency of impersonal constructions using impersonal it and existential there as well as passives; the use of these devices is indicative of a desire on the part of the addresser to be cautious and "hedgy" and to avoid specifying a causer or agent. In using these devices, the addresser also intends to give the addressees the impression that it is not the company that requires them to do something (e.g., fill out a form) but that they are agents of their own free will merely obeying some ulterior abstract necessity: $V_{3,4}$, VI_1, $VII_{1,4}$, VIII_1, X_1, XII_1,

d. preponderance of [-human] subject noun phrases adding to the impersonal character of the text: $II_{1,2}$, $III_{1,2}$, $IV_{1,2}$, $V_{1,2,3}$, VI_2, VII_2, etc.,

e. use of subjunctive in a that-clause: VI_1 - asked that you designate as opposed to the alternative: asked you to designate. This is a marked choice in English. The effect of the that+$V_{subjunctive}$ construction is such that the addressee is not the direct recipient of a request or command by the addresser but is left his own free agent. In other words, this structure has the illocutionary force of a suggestion whereas the structure asked you to designate would have the illocutionary force of a request in the context of this text.

textual means:

a. deliberate attempt to underplay the role of I. O. S. through putting I. O. S. in non-focussed position in prepositional phrases IV_2, $VIII_{1,2}$, XI_2,

b. deliberate overall organization of the text such that the addressees are first being presented with the change as a fait accompli and its many positive sides, and that they are only later (paragraph IX) being given the reasons (negative ones) for the change.

(4) Social Attitude

Consistent with the impersonal, distant relationship as outlined above, the social attitude of the addresser towards his addressees as reflected on the level of style, is a formal one:

syntactic means:

a. frequency of complex noun phrases showing both multiple premodification, postmodification, and discontinuous modification which add to the text's abstractness and impersonality. Examples may be found in nearly every sentence, therefore a specific listing is unnecessary,

b. deletion of conjunction if plus subject-auxiliary inversion: XII_1... than would have been possible, had those operations...,

c. completeness of clauses (no elliptical clauses); absence of contractions (cf. Medium),

d. frequency of impersonal constructions using it, there, and passives;

preponderance of [-human] subject noun phrases; use of subjunctive in a that-clause (for all of which see above Social Role Relationship).

lexical means:

a. presence of words and phrases marked [+formal] due to their restricted use in impersonal--in this case, business--situations: e.g., II_1 - declared, payable on and after, shareholders of record as of the close of; V_3 - expedite the distribution; IX_2 - precluded the maintenance of; XIII_1 - Very truly yours, a [+formal] letter closing formula, etc.

b. absence of interjections, qualifying modal adverbials and other subjectivity markers (cf. above, Medium).

textual means:

a. frequent use of passivization as a means of complex syntactic linkage specifically for preserving theme-rheme sequence (cf. above Medium).

(5) Province

Commercio-financial circular letter issued by the president of an international financing company to the company's shareholders. In this letter, the shareholders are being informed about changes in the set-up of the company. The preliminary label "language of commerce" with which one usually associates a preciseness in giving data of all kinds, textual cohesion, and explicitness, especially explicit allowance for possible alternative interpretations to avoid potential (costly) misunderstandings, can be further explained and justified by examining the use of the following linguistic features in this text:

lexical means:

a. use of precise technical terminology, i. e., special commercio-financial lexical items and collocations, e. g., II_1 - pro-rata, dividend, holding company; IV_1 - stockholder's equity; IV_2 - historical earnings performance, etc.

b. presence of phrases which precisely define the information given or explicitly state conceivable alternatives: II_1 - on and after December 20, 1971; to all shareholders of record as of the close of business on December 17, 1971; VI_1 - a bank (or broker); VI_2 - stamp (or seal),

c. absence of foregrounded words and expressions, and of any kind of figurative language.

textual means:

presence of strong textual cohesion due to the employment of several mechanisms of theme-dynamics and clausal linkage:

theme-dynamics:

a. repetition of lexical items, e. g., $II_{1,2}$ - dividend; $II_{1,2,3}$ - share; $III_{1,2}$ - contribute, contribution; $V_{1,2,3,}$ and VI_1 - certificate(s) etc.,

b. frequency of anaphoric referencing by means of pro-forms for noun phrases, adverbials, predicates, clauses or sentences, e. g., III_2 - in return for its contribution; in turn; that company; all of these shares; V_2 - That is; $V4$ - this, etc.

c. organization of thematic movement in sequences of theme-rheme to insure given-new ordering, e. g., II_{1-2}; V_{1-2-3}, V_4; VI_{1-2}, VII_{1-2}.

clausal linkage through logical connectors:

II_3 - of course; IV_2 - since; V_2 - That is, VIII_1 - as a result of; VIII_2 - therefore, etc.

Statement of Function

The function of the text consisting of the two components--ideational and interpersonal--may be summed up in the following way: the addresser's intention is (a) to inform the addressees of a collection of facts as precisely and efficiently as possible and to request action; (b) to establish a positive rapport with the addressees, to convince and reassure them of the appropriateness and advantages of certain moves by the company, to give the addressees a feeling of importance and power, and at the same time to always attempt to be indirect and non-committal as to the moves announced and their potential consequences.

This summary statement of the text's function has been derived by an examination of the ways in which the dimensions are marked in this text, and the manner in which they contribute to the two functional components:

On the dimension Medium, the written to be read mode supports the ideational component of the text's function by facilitating a condensed, uninterrupted and premeditated information flow unimpeded by any direct presence of the addressees in the act of communication. Similarly, on the dimension Participation, the lack of addressee participation, i. e., the infrequency of addressee-involving structures, also acts in support of the ideational component by making for a linear, non-alternating and premeditated organization of the message. However, on the same parameter, the few attempts at involving the addressees by addressing them directly, and by putting requests to them, do support the interpersonal component of the textual function.

On the dimension Social Role Relationship, the impersonality of the relationship reinforces the ideational component by promoting an economical transmission of facts disregarding the social circumstances of addresser and addressee. However, equally strongly supported on this dimension is the interpersonal component: the same linguistic devices which create the impersonality are also used to "manipulate" the addressees; e. g., the avoidance of a specification of a responsible causer or agent is used to give the addressees the illusion of their obeying an abstract necessity and not I. O. S. 's interests. Further, the attempt at flattering the addressees which we discovered on this dimension also obviously filters into the interpersonal component of the textual function.

The dimension Social Attitude, which we defined as formal, operates in support of the ideational component of the textual function in that the frequency of complex, abstract noun phrases and impersonal structures, and the exclusive presence of complete, well-planned and well-structured sentences provide for an efficiently condensed and objective information flow.

The dimension Province, marked by the use of clearly defined, automatized technical terminology, an explicit consideration of alternative interpretations of certain terms, and strong textual cohesion, clearly supports the ideational component of the text's function as well.

2. ST and TT Comparison and Statement of Quality

Mismatches on the following dimensions have been discovered as a result of the analysis of TT and the comparison of ST and TT:

Participation:

TT lacks the explicit involvement of the addressees in a few instances: $V_{1(2)}$ - as you know ≠ bekanntlich; VI_1 - your dividend certificate ≠ die Aktienzertifikate; VI_2 - Your bank ≠ die Bank; VII_1 your new company ≠ die Value Capital Limited.

Social Role Relationship

TT is in certain specified instances less reassuring and flattering, and less non-committal and diplomatically indirect vis à vis I. O. S. ' role and responsibility: IV_2 - TT uses active voice; this has the effect of stressing IOS as theme, which is undesirable in this context, because it is thus more strongly suggested that I. O. S. is important with respect to VCL's future earnings. In view of I. O. S.' fate, this is certainly not reassuring to the addressees. $V_{1(2)}$ - as you know ≠ bekanntlich: TT is less implicitly flattering to the addressees. $V_{3,4(3)}$ - your assistance is required... for your completion ≠ bitten wir Sie... auszufüllen. TT is more direct and forceful. ST expresses the action to be done by the addressees more abstractly and indirectly (nominally); the utterance in ST has the illocutionary force of a subtle suggestion, while the utterance in TT has one of a request. ST tries to suggest that it is not the company that wants something done, but that some external necessity suggests a course of action to the addressees. VI_1 - your dividend certificate ≠ die Aktienzertifikate: TT does not make an attempt to create in the addressees an idea of their own possessions and is thus less implicitly flattering. VI_1 - asked that you designate ≠ haben wir Sie gebeten: In ST, the addressees are not direct recipients of a request, but are left agents of their own initiative. The utterance has the illocutionary force of a subtle suggestion; TT lacks this nuance and is thus less careful and indirect; the illocutionary force in TT is one of a request. VI_1 - will be sent ≠ geschickt werden sollen: In ST, the relative clause is a non-restrictive one, i.e., the sending of the certificates follows automatically from the naming of the bank, and the sending is the company's responsibility. In TT, the relative clause has to be understood as a restrictive one, such that the instruction that the certificates should be sent to the designated bank, is the shareholders' responsibility. Hence ST is more reassuring, while TT undiplomatically throws the onus onto the shareholders. VI_2 - your bank (or broker) should indicate ≠ Sie müssen die Bank (oder einen Makler) bitten: The lack of the possessive pronoun renders the expression in TT less implicitly flattering; also, the illocutionary force of the utterance in TT is, mainly through the use of the modal müssen, one of an order. The addressees thus appear to be dependent on the addresser. Such an illocutionary force is directly opposed to the cautious and diplomatic tenor in ST. VII_1 - your new company ≠ die Value Capital Limited: TT is less implicitly flattering, i. e., it fails to suggest that the addressees are "owners of the company". VII_1 - ST's impersonal it-clause, which reinforces the non-committal and detached tenor of the text, is not matched in TT, which features Value Capital Limited as agent. TT gives an impression of greater certainty, which is unwarranted given the evasive, impersonal structure it is anticipated in ST. VII_4 - present intention ≠ z. Z. (zur Zeit). TT's expression z. Z. has the negative connotation of temporariness and fickleness, which is undesirable given the addresser's intention of reassuring his addressees and building up their good-will.

VIII_1 - ST's impersonal there-clause is rendered in TT by a "personalized" construction featuring I. O. S. as subject-agent. X_1 - new facilities being established ≠ von neuen Einrichtungen: TT suggests that these facilities are, at the time of utterance, already established.

TT loses the <u>be +V-ing</u> connotation of 'being set up right now', a subtle difference, but in TT the addresser again appears to be less non-committal, and carefully evasive. XI_1 - ST focusses on Value Capital Limited which is in theme-position; the role of I. O. S., from whose failures the addressees' attention is to be detracted, is thus underplayed. In TT, Value Capital Limited appears in non-focussed position <u>after</u> I. O. S. is mentioned.

<u>Social Attitude</u>

TT is in very few instances less <u>formal</u>, i. e. --consistent with the findings on the dimension <u>Social Role Relationship</u>--TT appears to be less distant, and more personal and direct:
II_4 - <u>er bleibt natürlich</u>. In this position, <u>natürlich</u> gives the sentence an almost colloquial tone. Initial position of <u>natürlich</u> or the use of the [+formal] <u>selbstverständlich</u> would have been more adequate.
V_3 - <u>your assistance is required</u> ≠ <u>bitten wir Sie</u>: TT is more personal, i. e., less socially distant and <u>formal</u>. VI_2 - <u>Sie müssen die Bank bitten</u> - a personalized, informal expression. VII_1 - ST's impersonal <u>it</u>-clause: <u>it is anticipated that</u> is not matched in formality by TT's more direct, non-impersonal structure.

<u>Province</u>

TT is, in a few instances, less clear, precise, and less textually cohesive than ST:

VI_2 - Ihre Unterschrift auf dem Dividenden-Zustellungsformular zu bestätigen - the prepositional phrase auf dem... is ambiguous; it may either be an adjectival or an adverbial phrase of location, i. e., it may either qualify bestätigen or Unterschrift. Thus TT appears to be less unambiguously clear. IX_1 - TT does not preserve the theme-rheme sequence as it starts the clause with the rheme thus losing the textual linkage to the preceding paragraphs. IX_2 - TT lacks ST's anaphoric noun phrase these operations (a consequence of the different thematic organization of IX_1 in TT). XI_1 beabsichtigt diese - undesirable ambiguity of the anaphoric pronoun diese's referent.

Overtly erroneous errors:

There are two mismatches of the referential meanings of ST and TT items:

II_2 - wrong selection: newly established holding company ≠ eine nach dem Recht der Bahamas neu gegründete Gesellschaft (Bahamische Holding Gesellschaft would have been more adequate). VII_1 - wrong selection: it is anticipated ≠ wird die Value Capital Limited. The choice of the future tense in TT does not express the uncertainty of an anticipation (the adverbial voraussichtlich should have been included).

Further, we discovered one breach of the target language system, to be subcategorized as a case of dubious acceptability:

III_2 - erhielt die IOS 6. 2 Mill. Aktien... die alle von der IOS... This is a confusing and illogical structure because I.O.S. is the subject of the main clause and it appears in a prepositional phrase in a passivized relative clause. Hence passivization serves no real purpose as it does not omit the agent. We claim that this structure is counter-intuitive, and of dubious acceptability. The following similar example seems to confirm our assumption: Each of us received $20 which was spent by each of us on the spot. This example--and III_2 in the present text--is only acceptable if the agents in the main clause and the passivized relative clause are non-identical.

Statement of Quality

The comparison of ST and TT along the eight parameters shows that there are mismatches on all dimensions of language use but Medium; however, by far the greatest number of mismatches occur on the Social Role Relationship parameter rendering TT in the specified instances less flattering to the addressees, less diplomatically polite and deliberately non-committal, i.e., blunter and more direct. Clearly, the interpersonal component has been altered through these mismatches. The few mismatches on the dimension Participation which result in TT's involving the addressees less directly and explicitly in a few (for the addressees positive) instances also detract from the interpersonal functional component. The few mismatches on Social Attitude which render TT less formal also alter the interpersonal component of the textual function by making TT less socially distant, and carefully polite. The mismatches on Province, which result in TT being less unambiguously clear and textually cohesive, as well as the three overtly erroneous errors affect the ideational component of ST's function by detracting in these few instances from a clear and efficient passing on of information.

From this configuration of mismatches, it becomes clear that, while the ideational component of ST's function is violated to a minor degree only, ST's interpersonal functional component is violated to a considerable extent as evidenced by the pattern of mismatches along the dimension of Social Role Relationship. Thus, we may say that with regard to the addresser's implicit attempt at giving the addressees a feeling of importance and his desire to be non-committal, indirect, and diplomatic about the consequences of the changes in his company, TT has serious shortcomings which we have specified in detail above.

III. JOURNALISTIC ARTICLE (ST English; TT German, see Appendix, pp. 291-96.

1. Analysis of ST and Statement of Function

Dimensions of language user:

(1) Geographical Origin: non-marked, Standard American English

(2) Social Class: non-marked, Educated Middle Class

(3) Time: non-marked, contemporary American English

Dimensions of language use:

(1) Medium: complex: written to be read as if heard. There are at least two ways in which this text may have been produced: a) the text is an adaptation of lecture notes or even an (edited) transcript of a lecture given by the addresser, or b) the text has been specially prepared to appear as though it originated in the manner of a) above because of the addresser's assessment of the addressees' preferences.

The above considerations are substantiated by the following linguistic means:

syntactic means:

a. presence of anacolutha: II_1, IV_1

b. presence of elliptical structures: $II_{3,4}$

c. presence of loosely-structured clauses featuring parenthetical and appositional structures either inside the main clause or extraposed, thus creating an impression of lack of premeditation, typical of the spoken mode: IV_1, VI_2, $VIII_{2,3,4}$.

textual means:

a. the text is predominantly etic, i. e., showing links to the particular participants in the situation in which it is embedded through the frequent use of deictic personal pronouns, i. e., we, involving addresser and addresses together, and you in direct address. See especially paragraph II, in which the addressees' physiognomy is referred to for illustration purposes,

b. looseness in the logical structuring of the text, which is indicative of the lack of premeditation typical of the spoken mode (and which may have been introduced deliberately into this text to simulate this Medium).

(2) Participation: complex: monologue with direct address and personalized instructions indicative of addressee participation.

syntactic means:

a. use of first person plural personal and possessive pronouns as inclusive terms, involving the addressees directly in order to heighten their interest in the subject matter: I_1, $III_{1,2}$, IV_1, VII_2, $VIII_{2,3}$,

b. use of second person singular personal and possessive pronouns as direct address forms: $II_{1,2,3,4}$,

c. presence of rhetorical, addressee-directing utterances such as: VIII_1 - What brought the split about?: A rhetorical question through which the addressees are invited to participate in the argument put to them. VIII_3 - we cannot simply say: which constitutes an admonition of the addressees.

(3) Social Role Relationship:

Asymmetrical role relationship: addresser has professional authority over the addressees.

Position role of addresser: professor of anthropology.

Situational role of addresser: writer of an article for the general lay public about his field of specialization.

The role relationship in this text may be characterized as follows: the addresser is fully aware of the "authority gap" between himself and his addressees in terms of knowledge of his special field, and he does not make any attempt at concealing this fact. This results in a sometimes slightly condescending tone. The following linguistic means have suggested this characterization:

syntactic means:

a. presence of structures in which instructions given to the addressees acquire a connotation of mild condescension: VII_2 - or between animals properly called: The addresser informs the lay public of the true way of referring to a certain type of animal in a schoolmasterly manner.

VIII_1 - What brought the split about?: Rhetorical question exemplifying the distinction between the informed and the uninformed.

VIII_3 - we cannot simply say: The addresser points out to the unenlightened that things in his field are not as simple as their common sense might suggest they are.

textual means:

a. insertion of a whole paragraph (II) with clearly educational illustrative intention.

(4) Social Attitude:

Consultative-casual, an informal style which might be glossed as 'conversational, friendly, chatty'. This style level seems to be consistent with the role of an instructor who adopts a mildly condescending tone vis à vis his addressees, i. e., the addresser "steps down" to reach the addressees at what he assumes is their level:

syntactic means:

a. presence of anacolutha, elliptical structures as well as parenthetical and appositional structures (cf. above *Medium*),

b. simplicity of noun phrases, i. e., lack of multiple premodification or postmodification,

c. use of *'s-genitive* with a [-human] object. This results in personification of the object and achieves an informal, personalized style level: I_2 - *India's Siwalik Hills*.

lexical means:

a. use of abbreviations for educational institutions· I_2 - *of Yale*, V_1 - *at Yale*,

b. presence of words and phrases marked [-formal] due to their common occurrence in more intimate social situation, e. g., II_1 - *these things*; III_2 - *belong in* (instead of *belong to*); IV_1 - *put away in a drawer*; V_1 - *was looking... at* (instead of *investigating* or *examining*); VII_1 - *on one hand* (omission of article *the*); VII_2 - *anything on the human side*; VII_3 - *looking for* (instead of *investigating*, etc.); VIII_1 - *what* brought the split about?.

(5) Province:

Journalistic science article written by a specialist for the general, non-specialist public. The article is published in a general, "Readers Digest" type magazine which is characterized by its instructional-informative nature. Descriptions of scientific discoveries are not so much factual reports but attractive stories. There is an all-pervading tendency of personalization, dramatization, and concretization of scientific facts. Typical of this "popularization of science" is a concern with linking general life experiences to abstract scientific notions. The following linguistic means are evidence for this description:

syntactic means:

a. use of be+Ving forms suggesting an interest in the process of discovery involving a human being (as opposed to a concern with the bare facts of the discovery): V_1, VI_2, VII_3,

b. use of s-genitive for personalization of [-human] noun phrase (cf. above Social Attitude): I_2 - India's Siwalik Hills,

c. use of the instantaneous present to achieve a dramatic, theatrical quality: VII_2 - thus we also see (the logical connector thus also adds to the dramatic forces of the clause),

d. use of a rhetorical question for dramatic force (cf. above Social Role Relationship): VIII_1,

e. omission of the article preceding a noun in apposition. This results in giving the appositive the status of a title and achieving a bombastic, dramatic effect: VII_1 - Dryopithecus, ancestor of the apes;

f. use of personal and possessive pronouns (cf. above Participation) whenever the addressees are being invited to relate scientific facts to their own range of experience: I_1/III_2 - our ancestor/our ancestry, and entire paragraph II.

lexical means:

a. use of figurative language, e.g., III_1 - as though he had just set his foot on a path (personification of species); IV_1 - the tide of scientific opinion...was against Ramapithecus (cliché metaphor plus personification); VI_1 - Simons rescued...Ramapithecus from burial (personification: only animate beings can be buried), etc.

b. use of scientifically imprecise words and phrases which are typical of the Province of popularized science text, e.g., I_1 - and pointed to some man-like features; II_1 - these things; IV_2 - after almost 30 years; VI_1 - other pieces of Ramapithecus; VI_2 - in various places from the U.S.A. to India...a few more fragments; VII_2 - anything on the human side, etc. All these items provoke a logical follow-up question: Which/what exactly...?

c. popularized way of giving bibliographic references, i.e., lack of precision in the data given: I_2 - G. E. Lewis of Yale; V_1 - Elwyn Simons at Yale; IV_2 - after almost 30 years, L. S. B. Leakey found a similar fossil at Fort Ternan. Reference is being made to the place where the researcher worked but not to the publication in which he describes his findings.

textual means:

a. use of an introductory formula (as in a fairy tale) to achieve dramatic force: V_1 - it happened that at the same time;

b. use of cleaving as a device for giving thematic prominence to the new element in a clause and adding a dramatic note to the utterance: I_1 - It was out of... that... and, in fact it was;

c. presence of textual cohesion through repetitions: III_1 - foot; IV_1 - tide(s), facts; and iconic linkage: I_1 - it was... it was; $II_{3/4}$ - an ape's are longer... yours is straighter. These features add to the attractiveness of the text and thus help to catch the addressees' interest.

Statement of Function:

The function of the text consisting of an interpersonal and an ideational component may be summed up in the following way: the addresser's intention is to inform and instruct the addressees about scientific facts in such a way that the material presented to the addressees is made "non-technical", attractive, interesting, and easily digestible in order to suit the addressees' level of knowledge and understanding of the subject matter.

The interpersonal component of the textual function is well marked on each dimension, whereas the ideational component is never visibly marked, but is, of course, implicitly present because the text obviously aims at passing on factual information to the addressees. The individual dimensions operate in the following way: On the Medium dimension, we found that the text has a complex mode: written to be read as if heard. This mode acts in support of the interpersonal component of the text's function by promoting a direct involvement of the addressees, suggesting that the addresser is speaking to the addressees (i. e., implying his immediate presence). The interpersonal functional component is also supported by the dimension Participation because of the anticipated or implied addressee participation manifest in the frequent use of personal and possessive pronouns and the presence of addressee-directing utterances in the text. Similarly, on the dimension Social Role Relationship, the presence of structures showing a connotation of condescension and the insertion of a whole paragraph of addressee-related illustrations of facts also clearly support the interpersonal functional component. The Social Attitude dimension is marked for consultative-casual style, a style level suitable for informally passing on information to a lay public, i. e., specially geared to the addressees' assumed need of a colloquial presentation. This dimension therefore also filters into the interpersonal functional component. On the dimension Province, the attempt at dramatizing and personalizing scientific facts also promotes the interpersonal component by making the material attractive and palatable to the addressees.

2. ST and TT Comparison and Statement of Quality

Mismatches on the following dimensions have been discovered as a result of the analysis of TT and the comparison of ST and TT:

Medium:

TT has fewer features characterizing the spoken component of the complex medium written to be read as if heard:

a. TT lacks anacolutha: II_1, IV_1,

b. In two instances, TT lacks parenthetical and appositional structures which, in ST, express the type of afterthought or "in-between commentary", typical of the lack of premeditation in the spoken mode: $VIII_{2(3), 3(6)}$.

Participation:

TT appears to be less concerned with deliberately involving the addressee:

a. lack of personal pronoun we, i. e., lack of addressee - inclusion: IV_1, VII_2, $VIII_{3(5)}$,

b. lack of second person singular personal and possessive pronouns: $II_{1, 2, 3, 4}$. The use of wir (for you) in II_1 invites addressee participation less markedly. The use of Mensch (for you) in II_3 puts the utterance onto a more generalized, i. e., less personalized level, which is not desirable here,

c. absence of rhetorical, addressee-directing utterance: VIII_3 - the utterance in TT lacks the subtle overtones of the utterance in ST where the addressees are being warned against having a too facile approach to the subject matter.

Social Role Relationship:

TT does not exhibit ST's slightly condescending tone. Also, the relationship projected in TT is a more symmetrical one, witness the following linguistic means:

a. lack of connotation of condescension which we established to be present in ST: VII_2 - the phrase properly called is omitted in TT; VII_3 - whole utterance is ommitted in TT. This is perhaps the most striking illustration of the fact that the social role relationship as portrayed in TT is markedly different: the jovial, rather trivial remark in VII_3, which is clearly designed to make the addresser's special field palatable to the ignorant lay public, is omitted in TT. TT thus appears to indicate a more symmetrical relationship. $VIII_{3(5)}$ - ommission in TT of the personal pronoun, i. e., use of an impersonal es-structure; TT is therefore more neutral and less condescending. Further, the naive value judgement expressed in better is omitted and the meanings of better and more successful are collapsed into vorteilhafter.

Social Attitude:

TT's style level is, in a considerable number of instances, more formal:

syntactic mismatches:

a. lack of anacolutha and parenthetical structures (cf. above, Medium); II_2/II_4 - Derjenige des Affen, jene der Affen: demonstrative anaphoric pronoun marked [+formal] in German; III_2 - use of subjunctive in TT and of conjunction obschon, both of which are marked [+formal] ; use of past tense instead of present perfect, the former differing from the latter in terms of formality; presence of extensive prenominal modification in TT: in eine vom Dryopithecus abweichende Richtung, which renders TT more abstract and formal; IV_3 - das Fossil, als eine weitere Art von Dryopithecus abgetan: -ed participle clause in which the antecedent head is identical with the deleted subject of the -ed post-modifying clause. The participle is firmly linked with the passive voice, which makes the expression impersonal and [+formal] . ; VIII_5 - es wäre... gleichsetzen zu wollen: impersonal es- structure plus infinitive in TT, which is typical of a formal style level.

lexical mismatches:

$II_{4(5)}$ - this length makes an ape's face projecting ≠ die Länge der Molaren bedingt, dass: the structure is marked as [+formal] in German; $III_{2(3)}$ - So Lewis thought ≠ dies bewog (bewiegen is strongly marked as [+formal] in German); VII_2 - anything on the human side ≠

Arten mit Ansätzen von menschenartigen Merkmalen: TT's phrase is much more precise and formal; VIII_2 - evolution has reasons ≠ Die Evolution folgt einem Plan; VIII_7 - lichte Wälder, gewisse, teils: all of these items are marked [+formal] in German.

Province:

TT shows in many instances fewer traces of personalization, dramatization, and concretization through illustrations and imagery. TT is therefore less true to the Province of "popularized science text"; it is also less journalistically attractive, and less vague and imprecise in its descriptions of scientific facts. Consider the following mismatches:

syntactic mismatches:

a. lack of personal and possessive pronouns rendering the text less addressee-oriented (cf. above Medium),

b. TT lacks equivalent for be+Ving form, e.g., V+a modal adverbial such as gerade, nun, etc., thus failing to emphasize the process of discovery by a human being: V_1, VI_2, VII_3 (altogether omitted in TT),

c. dramatic quality achieved in ST through deletion of the definite article preceding a noun phrase in apposition is lost in TT: VII_1 (an equivalent structure in German is available).

lexical mismatches:

a. lack of scientifically imprecise words and phrases: II_1 - omission of an equivalent structure for these things in TT; II_3 - molar teeth ≠

Molaren, a scientific term in German (as opposed to the general term Backenzähne); VII_2 - anything on the human side ≠ Arten mit Ansätzen von menschenartigen Merkmalen (cf. above, Social Attitude); apes ≠ Affen und Menschenaffen,

b. lack of, or use of less evocative, figurative language: $III_{1(2)}$ - path diverging ≠ abweichende Richtung; IV_1 - tide of scientific opinion ≠ Meinungen der Wissenschaft; VI_1 - rescued... from burial ≠ verhinderte... dass: VIII_2 - Evolution has "reasons" ≠ Die Evolution folgt einem Plan: i. e., TT is far less personalized, Plan, in this case, being something pre-existent and impersonally fixed.

textual mismatches:

a. lack of double cleaving in TT which adds dramatic quality to the ST utterance, and lack of iconic linkage: I_1 - TT has foregrounded word-order only in the second part of the sentence, therefore the emphatic effect of iconic linkage is lost,

b. lack of equivalent dramatizing introductory formula in TT for V_1 - It happened that,

c. omission of German equivalent for the logical connector thus in VII_2, which adds to the utterance's dramatic effect (although it really lacks a logical foundation).

Overtly Erroneous Errors:

There is one mismatch of denotative meaning to be subclassified as a wrong selection: $II_{4(5)}$ - makes an ape's face projecting, yours is straighter ≠ bedingt, dass das Gesicht der Affen--im Vergleich zum menschlichen--anders ist.

Statement of Quality:

The comparison of ST and TT along the situational parameters shows that there are mismatches on all five parameters of language use. Our analysis of ST has shown that, while the interpersonal component of the textual function is marked on all dimensions, the ideational component is--although implicitly present--not specifically marked. This relative markedness of the two components is different in TT.

On the dimension Medium, we found that ST's mode written to be read as if heard is not always matched in TT, which appears to lack several "spoken mode elements". On this dimension, the interpersonal component is less marked, whereas the ideational component is strengthened because the informational content is transmitted more straightforwardly. Similarly, on Participation, TT appears to be less geared to elicit addressee participation; therefore, the interpersonal component is weakened while the ideational one is strengthened through a greater concentration on the information to be transmitted. On the dimension Social Role Relationship, the addresser's attitude towards the addressees appears to be less condescending, but more neutral and symmetrical. Again, the ideational component is stronger in that TT is more obviously designed to pass on factual information than to adapt the facts to the particular needs of the addressees.

On Social Attitude, the ideational functional component is again strengthened at the expense of the interpersonal one, since TT's style level is, in certain specified instances, less personalized and more formal.

On Province, TT appears to be less personalized, dramatized, and journalistically attractive than ST, but rather more precise and sober especially with respect to the use of scientific terms. Again, the interpersonal component of the textual function is violated while the ideational one is developed more strongly.

There is one overtly erroneous error, which detracts from the ideational component of passing on factual information.

Taken together, TT suffers from a distinct mismatch of both the interpersonal and ideational components of the textual function as revealed on all five dimensions of language use. The intention of the addresser to make his material attractive, interesting, and easily digestible for his addressees has not been realized in TT to the same degree as it has been in ST; the addresser's concern with passing on scientific facts is, on the other hand, clearly--and unwarrantedly--more visible in TT than in ST.

IV. TOURIST INFORMATION BOOKLET (ST German; TT English, see Appendix, pp. 297-303.

1. Analysis of ST and Statement of Function

Dimensions of language user:

(1) Geographical Origin: non-marked, Standard High German

(2) Social Class: non-marked, Educated Middle Class

(3) Time: non-marked, contemporary German

Dimensions of language use:

(1) Medium: simple: written to be read

syntactic means:

a. absence of anacolutha, elliptical clauses and contractions,

b. absence of contact parentheses and comment parentheses typical of the spoken mode.

lexical means:

a. absence of interjections, qualifying modal adverbials, spoken language markers like Sehen Sie, Wissen Sie, Hören Sie mal, etc., and other emotive subjectivity markers.

textual means:

a. the text is totally emic, lacking temporal, local, and personal deictic reference to the situation of utterance. Because the situation does not support the organization of the message, the text is highly elaborate and explicit.

(2) Participation: complex: predominantly monologous with a few traces of indirect, implied addressee participation.

syntactic means:

a. absence of first and second person personal and possessive pronouns making for a predominantly non-participatory type of text, with one exception: I_2 - sind uns bekannt, where, due to the inclusive wir, both addresser and addressees are being involved,

b. the attempt to elicit addressee participation is, however, noticeable in the presence of utterances displaying an illocutionary force of an indirect, subtle invitation to the addressees to look at Nürnberg's places of interest: VI_3 - ist... nachzuspüren: suggesting that addressees themselves explore these places; $VII_{1, 2, 3, 4}$ - the entire paragraph deals with the addressees as potential "guests" of the city: VIII_4 - Auf eine Spezialität ist die Gastronomie... preiswert essen und trinken; Illocutionary force: 'come, eat and drink here, meals and drinks are well worth their price; IX_2 - bieten... laden ein zu: illocutionary force of an indirect invitation to the addressees; X_2 - kann der Gast auf seine Rechnung kommen: praising the advantages of being a "guest" in Nürnberg results in an illocutionary force of an indirect invitation.

(3) Social Role Relationship

Symmetrical role relationship;

Position role of addresser: textwriter (anonymous).

Situational role of addresser: quasi-representative of the city of Nürnberg, and host to potential visitors.

The role relationship is an impersonal one, since the addresser does not betray his identity, and does not give specific identities to his addressees. This neutrality and impersonality, of course, widens the circle of potential visitors to Nürnberg. Addressees are thus the general-anonymous public potentially visiting the city or already in the city and eager to get to know it.

As indicated above (cf. Participation), there is a distinct attempt on the part of the addresser to make the addressees become visitors of the city of Nürnberg, or become convinced of its beauties. This intention is also given expression in the addresser's attempt to flatter the addressees by presupposing some cultural knowledge about Nürnberg on their part. Since it is quite likely that the addressees do not know anything about Nürnberg, they will be flattered by the implication that they do.

This description of the role relationship in this text is justified by the following instances in the text:

syntactic means:

a. absence of second person personal and possessive pronouns (cf. above Participation) promoting neutrality and impersonality of the text,

b. presence of utterances with an illocutionary force of indirect invitation (cf. above Participation) illustrating the addresser's attempt at persuading the addressees to visit Nürnberg,

c. use of indefinite article preceding proper name: IV_2 - eines Albrecht Dürer, eines Veit Stoss (glossed as 'somebody like'), which expresses the presupposition that the names are known to the addressees.

textual means:

a. in two instances, references to cultural figures and artifacts associated with Nürnberg belong to the theme of the utterance in which the reference occurs. Hence there is a presupposition that such cultural references are familiar to the addressees. This presupposition clearly flatters the addressees: I_3, V_3.

(4) Social Attitude: consultative-formal

syntactic means:

a. absence of elliptical clauses, anacolutha and contractions (cf. above Medium),

b. frequent use of s-genitive instead of prepositional phrase genitive, the former being marked [+formal] in contemporary German, e.g., I_2 - Lieder geistlichen und weltlichen Inhalts; II_1 - Nürnbergs Stadtantlitz; II_3 - Fülle reizvoller Kontraste; IV_2 - eines Albrecht Dürer; Baugesinnung dieser Tage,

c. presence of impersonal zu-infinitive structure: VI_3 - ist... nachzuspüren, marked [+formal] in German.

lexical means:

a. absence of subjectively qualifying modal adverbials, interjections, and other emotive subjectivity markers (cf. above Medium),

b. frequency of words and phrases marked [+formal] due to their usual occurrence in situations characterized by the social distance between the communication partners, e.g., I_6 - befindet sich im Besitz; II_1 - Stadtantlitz; ist... gezeichnet; II_3 - eindrucksvoller Spielarten; IV_2 - ihr kostbares Erbe; V_1 -Tand (=[+archaic]); V_2 - kündet von; VI_2 - bergen Kunstwerke; VII_2 - darein (=[+archaic]), cataphorically used with verbs that need an accusative object, IX_2 - entfalten, etc.

(5) Province

This is an excerpt from a tourist information booklet written by a professional script writer for the Verkehrsverein Nürnberg, a local tourist information centre, for the purpose of attracting tourists to Nürnberg by informing them about the characteristics of that city. The addresser gives the addressees an exclusively favourable impression of the city since it was his commission to do so. The result of these circumstances of production and of the textual Province features is a good measure of exaggeration and pretension--as in advertising--and this text has, of course, obvious affinities to advertisements. The following linguistic means characterize the text's Province:

syntactic means:

a. frequencies of superlatives, comparatives, and intensifiers: I_2 - über 4000; viele seiner Werke; II_1 - mehr als 900jährigen Geschichte; V_1 - in alle Land; V_3 - der erste Globus und die erste Taschenuhr; V_3 - nur einige bleibende Beispiele, a coquettish understatement suggesting that there are many more; VI_2 - von unschätzbarem Wert; VII_2 - ihren ganzen Ehrgeiz, etc.

lexical means:

a. use of figurative language--often cliché images--alliteration, rhyme, and lexical items marked [+emotive] or [+archaic] expressing the desire of the addresser to make the text attractive and "poetic":

- personification of Nürnberg throughout the text, i. e., use of the noun Nürnberg as subject of verbs that are normally used with [+human] subject noun phrases, e. g., VII_1 - Nürnberg verwöhnt seine Gäste;

- I_1 - Blütezeit; I_4 - Vaterstadt; II_1 - Stadtantlitz, Sonnenstrahlen und Stürmen einer mehr als 900jährigen Geschichte (imagery and alliteration); III_2 - sind Geist und Lebensstil vergangener Epochen lebendig (personification); V_3 - bieten nur einige bleibende Beispiele (alliteration); VII_2 - darein ([+archaic]); VIII_1 - mit lukullischen Köstlichkeiten, invoking the image of Lucullus, a Roman general famous for his luxurious and opulent meals, here pretentiously used, as the ensuing list of delicacies suggests, in fact, local dishes of a more frugal nature; VIII_3 - Duft der weiten Welt (cliché image taken from a

German cigarette commercial), etc. ,

b. preponderance of lexical items which have positive connotations.

textual means:

a. strong textual cohesion, which foregrounds the text such that its textual shape attracts the attention of the addressees, is achieved through the following devices of theme-dynamics and iconic linkage:

theme dynamics:

a. repetitions of lexical items: all paragraphs (except I) start with Nürnberg. See also I_1 - Blütezeit... Zeit... Zeit,

b. the contrasting "theme": "old versus new" expressed in various ways (e.g., Mittelalter und Neuzeit, Geschichte und Gegenwart) is carried through paragraphs I to VI,

c. all paragraphs (save I) start with short sentences which give a brief introductory presentation of a particular feature of Nürnberg, as the "theme" of the paragraph. The rest of the paragraph is then an elaboration of this "theme",

d. thematic movement organized in sequences of theme-rheme to ensure given-new ordering: I_{1-2}; I_{4-5}; II_{1-2}; VII_{2-3}; VIII_{3-4}.

iconic linkage:

a. II_2 - iconic linkage between three coordinated noun phrases. This structural parallelism also mirrors, on the content plane, the contrast between "old" and "new"; $II_3/V_3/VI_3/VII_3VIII_2$ - iconic linkage between two coordinated noun phrases: X_2- sei es... sei es; iconic linkage between two correlative clauses.

Statement of Function:

The function of the text consisting of an ideational and an interpersonal component may be summed up in the following way: the text's function is a) to inform the addressees about the characteristics of the city of Nürnberg, and b) to induce and persuade the addressees to come and see Nürnberg by describing its characteristics so as to impress and tempt.

This summary statement of the textual function has been derived through an investigation of the particular ways in which the dimensions contribute to the two functional components.

On the Medium dimension, the written to be read mode supports the ideational functional component by facilitating a condensed, complete, and premeditated information flow. On the dimension Participation, the predominantly monologous, non-participatory character of the text, which also allows for a fully premeditated, non-alternating, and well-organized flow of information, supports the ideational component as well. However, the interpersonal component is also supported on this dimension to a minor degree because of the addresser's attempt to elicit addressee participation through the use of some utterances displaying the illocutionary force of a subtle invitation. On the dimension Social Role Relationship, the impersonality of the relationship supports the ideational component of the text's function because the information flow is unimpeded by social considerations involving addresser and addressees. However, on the same dimension the attempts to persuade the addressees to come and see Nürnberg, and to flatter them clearly support the interpersonal functional component.

On the Social Attitude dimension, the consultative-formal style level seems to support the interpersonal functional component because, in the context of this text, this particular style level adds a special pseudo-poetic flavour to the text which is to impress the addressees. On the dimension Province, the frequent use of superlatives, comparatives, and intensifiers, of figurative language, rhetorical devices such as alliteration, and of the textual device of foregrounding, clearly contributes tomaking the text more convincing to the addressees, i. e., they support the interpersonal functional component. The ideational component is not visibly marked on this dimension but is, of course, implicitly present given the Province of this text as characterized above (p. 118).

2. ST and TT Comparison and Statement of Quality

Mismatches on the following dimensions have been discovered as a result of the analysis of TT and the comparison of ST and TT:

Participation:

TT shows fewer traces of an attempt to elicit addressee participation than ST: $VI_{3(2)}$ - ist dem zeitgenössischen Schaffen nachzuspüren ≠ contemporary art is produced and displayed: lack of illocutionary force of an invitation in TT; VII_3 - TT lacks equivalent for Gastfreundschaft, thus also losing the illocutionary force of persuading addressees to become "guests" of the city; VIII_4 - Auf eine Spezialität ist die Gastronomie... TT omits entire clause. Crucial is the omission of Gastronomie, which again shows that there is less of an attempt in TT to imply that addressees are potential guests of Nürnberg; IX_2 - bieten... laden... ein: No equivalent terms in TT; the utterance in TT lacks the illocutionary force of an invitation.

Social Role Relationship:

While maintaining the impersonality of the role relationship, TT fails to flatter the addressees in two instances, because the assumption of the addressees' knowledge of facts about Nürnberg has not been upheld in TT: I_1 - addition of and their best-known representative as an explanatory note to Hans Sachs; $V_{3(2)}$ - explanation in TT of Männleinlaufen and Englischer Gruss, i.e., TT lacks the presupposition of the addressees' knowledge and the resultant flattery of the addressees.

These two mismatches are examples of the case where a reference in ST to the particular cultural heritage of the source language community needs to be explained to the TT addressees, for whom this culture is alien. Therefore, these mismatches cannot be classed among covertly erroneous errors but must be regarded as changes necessitated by the differences in the cultural background between the two language communities (see below, Chapter VI, pp.196-201) for a more detailed discussion of cultural problems involved in the evaluation of translation adequacy).

Social Attitude:

TT appears to be less formal in certain instances, and less carefully designed to impress the addressees: I_4 - Vaterstadt ≠ home town: home town is too little foregrounded and too casual; II_2 - the pride of these Nurembergers: this phrase is too casual and even slightly derogatory (civic pride, for instance, would have been more accurate given the consultative-formal style level); $IV_{2(1)}$ - like that of Albrecht Dürer... for example Veit Stoss: both these phrases are more informal than the (foregrounded) German use of the indefinite article plus proper name; IV_2 - macht jedoch auch die Baugesinnung ... sichtbar ≠ a glance..makes it clear...that Nuremberg also keeps: greater informality in TT; VIII_1 - lukullische Köstlichkeiten ≠ local delicacies: the German phrase is more foregrounded and unusual; X_2 - sei es...sei es: this [+formal] correlative conjunction has no equivalent in TT's simple or.

Province:

As we have already noticed above on Social Role Relationship and Social Attitude, TT's overall tone is more sober and factual. TT also lacks ST's extensive use of figurative language, and it lacks the textual devices of foregrounding; as well as two instances of exaggeration by means of using intensifiers.

syntactic mismatches:

VII_2 - setzen ihren ganzen Ehrgeiz darein ≠ are eager to: lack of intensifier; X_3 - Grosstadt ≠ city: lack of intensifying adjective.

lexical mismatches:

II_2 - loss of personification of Halbmillionenstadt; $IV_{2(3)}$ - Die Stadt... macht... die Baugesinnung... sichtbar ≠ a glance... makes it clear that: Loss of personification of the city of Nürnberg; V_1 - Tand... Land ≠ wares... world: loss of rhyme in TT. This is a case of untranslatability, so this mismatch will not be regarded as an error. VII_1 - Loss of personification of Nürnberg; VII_2 - its citizens (instead of her citizens) is too sober and neutral and, again, misses out the personification of Nürnberg, which is a dominant trait in ST; VIII_1 - lack of personification of Nürnberg in TT; $VIII_{2(1)}$ - Geschichte und Geschichten gemacht: loss of pun in TT. This mismatch cannot be regarded as an error as in the translation of puns the limits of translatability are reached; VIII_3 - Duft der weiten Welt: this culture-specific allusion to a German advertising slogan cannot be rendered as such in TT. Again, this mismatch will not be regarded as an error; $VIII_{4(3)}$ - Auf eine Spezialität ist die Gastronomie besonders stolz: the entire clause is omitted in TT which results in a loss of the wordplay with Spezialität--a wordplay which is also possible in English. This omission clearly makes for a more sober and factual tone in TT; $IX_{2(4)}$ - Fächer ≠ range: loss of image; further, loss of personification of Innenhöfe, Ballsäle, Theater in TT; X_2 - vom frühen Abend bis spät in die Nacht ≠ far into the night: TT's phrase is less elaborate, i. e., shorter and more sober; X_2 - kann der Gast auf seine Rechnung kommen: a wordplay, whose loss in TT cannot be regarded as an error because of untranslatability.

textual mismatches:

I_2 - loss of theme-rheme sequence in TT resulting in lack of textual cohesion; I_{4-5} - total loss of textual cohesion in TT through a disruption of the theme-rheme sequence: in TT, there is no link at all between the poem mentioned in I_4 and the title quoted in I_5, whereas ST has a theme-rheme sequence plus an anaphoric demonstrative pronoun in I_5 to provide a linkage between I_4 and I_5; II_2 - lack of iconic linkage of noun phrases in TT; II_3 - lack of logical connector so and lack of iconic linkage of noun phrases; III_1 - omission in TT of paragraph-initial Nürnberg resulting in a loss of repetition, as all paragraphs (save I) start with Nürnberg; IV_1 - omission not only of paragraph-initial Nürnberg in TT, but of entire sentence which, in ST, repeats the contrasting "theme": "old versus new"; $VI_{3(2)}$ - loss of iconic linkage of noun phrases in TT.

Overtly Erroneous Errors:

There are three mismatches of the denotative meaning of ST and TT items to be subclassified as wrong selections: VII_2 - weltoffen ≠ man of the world: the English phrase has, apart from the intended meaning of 'cosmopolitan', an unwanted meaning component of 'being unshockable'; VIII_1 - mit lukullischen Köstlichkeiten ≠ with local delicacies (cf. above, mismatches on Social Attitude); X_2 - the contrast in German between Kneipe and Bar is not matched in TT by the contrast between pub and bar as these items are not in [(±) elegant] contrast in their denotative meanings. (Cocktail bar would have been more appropriate.)

Statement of Quality:

The comparison of ST and TT along the eight parameters has shown that there are mismatches on all parameters of language use except Medium. On Participation, TT appears to be less addressee-involving, which clearly detracts from the interpersonal functional component. On Social Role Relationship, TT is less potentially flattering to the addressees; again, the interpersonal functional component is violated. However, as we pointed out above (p. 124), this mismatch is an unavoidable one because of the existence of differences in the cultural heritage between the two language communities. The mismatch cannot therefore be regarded as an error.

On the dimension Social Attitude, TT appears to be less formal and less deliberately designed to impress the addressees. Again, the interpersonal functional component is violated.

By far the greatest number of mismatches occurred on Province, where we established that TT fails to use intensifiers, figurative language, and cohesion devices. These mismatches clearly also weaken the interpersonal functional component.

Taken together, as concerns the ideational functional component, TT seems to be deficient only in terms of the three overtly erroneous errors mentioned above. The interpersonal component, however, i. e., the attempt to induce addressees to come and see Nürnberg by describing its characteristics in an impressive, pleasing, and attractive manner, is violated on four dimensions in the instances specified above.

V. RELIGIOUS SERMON (ST German; TT English, see Appendix, pp. 304-13.

1. Analysis of ST and Statement of Function

Dimensions of language user:

(1) Geographical Origin: non-marked, Standard High German

(2) Social Class: non-marked, Educated Middle Class

(3) Time: non-marked, contemporary German

Dimensions of language use:

(1) Medium: complex: written to be spoken/written to be read as if heard, depending on whether the present form of the written text preceded or followed the original speech of which the text purports to be a record. If the text was written in its present format and read as such on a particular later date, then the text is clearly written to be spoken. However, in the event that the written format of the text was prepared after the spoken presentation, then the categorization written to be read as if heard applies.

There is an overall impression of spontaneity and non-premeditatedness. This impression has been achieved through the following linguistic means:

syntactic means:

a. use of a contact parenthesis V_4 - nicht wahr; a comment parenthesis VI_3 - wie es heute; and an interjection in apposition III_{13} - o Wunder, and presence of extraposited appositives giving the impression of "non-preparedness", which necessitated the addition of "afterthoughts", e.g., II_2 - am Telefon nämlich; VI_4 - weder durch die Fasnacht...; VI_5 - jetzt in...; VI_6 - wie wir es,...,

b. occurrence of anacolutha, e.g., II_2 - unterbricht und stört mich... etc.; III_9 - und so auch; III_{12} - mit ihm... nicht; III_{13} - und mit...,

V_7 - deine äussere; and elliptical clauses: III_2 - Gott? ; III_3 - Ja, Gott! IV_8 - ruft er... ; IV_9 - Alles in Allem tatsächlich... ; VI_{10} - Und darum...

c. frequency of clause-initial and resembling spoken narrative: e.g., $II_{6,7,8}$; III_5; IV_1,

lexical means:

a. frequency of qualifying modal adverbials, e.g., II_2 - wohl, gerade, einmal; II_6 - schon; II_7/III_6 - eben; III_5 - ja; III_{12} - freilich; V_6 - nun eben, etc.

textual means:

a. this is an etic text, marked by the presence of temporal, local, and personal deictics which link the text to the situation of production and reception:

- use of personal pronouns throughout the text,
- use of local deictics: V_3 - da draussen; V_6 - in diesem Hause; VI_6 - draussen in der deutschen Bundesrepublik; wir...in der lieben Schweiz; wir...in Basel,
- use of the definite article with names of specific Swiss phenomena pointing to the environment in which both addresser and addressees find themselves: VI_4 - die Fasnacht; die Mustermesse,
- use of temporal deictics: V_4 - jetzt; VI_4 - kürzlich,

b. ample use of repetition to provide redundancy, which marks the spoken mode (see below, p.134 Province for details).

(2) Participation: complex: monologue with anticipated involvement and participation of addressees who were present in the original communicative situation. The impression of the addressees' being constantly invited to participate--at least mentally--is reached through the following linguistic means:

syntactic means:

a. presence of direct address through the use of second person singular personal and possessive pronouns throughout the text, and presence of the vocative phrase: I_2 - liebe Brüder und Schwestern,

b. use of a contact parenthesis interspersed in a clause: V_4 - Aber, nicht wahr, du denkst jetzt... anticipating addressee response (cf. above, Medium),

c. quick alternation between declarative, interrogative, imperative, and exclamatory sentences. This frequent change strongly suggests addressee involvement and gives the impression of a dramatic dialogue, e.g., III_{1-5}; IV_{1-5}, IV_{8-11}.

(3) Social Role Relationship:

Asymmetrical role relationship: addresser has spiritual authority over the addressees.

Position role of the addresser: minister and teacher.

Situational role of the addresser: preacher visiting the inmates of a prison.

Despite the existing asymmetrical role relationship, the addresser does not always display the authority he has over the addressees; he sometimes tries to deliberately make this relationship more symmetrical by expressing his solidarity with the addressees, his sympathy for them, and his conviction that all men--including the prisoners--are equal before God.

syntactic means:

a. specific use of personal and possessive pronouns:

- use of first person singular personal pronoun, $II_{2,4,5,6,7}$: the addresser presents himself as an example and he deliberately puts himself on the same level as the prisoners,

- use of first person plural personal and possessive pronouns: III_6 - (du und ich)... wir alle (again stressing the equality of addresser and addressees by equating du and ich with wir alle); III_9 - mit uns (mit dir und mir); III_{10} - unser Vater, unser Bruder, etc.

- use of second person singular personal and possessive pronouns throughout the text: du is used in a peculiar way, as it really stands for the second person plural pronoun ihr, because of its lack of referential specificity. Du is used because it conveys a strong emotive connotation of brotherhood and community between each individual addressee, and the addresser,

b. the position role of minister and teacher is manifest in the particular illocutionary forces which utterances acquire in the text, e.g., those of explanation: $II_{3,5-8}$, III_{6-14}; assertion: IV_6, V_1; order: $IV_{4,5,11}$; $VI_{7,10}$; and consolation: $V_{3,8}$, $VI_{1,2}$,

lexical means:

use of particular formula of addressing the prisoners in which solidarity is expressed (cf. above Participation): I_2 - liebe Brüder und Schwestern.

(4) Social Attitude: consultative, i.e., the "highest" level of Joos' informal styles, a conversational, colloquial, addressee-involving style level.

syntactic means:

a. presence of contracted forms: II_3 - in unserm Text; III_{12} - mit unsrem Nächsten,

b. use of demonstrative pronouns, der, die, as substitutes for personal pronouns, which gives the text an informal, colloquial note: II_5 - aber der fragt nicht lange; III_6 - Der mich da anruft; VI_6 - die draussen.

c. use of contact and comment parentheses, anacolutha, elliptical clauses, and clause-initial and (cf. above Medium), all of which add to the conversational, "chatty" tone of the text.

lexical means:

a. frequency of qualifying modal adverbials (cf. above Medium) marking subjectivity and informality,

b. absence of lexical items marked [+formal]; especially noticeable is the absence of (Latin-based) religious terminology. Only those specifically religious terms which are readily understood by non-specialists are employed in the text.

(5) Province:

The Province of this text is that of a religious sermon delivered by a minister in a Basel prison and intended for the inmates of the prison. The following linguistic means were found to be characteristic of the emotive-expressive "language of religion" used in this text:

graphical means:

a. presence of capitalized words referring to deity, man as an individual, or humanity as a whole. Capitalization is also frequently used to emphasize particular lexical items, e.g., II_8 - das Eine und Einzige,

b. use of italics to emphasize certain words and phrases, e.g., III_3 - Gott; VI_3 - gemeinsame und allgemeine, and to give prominence to the excerpt from the Bible: I_1, II_1, V_1.

syntactic means:

a. exclusive use of the present tense to express the "eternal truth" of what is being stated,

b. frequency of the copula sein. This is typical of the multitude of existential, descriptively-identifying statements of a religious-philosophical nature: II_8, III_{6-14}, $IV_{7, 10, 11}$, etc.

c. presence of quick alternation between declarative, interrogative, imperative, and exlamatory sentences (cf. above, Participation). This achieves a dramatic and emotive effect.

d. occurrence of the sequence: demonstrative pronoun plus possessive pronoun as pre-head nominal modifiers: V_8 - diese deine persönliche Not... in dieser deiner besonderen Not. This structure is a means of achieving emotive emphasis.

lexical means:

a. use of specifically religious words and phrases throughout the text: Gott, der Herr aller Dinge, der Nächste, etc.,

b. presence of figurative language: VI_5 - wie in grossen Geschwüren; VI_6 - ein bisschen den Regenschirm aufspannen; and frequent use of intensifiers and superlatives: II_7 - eine einzige wirklich wichtige Geschichte; II_8 - das Letzte... das Erste... das Eine and Einzige; III_8 - die ganze Welt; III_{13} - in grosser Geduld...grosser Strenge; $IV_{6, 9}$ - tatsächlich, etc.

textual means:

presence of the particular religious trait of explaining, interpreting, and modifying a certain biblical "theme" which is introduced initially (I_1), and which runs like a unifying thread through the entire text. This phenomenon gives the text a particularly strong textual cohesion. In detail, the means of textual cohesion and, in the case of this particular text, of emphasis, include the following:

theme dynamics:

a. repetition of lexical items which occur in the excerpt from the Bible, and which act as "key words" with vastly different collocational potential and rich connotations. The repeated employment of these key words throughout the text facilitates a full exploitation of their various meanings: anrufen: $II_{1, 2, 4, 7, 8}$; $III_{6, 14}$; $IV_{1, 9, 11}$

Not: entire paragraphs V and VI,

b. frequent use of paraphrase with partial synonymy: III_4 - so viel gebraucht... so abgegriffen; III_{13} - nicht fallen lässt.. nicht entrinnen lässt, nicht loswerden... nicht abspeisen; IV_8 - sagt er uns, ruft er uns zu; $VI_{8/9}$ - geht dich... an... bist auch in... gehörst auch dazu,

c. presence of emphatic, foregrounded word order to mark the theme of a clause: II_7; $IV_{4, 5, 6, 11}$,

d. use of cleaving to achieve emotive emphasis of a particular clausal element: $III_{6, 7, 9, 13, 14}$; V_5; VI_{3-6},

e. frequency of cataphoric referencing, also rendering the text both more cohesive and emphatic, e.g., III_6 - der... das ist der Andere; III_7 - der, dem; III_8 - ihm, der; III_9 - der, der es; IV_9 - dieses Eine; VI_2 - es; VI_3 - das ist... dass, etc.,

iconic linkage:

III_{10-14} - iconic linkage of subject and copula in five sentences: er ist; IV_{11} - iconic linkage between four clauses; $VI_{5/6}$ - iconic linkage between main clauses followed by a relative clause, including word-for-word repetition of lexical items: Sie ist eine Not; VI_5 - iconic linkage between adverbials of place: jetzt in.

Statement of Function

The function of the text consisting of an interpersonal and an ideational component may be summed up in the following way: the addresser's main intention is to affect or change the state of mind and the behaviour of the addressees by consoling, comforting, moving them, and by converting them to his own religious beliefs. In trying to do this, the addresser also imparts religious knowledge to the addressees.

The interpersonal functional component is the dominant one in this text, being strongly marked on all the dimensions of language use. The ideational functional component, while implicitly present, is never specially marked. The individual dimensions operate in the following way: On the dimension Medium, the written to be spoken/written to be read as if heard mode, which accounts for the text's apparent spontaneity, immediacy and non-premeditatedness, clearly supports the interpersonal functional component. On the dimension Participation, the addresser's frequent attempts at involving the addressees also obviously supports the interpersonal functional component. On the dimension Social Role Relationship, we have shown that the addresser, on the one hand, attempts to underplay the existent asymmetrical role relationship as evidenced in the particular use of pronouns and formulae of address in the text, and that he, on the other hand, fully uses his authority in order to instruct, explain, give orders, assert and console (witness the variety of types of illocutionary acts performed in the text). Given this description, the dimension clearly operates in support of the interpersonal functional component.

The predominance of a consultative style level on Social Attitide--a conversational, addressee-involving style level--also supports the interpersonal functional component. Lastly, on the dimension Province, the presence of intensifiers and superlatives, of simulated dramatic dialogues, and of manifold devices for achieving textual cohesion and emotive emphasis, all seem to act in support of the interpersonal component as well. The text is thus clearly designed to produce an emotional effect on the addressees.

2. ST and TT Comparison and Statement of Quality

Mismatches on the following dimensions have been discovered:

Medium:

Exclusive use in TT of uncontracted forms of negation, which makes the text less adequate for the written to be spoken/written to be read as if heard mode. Lack of anacoluthon: II_2. The etic character of the text is not preserved in TT in one instance: VI_4 - the translations of the terms Fasnacht and Mustermesse (carnival and trade fair) do not make it clear that the terms are deictic ones pointing to locally known events. Leaving the German terms and adding an explanatory footnote would have been more appropriate in that it would have preserved the text's "local situatedness".

Social Role Relationship:

The addresser's attempt to equalize the asymmetrical role relationship by expressing his solidarity with the addressees through the use of the solidarity pronoun du which is, in German, in opposition to Sie, is not as noticeable in TT because the English pronoun you cannot specify a marked solidarity relationship. This mismatch cannot, of course, be regarded as an error because it is due to differences in the two language systems.

Social Attitude:

TT appears to be more formal in a number of instances:

syntactic mismatches:

a. use of uncontracted forms of negation with not which adds to the formality of the text (cf. above Medium),

b. lack of anacoluthon II_2 (cf. above Medium).

lexical mismatches:

a. modal adverbials used in TT are sometimes more formal than their "equivalents" in ST: $II_{6(7)}$ - was könnte ich schon für ihn tun ≠ what indeed could I: the use of indeed in post-position is more rhetorical and formal than ST's conversational, colloquial sequence (What could I really do for him? might be more adequate in terms of formality); III_6 - der eben ganz anders ist ≠ who is indeed utterly different: Indeed in collocation with utterly marks this phrase as slightly stilted and certainly more formal than the conversational German clause; IV_1 - eben er ≠ this very one; TT is again too rhetorical and formal (He himself might have been more adequate given ST's level of formality),

b. other lexical mismatches include the following: $II_{2(3)}$ - fängt an ≠ begin + $V_{infinitive}$, which is more formal than, e.g., start + V-ing (start asking me would then have been a more adequate alternative); III_8 - Mücke ≠ gnat: The English word is rare and foregrounded, thus not adequate for a "normal", conversational style level; III_{13} - lieb hat und behält ≠ loves and sustains: The English expression is too deliberately "biblical" and pompous, thus again not adequate for the desirable conversational style; V_4 - Aber, nicht wahr, du denkst jetzt ≠ But is it not the case that: The English clause is far too formal (alternative: But aren't you now); VI_4 - Olympische Spiele ≠ Olympiad: The English term is foregrounded and more formal (Olympic Games, the non-foregrounded term would have been more adequate); VI_6 - ein bisschen den Regenschirm aufspannen ≠ spread out the umbrella a little: The English expression is unnatural to the point of bizarreness (a more conversationally natural phrase would be: put up your umbrella a little).

Province:

lexical mismatches:

VI_3 - ihre gemeinsame und allgemeine Not ≠ this its common and general trouble: Both gemeinsam and allgemein have greater connotative and emotive value than common and general (suggested alternative: collective and universal),

textual mismatches:

a. lack of devices of theme dynamics: lack of repetition: III_8 - ohne den Alles nicht wäre und auch du wärst: Lack of repetition of equivalent of copula sein in TT; $III_{9, 12}$ - gut meint und gut macht/gut meinen und machen ≠ means well and does good, mean well or do good: Lack of repetition of good in TT; lack of theme-rheme sequence: $II_{7(8)}$, $IV_{5, 6, 11(12)}$,

b. lack of iconic linkage: $IV_{11(11, 12)}$: TT lacks the structural parallelism in the last two clauses, such that the pattern of four structurally parallel clauses (with foregrounded word order) is disrupted in TT.

Overtly Erroneous Errors:

There are two mismatches of the denotative meaning of ST and TT items, to be subclassified as wrong selection: IV_8 - was aber sagt er uns, ruft er uns zu ≠ But what does he say to us if he calls us?:

if should be replaced by when. The use of if destroys the immediacy and strong likelihood of God's calling man. ST presupposes that God calls; TT expresses God's calling in the form of a conditional clause which destroys this presupposition. III9 - gut meint ≠ means well: Mean well is used in English to signal someone's good intention when this intention is in contrast to an inadequate achievement. Therefore, a possible implication of the use of the expression God means well is that he, in fact, treats us badly. The whole tenor of ST suggests, however, that this is not part of the addresser's intention (suggested alternative: (the Lord) wants what is best for us and does what is best for us, which also achieves the desirable repetition).

Statement of Quality

The comparison of ST and TT along the eight situational dimensions has shown that there are relatively few mismatches on the dimensions Medium, Social Role Relationship, and Province, and a considerable number of mismatches on Social Attitude.

On Medium, TT appears to be less "spoken" than ST, i. e., in a few instances, the emotive effect of (simulated) spontaneity and ad-hoc oral formulation is lost in TT. This deficiency detracts from the interpersonal functional component. On Social Role Relationship, the non-availability of a direct equivalent of the [+intimate] German du in English because of system differences between the two languages also affects the interpersonal functional component: TT appears to be less overtly marked for a relationship of solidarity. TT also exhibits less clearly the addresser's attempt to convert the existing asymmetrical relationship into a symmetrical one. On the dimension Social Attitude, we found that TT's style level is, in a considerable number of instances, more formal than ST's. The interpersonal effectiveness of the text is again potentially weakened because of the distant and impersonal nature of a formal style level. On Province, we demonstrated that TT is, in certain instances, less foregrounded, exhibiting to a lesser degree the emphatic effects displayed in ST. The lack of repetition, of foregrounded word order and of iconic linkage also detract from the interpersonal functional component by clearly lessening the potential emotive impact of the text.

The ideational functional component has been violated in TT only through the presence of the two overtly erroneous errors. The strongly marked interpersonal component, however, has been violated on four dimensions of language use in the instances specified above.

VI. POLITICAL SPEECH (ST English; TT German, see Appendix, pp. 314-21.

1. Analysis of ST and Statement of Function

Dimensions of language user:

(1) Geographical Origin: non-marked, Standard British English

(2) Social Class: non-marked, Educated Middle Class

(3) Time: non-marked, contemporary English

Dimensions of language use:

(1) Medium: complex: written to be spoken/written to be read as if heard, see description of this medium under Religious Sermon (above, p.129). In the present text, the following linguistic means are used to mark this medium:

syntactic means:

a. presence of an elliptical sentence: II_2,

b. use of contact and comment parentheses creating an impression of spontaneity and subjectivity: I_2 - believe me; III_1 - and I know you will not; V_5 - I won't say; V_8 - I will not say,

c. presence of sentences featuring several either syndetically or asyndetically coordinated (often elliptical) clauses. Such structural organization resembles the loosely additive clause linkage typical of the spoken mode, in particular the public address, in which building clause on clause and phrase on phrase for a cumulative effect is a common rhetorical feature: I_2, II_1, IV_3, $V_{1,6,8}$.

textual means:

a. this is an etic text, marked by the use of personal and temporal deictics which link the text to the situation of utterance:

- use of first person singular personal pronoun I and second person plural personal pronoun <u>you</u> throughout the text,

- use of a deictic temporal adverbial: I_1/II_1 - <u>now</u>,

b. use of repetition to provide redundancy--typical of the spoken mode (cf. description under <u>Province</u> below, p. 150).

<u>(2) Participation:</u> complex: monologue with calculated, anticipated addressee participation. The addressees were present in the original communication situation; in the text, they are being constantly and directly involved by the addresser. This can be seen by the use of the following linguistic means:

<u>syntactic means</u>:

a. presence of direct address forms, i.e., second person plural personal and possessive pronouns, e.g., I_2, III_1, V_2, etc.,

b. use of first person plural personal and possessive pronouns <u>we</u> or <u>our</u> as "inclusive" terms to achieve addressee involvement, e.g., II_1, III_4, $V_{1,3,4}$, etc.,

c. presence of simulated dialogue to anticipate and direct addressee response. The individual addressees are being deliberately used as "fictus interlocutor"--I_2--and, in certain instances, the addressees' desirable beliefs and behaviour are explicitly stated: III_1, $IV_{1,2,3}$, $V_{2,8}$.

(3) Social Role Relationship:

Asymmetrical Role Relationship: addresser has political and administrative authority over addressees by virtue of being the Prime Minister of Great Britain and the addressees being citizens of that country. The addresser has also the moral and military authority of a leader of a country at war.

Position role of the addresser: Prime Minister and military leader of a country at war, of which the addressees are citizens.

Situational role of the addresser: Visitor to a town of which the addressees are inhabitants and public speaker delivering an address in front of the town hall.

In order to underplay his leadership, the addresser identifies with his audience, i.e., he deliberately tries to downplay the existing asymmetrical relationship stressing his solidarity with the addressees. The addresser attempts to create in the addressees positive sentiments about the war by directing their attentions and emotions to a cause which they are morally obliged to pursue as fellow countrymen (fellow countrymen of the addresser who already pursues this cause). The addresser's dual role as both leader and fellow countryman is expressed by the following linguistic means:

syntactic means:

a. close juxtaposition of first person singular, second person plural, and first person plural personal and possessive pronouns plus a number of universal pronouns such as: all, all of us, everyone of you, etc. to create an impression of togetherness, solidarity, and of belonging to "one great family", suggesting that the addressees are members of that family, and that their contribution to the efforts of that "family" are needed. The pronoun we is an "inclusive" term standing for all Englishmen over and above the addresser and the addressees: I_2 - all, I, you, everyone of you; II_1 - we, I, our; III_1 - I, you, us (shift within one single sentence): V_5 - we, our, all of us, I,

b. the role of leader is expressed in utterances with the illocutionary force of an order or exhortation: $III_{1,4}$; $IV_{1,2,3}$,

c. the addresser's attempt at urging the addressees to keep up their morale is expressed in utterances with the illocutionary force of a promise: I_2, IV_3, V_8 or of an act of flattery: I_2, $IV_{2,3}$, V_1.

lexical and syntactic means:

a. use of a consultative-formal style level (cf. below Social Attitude) to stress the addresser's position role as leader.

(4) Social Attitude: consultative-formal, a rhetorical, slightly pompous style level with a very few casual interspersions, e.g., I_2 - doing their bit; V_5 - I won't say.

syntactic means:

a. absence of contractions (one exception, see above: V_5 - won't), non-deletion of prepositions or prenominal modifiers in conjoining: I_2 - in the air... in the coal mines; IV_2 - upon our strong right arms, upon our... upon our; V_6 - the cause of freedom and of justice,

c. propensity for "long-windedness", i.e., deliberate (sometimes tautological) explicitness: I_2 - each and everyone; II_1 - the month of November; III_1/IV_1 - the good fortune that has come to us/good tidings came to us (instead of: our good fortune/good tidings for us); V_4 - leaving the entire burden to the borne by the Russians (instead of leaving... to the Russians); the whole of this year; V_5 - we are all of us,

d. extremely long sentences revealing careful planning for rhythmical effects: I_2, II_1, $V_{1,8}$,

e. frequency of passive and impersonal constructions: I_1, III_3, IV_2, $V_{1,3,4,8}$.

lexical means:

a. use of (often Latin-based) words and phrases foregrounded for non-everyday use, e.g., I_2 - glorify, dignify; II_1 - victorious, redoubtable blows; efforts crowned with a considerable measure of success; IV_1 - rejoice at, good tidings; IV_3 - virtues which our island race has cultured and nurtured; V_8 - inevitably and inexorably forward to victory.

(5) Province:

The province of this text is that of an exhortatory, persuasive and morale-boosting speech delivered by a political leader, in time of war, to the civilian population of an English town.

syntactic means:

a. use of utterances with an illocutionary force of exhortation, (cf. Social Role Relationship above),

b. use of present perfect tense for past time reference throughout the text. This tense stresses the current relevance of what is reported by the addresser, thus adding to the emotive force of his statements,

c. presence of the rhetorical device of cumulatively stringing together a series of (either syndetically or asyndetically coordinated) clauses in one single sentence, a device for achieving an emotive effect (cf. Medium above),

lexical means:

a. frequent use of value adjectives and nouns, which are often vague and abstract, to suit the exhortatory and persuasive intent of the addresser: I_2/II_2 - great; III_4 - strength; IV_2 - strong, honest, hard-working, courage; IV_3 - virtue; V_5 - cause; V_6 - freedom, justice, mercy, tolerance, iron-bound tyranny, weak, strong, etc.,

b. use of a euphemistic phrase, designed to belittle the hardships of war: II_1 - this present unpleasantness,

c. frequency of intensifiers, comparatives, and superlatives:

I_2 - all, greatest, ever; II_1 - a good deal, better, considerable; III_1 - harder; III_2 - most tense; III_4 - all our strength; IV_2 - the whole course; IV_3 - many, all; V_1 - very hard fighting; V_4 - so much fighting, entire, immense, the whole of... a large part of, etc.

d. use of figurative language: I_2 - one great family, rowing my weight in the boat; IV_3 - virtues which our island race has cultured and nurtured; V_1 - the violence and military power of the enemy has been beaten down and driven into the sea; V_4 - burden to be borne by the Russians; V_6 - iron-bound tyranny; V_8 - the fruits of victory.

textual means:

creation of strong textual cohesion by means of devices of theme-dynamics, iconic linkage, and logical clause connection. This textual cohesion is designed to heighten the emotive effect of the text on the addressees.

theme dynamics:

a. repetition of lexical items which are key-words or "themes":

- paragraphs I and II start with now,

- I_2 - all; $II_{1,2}$ - month; IV_2 - we count upon our; IV_3 - virtues; V_5 - defending; $V_{6,7,8}$ - cause; V_8 - world,

b. use of paraphrase with partial synonymy for emotive emphasis, e. g., I_2 - standing together, helping each other, taking their share, all... each... every one; doing their bit, bearing their part, bearing his or her part, rowing... weight in the boat; II_1 - affairs have prospered, been victorious, etc.

iconic linkage:

I_2 - iconic linkage of elliptical clauses: some in the air, some in the coal mines... some in the homes; II_1 - iconic linkage of prepositional phrase in which our; IV_2 - iconic linkage of prepositional phrase upon our; V_5 - iconic linkage of main clauses they are... we are; V_6 - iconic linkage of main clauses: that cause... that cause; $V_{7/8}$ - iconic linkage of main clauses: That is... That is.

logical clause connection:

frequent use of the adversative conjunction but to highlight contrasts, and, specifically, to introduce the main exhortatory import of the speech in contrast to information which might produce undesirable attitudes (e.g., relaxation of effort): II_1, III_1, IV_1, V_{1-5}.

Statement of Function

The function of the text consisting of an interpersonal and an ideational component may be summed up in the following way: the addresser's intention is (a) to inform the addressees about the course of the war in which their country is currently engaged, and, more importantly, (b) to express the addresser's personal views and feelings about this war, and to affect a change in the addressees' behaviour such that they display a greater willingness to endure the war and make sacrifices for their country.

The interpersonal functional component is strongly and exclusively marked on the situational dimensions; the ideational component is never overtly marked but is, of course, latently present in that the addresser does impart factual information to the addressees in the text. The individual dimensions were found to operate in the following way:

On the dimension Medium, the deliberate creation of an impression of spontaneity and subjectivity supports the interpersonal functional component, i. e., the text gains in emotiveness and direct appeal. On Participation, the addresser's frequent attempts to involve the addressees--especially by using a simulated dialogue--also support the interpersonal functional component.

On Social Role Relationship, the presence of utterances with an illocutionary force of exhortation, flattery or promise as well as the specific way the personal and possessive pronouns are being employed in the text clearly operate in support of the interpersonal functional component. Similarly, on Social Attitude, the presence of a formal "pompous" style level which is used to impress the addressees also supports this component.

On the dimension Province, the frequent use of value adjectives and nouns, of comparatives, superlatives, and intensifiers, as well as the deliberate employment of the textual devices of repetition, paraphrase with partial synonymy, iconic linkage, and clausal linkage with the adversative but to create emotive contrast--all of these features act together to support the interpersonal functional component.

2. ST and TT Comparison and Statement of Quality

Mismatches on the following dimensions have been discovered following the analysis of TT and the comparison of ST and TT:

Medium:

In a few places, TT exhibits fewer features of the spoken mode: II_1 - omission of a German equivalent for now as temporal deictic marker indicating the time of utterance; $II_{2(4)}$ - omission of elliptical sentence in TT; III_1 - interspersed contact parenthesis and I know... is broken up in TT, i. e., part of the parenthetical structure has been integrated into the main clause. The impression of ad-hoc formulation and spontaneity is thus lessened.

Social Role Relationship:

In a few instances, TT appears to be stressing solidarity and togetherness to a lesser degree than ST. TT also lacks addressee flattery in some instances: $I_{2(3)}$ - all doing their bit ≠ alle tun ihr kleines Stück Arbeit: The original connotation of smallness of the word bit is, to a large extent, no longer vigorous in the set collocation do one's bit. In the German clause, however, the notion of smallness is stressed through the use of the word klein; thus the relative insignificance of the addressees' contribution is highlighted. The German phrase therefore works against the addresser's attempt to flatter the addressees (*Jeder tut das Seine* would be a more appropriate alternative); $I_{2(3)}$ - *Am I rowing my weight in the boat* ≠ *Habe ich zumindest das getan was ich tun muss?*: There is an (undesirable) connotation of an external force or constraint in TT because of the use of a modal auxiliary of obligation, and the use of the downtoner *zumindest*. Therefore, this expression also acts against the addresser's attempt to flatter the addressees; $I_{2(4)}$ - *bearing their part* ≠ *hat... seine Pflicht getan*: *Pflicht* has the (undesirable) connotation of an imposed duty, which is not compatible with the addresser's intention of identification with the addressees and of boosting their self-confidence.

Further, throughout the text, the addresser's effort of showing solidarity is counteracted by the employment in TT of the distant "power-pronoun" *Sie* as opposed to *du/ihr*. Since there is no obligatory distinction between equivalent pronouns in English, ST is less explicitly distant but rather ambiguous as to the presence of "power" or "solidarity" pronouns.[1] The choice of *ihr* in TT would have been even less appropriate given the lack of intimacy between the addressees and the addresser. Since this mismatch is due to system differences between the two languages, it cannot be treated as an error.

---

[1]These terms were coined by Brown and Gilman (1960).

Social Attitude:

TT is less formal and rhetorically pompous in a few instances: $II_{1(2)}$ - month of fogs and gloom ≠ nebliger und düsterer Monat (ein düsterer Nebelmonat would be a more appropriate alternative); $V_{2(3)}$ - I do not doubt of ≠ Ich zweifle nicht an (a more appropriate alternative would be ich hege keinen Zweifel an, which matches the level of formality better than the everyday word zweifeln); $V_{4(6)}$ - the entire burden to be borne ≠ die gesamte Last den Russen überliessen (die gesamte Bürde die Russen alleine tragen lassen would have been more adequately formal).

Province:

syntactic mismatches:

IV_1 - use of a hypothetical if-clause in ST in keeping with the addresser's intention of preparing the addressees for impending hardship by deliberately presenting good news as being remote. In TT, both the use of the present tense and the omission of an equivalent word for unexpected act against an adequate expression of this intention;

- frequent use of past tense in TT for ST's present perfect tense, which has the disadvantage of losing the connotation of current relevance intended in ST as a stimulans for future efforts to be made by the addressees: $II_{1, 2(3, 4)}$, $IV_{2, 3}$, $V_{4(6)}$.

lexical mismatches:

I_2 - one great family ≠ einegrosse Familie: ST stresses the idea of unity, i. e., the fact that the people are "one" despite great diversity. The indefinite article in TT is not sufficient for expressing this connotation (eine einzige grosseFamilie would be more adequate);

$I_{2(3)}$ - Am I rowing my weight in the boat? ≠ Habe ich zumindest das getan,was ich tunmuss?: Loss of figurative language; $II_{1(3)}$ - our kith and kin ≠ unsere Verwandten: TT's expression is too little foregrounded and thus less emotively effective (Fleisch und Blut would be a more adequate alternative).

textual mismatches:

$I_{2(4)}$ - bearing their part, each and every one bearing his or her part ≠ hat jeder seine Pflicht getan: Omission of repetition and paraphrase in TT; II_1 - TT lacks repetition of paragraph-initial now; IV_2 - TT lacks repetition of an equivalent expression for we count upon;

$V_{6(8)}$ - TT omits double repetition of an equivalent expression for That cause is the cause (e. g., DieseSache ist) using a slightly different phrase: es ist die Sache, although in V_9 and V_{10} the clause is repeated as Das ist die Sache. The emotive effect of a fourfold repetition is thus lost in TT.

Overtly Erroneous Errors:

There are two mismatches of the denotative meaning between

an ST and a TT item, subclassified as a wrong selection of a TT element and a wrong combination of TT elements; $V_{1(2)}$ - there are still twenty miles to go ≠ zwanzig Meilen haben wir noch zu gehen: The English verb go has a much wider semantic coverage than the German verb gehen, which is here restricted to the meaning 'go on foot'. To match the generality of go, verbs like zurücklegen or überwinden might have been more adequately chosen, or, in this context, a clause like Wir sind noch zwanzig Meilen von unserem Ziel; the violence and military power of the enemy has been...driven into the sea ≠ die Gewalt und militärische Stärke des Feindes...gebrochen ist, bis er in die See getrieben wurde.

Further, there is one case of a breach of the target language system, a case of ungrammaticality: V_6 - In diesem Monat...da war es ein Gefühl der Freude: This construction is only possible in German as a main clause in a cleft sentence, e.g., da war es ein Gefühl der Freude, welches sie anspornte: As it stands, the clause in the text is not followed by a relative clause and is thus ungrammatical.

Statement of Quality:

The comparison of ST and TT along the situational dimensions has shown that there are very few mismatches on Medium, Social Attitude, and Social Role Relationship, but more numerous mismatches on Province.

On Medium, TT was shown to be less close to the spoken mode than ST in three instances. In these instances, TT loses the emotive effect of simulated spontaneity, which clearly detracts from the interpersonal functional component. On Social Attitude, TT appears, in very few instances, to be less formal and rhetorically pompous, i. e., less designed to impress the addressees, and on Social Role Relationship, the addresser's attempt to stress his solidarity with the addressees and to flatter them is in a few instances less pronounced in TT. On both dimensions, the interpersonal component is clearly violated. The more numerous mismatches on Province, i. e., omission of figurative language, repetitions, and iconic linkage also detract from the interpersonal functional component.

The ideational component of the text's function which is not overtly marked on any dimension is only violated in two instances, i. e., through the overtly erroneous mismatches of the denotative meanings of ST and TT items. The strongly marked interpersonal component is, however, as we have seen, violated on four dimensions of language use in the manner specified above.

VII. MORAL ANECDOTE (ST German; TT English, see Appendix pp. 322-27.

1. Analysis of ST and Statement of Function

Dimensions of language user:

(1) Geographical Origin: non-marked, Standard High German

(2) Social Class: non-marked, Educated Middle Class

(3) Time: Early nineteenth century. The text was written in 1804. It is marked for temporal provenance in the following way:

syntactic means:

a. use of [+archaic] prepositions and conjunctions, e.g., III_1 - traf ... an dem Ackergeschäft an; III_2 - um 15 Kreuzer arbeite(n); V_2 - auf dass es dir,

b. use of the present subjunctive which is more infrequently used in contemporary German: I_4, III_2, IV_6, V_2,

c. use of future tense where present tense is more common in contemporary German: III_7, IV_{10},

d. use of demonstrative pronoun with anaphoric reference instead of personal pronoun which would be more typical in modern German: $IV_{1, 10}$,

e. use of a premodified nounphrase in the genitive case: I_4 - der Eltern Segen und Fluch,

f. substitution of the indefinite pronoun alle for jede: IV_6,

g. use of the second person plural personal pronoun in the accusative Euch as form of address.

lexical means:

frequency of [+archaic] lexical items and collocations, e.g., II_1 - Beherzigung; III_1 - Landmann, III_2 - Taglöhner; III_4 - Zwilchrock; III_5 - Dritteil, etc.

textual means:

use of indefinite cataphoric pronoun es: I_4, $III_{3,4}$ which is not common in contemporary German.

Dimensions of language use:

(1) Medium: simple: written to be read

syntactic means:

absence of anacolutha, elliptical clauses, contact and comment parentheses marking spoken language.

lexical means:

absence of interjections, qualifying modal adverbials, and spoken language signals like also, nun, etc.

textual means:

a. the text has a well-planned, logical structure: a frame (I, II, V) and two illustrative anecdotes (III, IV), which reveals the kind of premeditation typical of the written mode,

b. the text is emic, i. e., determined exclusively through text-immanent criteria. The text is thus independent of the enveloping situation of production and reception; also, as a product of fiction, the text creates its own timeless reality.

(2) Participation: complex: monologue with several cases of anticipated and directed addressee reactions.

syntactic means:

a. presence of two interrogative sentences: III_8 and V_1 and one imperative sentence: V_2, all directly involving the addressees,

b. indirect involvement of the addressees through the use of the impersonal pronoun man and the "inclusive" first person plural pronoun wir pointing to the universal relevance of the tales and, therefore, also including the addressees. This analysis is supported by the fact that the addresser presents the anecdotes as illustrations of a generally valid truth--a common trait in folk tales, e.g., I_1 - gar oft; I_4 - was gesagt wird und geschrieben ist; II_1 - unter anderen zwei Erzählungen.

(3) Social Role Relationship:

Asymmetrical role relationship: addresser assumes moral authority over the addressees.

Position role of the addresser: teacher and clergyman.

Situational role of the addresser: writer of didactic, moralizing tales.

The addresser tries to improve the moral behaviour of the addressees by providing them with examples of the moral behaviour of other people.

lexical means:

a. frequent use of value adjectives in the two anecdotes in order to cast moral judgement on the characters portrayed, thus explicitly revealing the role of "moral teacher": III_1 - einen fleissigen und frohen Landmann; III_4 - der brave Mann; III_6 - dem guten Fürsten; III_8 - artig gesagt und noch edler und schöner; III_9 - Rechtschaffenheit, wackeren; IV_3 - undankbaren; IV_4 - dem armen alten Greis; IV_7 - Murrkopf; IV_{10} - kalt und bösherzig.

textual means:

a. overall organization of the text into a frame and two anecdotes. The first part of the frame contains explicitly moralizing statements (see especially the sententious I_1) as well as instructions as to how the addressees ought to react to the ensuing two anecdotes: II_1.

Towards the end of the first anecdote, the addresser puts a rhetorical question to the addressees thus guiding their moral judgement. In the second part of the frame, the addressees are being questioned as to the nature of the lesson to be learned from the anecdotes, and a direction is given as to their future moral behaviour: $V_{1, 2}$.

(4) Social Attitude: consultative. A conversational style, designed to match the way the addressees would normally speak in everyday conversations.

syntactic means:

a. presence of direct speech: $III_{4, 5, 7}$; $IV_{9, 10}$.

lexical means:

a. absence of words and phrases marked either [+formal] or [-formal], typical of this "neutral" style. Preponderance of normal, everyday conversational expressions.

(5) Province

"Kalendergeschichte" ("Calendar-story"), written in 1804 for the Badischer Landkalender. (Later, in 1811, also published in Hebel's Schatzkästlein des Rheinischen Hausfreundes.) Since the fifteenth century, a "Kalender" has been a popular book with the lower, uneducated classes of people for which the "Kalender" frequently was the only book with which they came into contact. A "Kalender", apart from listing days, weeks, and months, also contained the so-called "Kalendergeschichte" or "Anekdote" (moral anecdote), i. e., a short, mostly moralizing, didactic tale. A moral anecdote was expressly designed to pass moral knowledge to the readers.

lexical means:

a. use of [+archaic] lexical items and collocations marking the Province as one which is no longer current (cf. above Time),

b. frequency of value adjectives typical of the Province of moral anecdote (cf. above Social Role Relationship).

syntactic means:

consistent use of the present tense in the two parts of the didactic frame to express the universal truth of the statements.

textual means:

presence of strong textual cohesion achieved through the following devices:

a. use of a didactic frame to envelop the moral "lessons" proper (cf. above Social Role Relationship),

b. presence of structural balance based on a cesura occurring in the middle of a phrase, clause, or sentence. The two halves are either in semantic opposition, in a semantic relationship of complementation, or they are near-synonymous in referential meaning, e.g., I_4 - was gesagt wird und geschrieben ist, Segen und Fluch; auf den Kindern ruhe und sie nicht verfehle; III_7 - fuhr fort und sagte, III_8 - the entire sentence exhibits this structural balance,

d. use of foregrounded word order (thematic fronting) for emotive effect: I_4, $III_{5,6,7}$, IV_2.

Statement of Function:

The function of this text consisting of an ideational and an interpersonal component may be summed up in the following way: it is (a) to express the addresser's beliefs about desirable moral behaviour, and (b) to influence or improve the moral principles and behaviour of the addressees by way of informing them about two instances of good and bad behaviour. Only the interpersonal functional component is marked on the dimensions; it is thus the dominant one for this text.

The individual dimensions operate in the following way: On the dimension Time, the text was shown to be marked for its early nineteenth century provenance. Taking contemporary speakers of the standard source language as our point of reference (cf. above, Chapter IV, p. 59), the text is clearly foregrounded for its temporal provenance. This foregroundedness gives the text its special, "fictional" character which operates in support of the interpersonal component of the text's function.

On the dimension Medium, the written to be read mode, especially the logical structure of the text, revealing advance-planning for a certain effect, acts in support of the addresser's moralizing intention, i. e., supports the interpersonal component of the textual function. On the dimension Participation, the attempts to break the monologous character of the text through the insertion of questions and commands, and the particular use of impersonal and personal pronouns for expressing the universal validity of the text's message, also support the interpersonal functional component. On Social Role Relationship, we have shown that the addresser tries to exercise his moral authority as a teacher/clergyman which is manifest in the use of an explicit exhortatory frame and in the frequent use of value-adjectives. This dimension also clearly operates in support of the interpersonal functional component. The consultative style level on the dimension Social Attitude may also be interpreted as supporting the interpersonal functional component in that this is a conversational, addressee-involving style level used in close contact with non-intimates (cf. above Chapter III, p.46), i.e., the style level is well adapted to the "interpersonal" relationship between addresser and addressees.

On the dimension Province, the presence of "genre"-typical value-adjectives, the use of the present tense in the didactic frame to stress the permanent truth of the lessons to be drawn by the addressees, as well as the presence of utterances with emphatic foregrounded word-order also seem to act in support of the interpersonal functional component.

2. ST and TT Comparison and Statement of Quality

Mismatches on the following dimensions have been discovered following the analysis of TT and the comparison of ST and TT:

Time:

Throughout the text, ST's temporal markedness is not matched by TT. There are too many individual instances of mismatching to give a complete list.

Social Attitude:

TT appears to be too formal and stilted in certain instances. (This may be interpreted as the translator's attempt to find some kind of "foregrounding" equivalence for the temporal markedness of the text: I_2 - es geht auch begreiflich zu ≠ and this procedure is understandable: TT is far too formal (suggested alternative: and that this is so is...); II_1 - darüber ≠ on this subject; III_1 - liess sich in ein Gespräch ein ≠ entered into a conversation: far too formal given ST's conversational tone; III_2 - täglich ≠ per day: too official and formal; III_3 - verwunderte sich darüber ≠ expressed his astonishment: again too formal; $IV_{1, 10}$ - dieser ([+archaic]) ≠ the latter: given TT's temporal non-markedness, the English item is too formal and business-like; IV_1 - im nämlichen Orte ([+archaic]) ≠ located in the same place and IV_2 - bei dürftiger Pflege ≠ though the care might be scanty: Both expressions in TT are too stilted and formal.

Province:

lexical and syntactic mismatches:

lack of temporal foregroundedness of TT (cf. above Time).

Overtly Erroneous Errors

There are a number of breaches of the target language system. Firstly, there are three cases of ungrammaticality: I_3 - the children learn it: children is, in this case, a generic noun which should not be preceded by a definite article; III_8 - beautifully thought and acted; Ungrammatical without an addition of prepositions (alternative: thought out and acted upon); IV_{10} - As an emergency for the future: Two correct alternatives are: for a future emergency, or against the future time.

Secondly, there are three cases of dubious acceptability: I_1 - people are treated by their children in old age just as: An unnatural separation of the qualifier in old age from the noun phrase it modifies; III_2 - After a few questions: More natural would be: After having asked a few questions; IV_5 - he did not find everything as he wished it: Omission of to be or had hoped it would be, etc.

Statement of Quality:

The comparison of ST and TT along the situational dimensions has shown that there are complete mismatches on Time and on Province, on which the temporal mismatch was crosslisted, and a number of mismatches on Social Attitude. The deviations on the Time/Province dimensions alter the text's "genre" of a temporally conditioned Kalendergeschichte; this lack of temporal foregroundedness clearly detracts from the text's interpersonal functional component. On the dimension Social Attitude, the unwarranted formality and stiltedness which we discovered in TT in certain instances also detracts from the same functional component in that TT, lacking the conversational tone, exhibits greater social distance and impersonality. The overtly erroneous errors, all of which are breaches of the target language system, also detract from the interpersonal functional component by making the text less attractive to read and thus less potentially convincing.

VIII. COMEDY DIALOGUE (ST English; TT German, See Appendix, pp. 328-44

1. Analysis of ST and Statement of Function

Note: Because the text is part of a play, it has two components: (1) a record of speech between two interlocutors, and (2) a frame inside which (1) takes place. The frame contains two different types of descriptions: one which elaborates on the way the text should be spoken by actors, i. e., a commentary on ways of enunciation, and one which describes the physical activity which either accompanies or links portions of (1), i. e., stage instructions.

The existence of two "kinds" of texts is manifest in the graphic conventions with italics being used for the two types of frame as well as for the names of the interlocutors whose utterances make up the record of speech. Because of these two textual components, we have chosen a more complicated numbering system using Roman numerals for paragraphs of the speech record, Arabic numerals for the sentences within the paragraphs, and numbering the parts of the frame from F_1 to F_n with S_1 to S_n standing for sentences within F_1 through F_n.

Dimensions of language user:

(1) Geographical Origin: non-marked Standard British English for the frame, the record of speech being marked as Hiberno-English. This geographical dialect is most strongly marked phonologically. However,

given the nature of our study, this component will not be considered.

syntactic means:

a. use of and or its contracted forms an' and 'n to replace other conjunctions. And thus expresses various semantic relationships between two clauses, e.g., LII_1 - My eyes are used to the darkness, now, 'n I can see (consequential); V_2 - An' the time galloping by? (concessive); LIII_3 - Why don't you keep your razor-blades in a safe place, an' not leave them (contrastive),

b. replacement of have by be in the formation of the present perfect: XIX_1 - Is the clock stopped?

c. use of the structure amn't I: XXIV_2, LIV_1,

d. replacement of V+ $have^{en}$ present perfect formation by be + after V_{ing}: XXIV_2 - Amn't I after looking; LV_1 - I'm nearly after mowing,

e. use of the time adverbial till as a subordinating conjunction of intention (e.g., so that): LIII_4 - Where is there a bit of old rag till I bind up my wounds?,

f. omission of relative pronoun plus switch of person: LI_3 - You're the kind of man, if you're not chained up, 'll pull,

g. use of ye for you: XLII_1, LV_1.

lexical means:

a. presence of a few Hiberno-English words and phrases: LI_3 - asundher; LI_4 - stop down; LIII_5 - I'm tellin you.

(2) Social Class: non-marked, Educated Middle Class for the frame, record of speech being marked as (urban, Dublin) lower class. As with the geographical dialect above, the class dialect is most strongly marked phonologically; again, this component will not be considered given the nature of this study.

syntactic means:

a. syntactic means listed above under Geographical Origin are also applicable here,

b. use of first person plural personal pronoun in place of first person singular personal pronoun: XL_2 - An' will you tell us,

c. use of the definite article plus the name of a part of the body: XXXVII_1 - keep the nose sticking up,

d. abundance of contractions and deletions of endings throughout the text,

e. frequent use of elliptical clauses throughout the text,

f. frequent use of and (an', 'n) as a "universal conjoiner" for both co-ordinating and subordinating clauses throughout the text.

lexical means:

a. use of casual address forms: XXIV_7, XXV, etc.: man, XLIX_2 - Eh, you up there,

b. presence of lexical items marked as substandard, e.g., V_3 - th' missus; XXXIII_3 - spuds.

(3) Time: non-marked, contemporary Hiberno-English.

Dimensions of language use:

(1) Medium: The text as a whole is clearly "written to be acted", i.e., the record of speech is written to be spoken as if not written by actors. However, the written text may also be read as a text "written to be acted". In this case, the medium is written to be read as if heard because in reading a play, the reader is aware of the fact that it is intended to be performed, and he acts out the play imaginatively. The latter case is the one relevant for our purpose of assessing the quality of a TT which will also be read (and evaluated).

We are here only analyzing the record of speech because the frame has merely a supporting role for the record of speech. In our assessment of translation quality, it is also only the record of speech that will be compared on Medium. The record of speech--written to be spoken as if not written/written to be read as if heard--is designed to simulate real-life, spontaneous language.

syntactic means:

a. multitude of contractions and deletions of endings (cf. above Social Class),

b. frequent use of and (an', 'n) introducing both coordinated and subordinated clauses (cf. above Geographical Origin and Social Class),

c. frequency of elliptical clauses, typical of oral conversational encounters where it is the situation that automatically disambiguates the incomplete utterances, and where it is often natural for the interlocutors to interrupt one another: II_1, III_1, $V_{1,2}$, X_1, etc.

lexical means:

a. presence of interjections: XXXVI_1, XXXVIII_1, XLIX_2 - Oh; XL_4, XLIX_2, - Eh?; LV_2 - uh.

textual means:

a. presence of songs which *per se* belong to the spoken mode: III_4, XXIV_6, XXVII_1, XXVIII_1, XXIX_2, XXX_1;

b. the text is totally etic on the level of fiction, i.e., there is ample reference to the enveloping fictional situation (which is to be "recreated" on the stage) by means of personal, local, and temporal deictics throughout the text,

c. ample use of repetition for redundancy throughout the text; frequently one interlocutor repeats what the other just finished saying, e.g., I_2-II_1; IV_1 - V_1, etc.

(2) Participation: simple: dialogue

On this dimension, too, we shall exclusively consider the record of speech, as the frame only acts to support specific parts of the record of speech in its performed version.

syntactic means:

a. predominance of first and second person personal and possessive pronouns to indicate direct interaction situation,

b. frequent switch in the text between declarative, interrogative, imperative, and exclamatory utterances, also indicative of the on-going interaction between two participant interlocutors, e.g., I_2 - II_1; IV_1 - $V_{1,2,3}$; VI_1 - VII_{1-4},

c. presence of question tags to elicit immediate response: V_3, IX_3, XIII_1, XV_1, XXII_1.

textual means:

interlocutors alternate constantly in speech.

(3) Social Role Relationship:

There are two distinct relationships: (a) the addresser (author) vis à vis the addressees (audience), and (b) one interlocutor (character) vis à vis the other one (in the record of speech).

In (a), the addresser tries to please, amuse, and entertain the addressees by representing a piece of ordinary domestic Irish life with which the addressees may either identify, or through which they are given the satisfying role of (secretly) witnessing fellow human beings in a very human situation--a domestic quarrel. For our investigation of the linguistic manifestation of a role relationship on this dimension, we shall restrict ourselves to considering (b), i.e., the relationship which is concretely manifest in the record of speech. This relationship acts, at the same time, as a means to give expression to the above described relationship of addresser vis à vis addressees.

Therefore, in dealing with (b) we shall implicitly deal with (a) as well.

Symmetrical role relationship: absence of authority between the two interlocutors or characters.

Position roles: friends on intimate terms.

Situational roles: participants in an argument.

<u>syntactic means</u>:

a. occurrence of elliptical clauses produced by the interlocutors' mutual interruption. This is a sign of an equi-status relationship: X_1, XII_1, XIV_1, XVI_1.

<u>lexical means</u>:

a. frequent use of expletives marking an intimate, very informal relationship: VI_1, XXII_1, XXXIII_3, XXXV_1, XLI_1, LI_2, LV_1,

b. presence of utterances with an illocutionary force of an abuse, an accusation, or an insult: VIII_1, XXII_1, XXXI_1, $LI_{3,4}$, LVI_1.

<u>(4) Social Attitude:</u>

For our consideration of the linguistic manifestation of <u>Social Attitude</u>, we shall concentrate on the record of speech and disregard the frame which merely acts to support the record of speech's effectiveness. The <u>Social Attitude</u> considered is that between the two interlocutors; it is <u>casual-intimate</u>, with interspersed elements of a <u>consultative-formal</u> style level.

<u>Casual-intimate style level</u>:

syntactic means:

a. frequency of elliptical clauses, of an' and 'n as "universal conjoiners" for both coordinating and subordinating clauses, and of contractions and deletions of endings (cf. above, Social Class and Medium),

b. use of first person plural personal pronoun instead of first person singular one: XL_2 (cf. above Social Class),

lexical means:

a. use of casual address forms,and items marked as being sub-standard (cf. above Social Class),

b. presence of informal interjections to signal non-comprehension or to establish contact: XL_4, XLIX_2 - Eh?.

Consultative-formal style level: there are a few interspersions of, in the context of the overall informal style level, pretentiously pompous phrases, i.e., V_3 - stand thou still there; VI_1 - expedite matters, VII_2 - it doesn't seem to strike you that; VIII_1 - pioneered me into doing; IX_2 - Barry Derrill, there's such a thing in the world as a libel; XIII_1 - I was doing callisthenics; XVII_1 - carry the conversation into a debate; XXV_1 - depositing it in the air; XXXVIII_1 - in the middle of an emergency.

(5) Province: The text is part of a one-act Irish Folk Comedy; most important for this Province is the effect of humour and the particular

Irish flavour of the play.

On this parameter, too, we shall restrict ourselves to a consideration of the record of speech. It should, however, be made clear that for its basic nature of comedy, the play's effect is strongly influenced by the frame, e. g., F_5 - he has struggled into the overall, where this clause reveals Darry's ineptitude even at the stage of preparation for housework, or F_{23}-S_1 - Darry dashes over to the fire; S_4 - rushing madly in, where S_1 and S_4 provide a humorous contrast between the previous long idleness and the sudden outburst of activity. Nevertheless, the frame is merely supportive of the text to be "read as if heard", which we shall here consider:

syntactic means:

a. presence of particular Hiberno-English syntactic features which give the play its Irish folk-character (cf. above Geographical Origin).

lexical means:

a. abundance of exaggerations and hyperboles to promote comical effects: $XXIV_{2,7}$, $XXXIII_{1,2}$, XXXVIII_1, XLII_1, etc.

b. use of figurative language and emotive-expressive words and phrases for comical effect, e. g., V_2 - the time galloping by; VII_4 - loitering...jiggling...plucking curious sounds; IX_3 - strutting in with a mandolin; XIII_1 - waltz'd in,

c. use of alliteration for greater emotive effect: V_3 - the meadow th' missus is mowing; VII_4 - loitering to look at you lying; XXIV_2 - twisting an' tearing,

d. presence of particular Hiberno-English lexical items (cf. above, Geographical Origin).

textual means:

a. frequency of repetition of previous statement of one interlocutor by the other. These repetitions are used to create a humorous effect (cf. above Medium),

b. presence of two contrasting and clashing style levels (cf. above Social Attitude). An air of grandiloquence and pedantry is introduced through the interspersed consultative-formal style elements. This creates a humorous effect,

c. a humorous effect is also achieved through the contrast between the utterances and the on-going activity (partially explained in the frame), or between an utterance and the true state of affairs as known to the audience, e.g., XVII_1 - I can't carry the conversation into a debate (the speaker has just managed to interrupt his interlocutor); $XXIV_{7,8}$ - You must have the hands of a gorilla... come over and wipe (contrast between the description of the hands of the interlocutor and the activity which these hands are supposed to engage in); L_1 - Nothing much-the washhand-stand fell over; etc.

Statement of Function

The function of the written text which consists of an ideational and an interpersonal component may be summed up in the following way: it is to enable the reader to reconstruct a piece of simulated reality depicting an everyday, very intimate domestic quarrel for his entertainment, and his pleasure. The text's ideational functional component is not marked on any of the situational dimensions; nevertheless, it is implicitly present in that the text, of course, informs the addressees about certain events taking place between two particular persons. However, the ideational component is clearly less important than the interpersonal one which is marked on two dimensions of the language user and on all five dimensions of language use. The individual dimensions operate in the following way:

On the dimensions Geographical Origin and Social Class, we established that the text (i. e., the record of speech) is marked for Hiberno-English and lower social class dialect. These two dimensions operate to support the interpersonal functional component because the dialectal features add to the text's emotive and humorous effects. On the parameter Medium, the written to be spoken as if not written/ written to be read as if heard mode also supports the interpersonal component because of the emotive effectiveness of (simulated) spontaneity and directness. On Participation, the nature of the text--a simple dialogue, which provides for constant alternation of the interlocutors and their continuous interaction, also filters into the interpersonal functional component because in the dialogue form, interest centres necessarily upon the dialogue participants as human beings.

On the dimension Social Role Relationship, we discovered that the relationship between the two interlocutors is one of great intimacy. This relationship also acts in support of the interpersonal functional component in that its linguistic manifestations enhance the text's expressiveness and humorous effect. The casual-intimate style level on Social Attitude, which is occasionally replaced by elements of a more formal nature, also supports the same functional component by enhancing the text's intimately personal and emotive quality. The interspersions of formal style elements support the interpersonal component as well, by being a source of humour. On Province, we described the text as being an excerpt from a one-act Irish folk comedy pointing in particular to its Hiberno-English features and the devices for creating humorous effects. These features also clearly act in support of the interpersonal component of the textual function.

2. ST and TT Comparison and Statement of Quality

We established mismatches on the following dimensions following the analysis of TT and the comparison of ST and TT:

Geographical Origin:

There is a total mismatch on this parameter (as far as the

grammatical and lexical devices are concerned), i. e., no attempt has been made in TT to find a German geographical dialect as a "match" for the Hiberno-English one in ST. It is, of course, true that differences in the cultural heritage of the two language communities make a transference of culture-specific phenomena sometimes impossible. However, culturally different but somehow "comparable" phenomena can be sought for a TT of a given ST. In the case of a geographical dialect occurring in ST, this means that a "comparable" dialect should be sought for TT. In the case of G. B. Shaw's Pygmalion, for instance, the London lower class dialect had been "translated" into lower class Berlin dialect, the two dialects being comparable because they share the distinctive features of "big city" and "lower class".[1]

By failing to select (features of) a German dialect, which is in some of the connotations it has for standard German speakers comparable to the Hiberno-English dialect vis à vis a standard English speaker, the translator failed to anchor the play in folk culture. The folk culture component is, however, as our analysis of ST has revealed, vital to the Province of this play.

Social Attitude:

The interspersed second style level (consultative-formal) is not

---

[1]See Chapter VI below, pp. 192-93, for a fuller discussion.

matched in TT in several instances: V_3 - stand thou still ≠ stehe still da: Not formal enough (suggestive alternative: stehe stille, oh Sonne); VIII_1 - pioneered into ≠ auf... angesetzt: TT is too colloquial; IX_2 - there's such a thing in the world as ≠ hast du schon mal was von... gehört: TT is much less pompous and pretentious; XIII_1 - callisthenics: this pompous, foregrounded lexical item is not matched by TT's everyday word Gymnastik; XVII_1 - carry the conversation into a debate ≠ in ne Debatte ausarten: Too informal in TT; XXV_1 - depositing it in the air ≠ stellst sie in die Luft (suggested alternative: deponierst sie in der Luft).

Province:

As has been mentioned under Geographical Origin, the Hiberno-English dialect has--at least on the grammatical and lexical levels--not been matched in TT. This means that, on the dimension of Province, the feature "folk play" is not matched in TT. Further, the comical and humorous effects of ST are not matched in TT whenever the interspersed second style level is absent in TT (cf. above Social Attitude). Moreover, there is a lack of alliteration in TT, which, however, cannot be regarded as an error because a denotatively equivalent alliterative expression in German is not readily available (cf. above, pp. 68-69).

Overtly Erroneous Errors:

There are two mismatches of the denotative meanings of ST and TT items to be subclassified as wrong selections: LIII_3 - 'an not leave them ≠ und lässt sie: TT misrepresents the English structure as meaning 'Why not [A and B] ?', when ST in fact contrasts A and B, the former being desirable and the latter totally undesirable. (suggested alternative: anstatt sie haufenweise); LIII_4 - TT uses the temporal adverbial bis for ST's till, which, in this context, is a subordinating conjunction of intention.

Statement of Quality:

The comparison of ST and TT along the situational dimensions has shown that there are mismatches on the dimensions Geographical Origin, Province, and Social Attitude. On Geographical Origin, we have found that TT lacks any comparable dialect features. This lack affects, of course, the strength of the interpersonal functional component. On the dimension Social Attitude, TT lacks, in many instances, the second interspersed style level, which is a source of humour in ST. Therefore, the interpersonal functional component is again violated. On the dimension Province, the feature of folk play has been changed in TT due to the lack of the dialect features; also some humorous effects are omitted in TT due to the lack of the consultative-formal style elements. Further, the poetic device of alliteration has not been, and could not have been, matched in TT. All these mis-matches on Province clearly detract from the interpersonal component of the text's function.

Taken together, the strongly marked interpersonal functional component of entertaining, amusing, and pleasing the addressees by presenting them with a piece of simulated reality, has been violated on three dimensions in the manner specified above. The implicit ideational component of the textual function has been violated only through the presence of the two overtly erroneous errors mentioned above.

CHAPTER VI

SOME THEORETICAL CONSEQUENCES OF THE MODEL

In this chapter, we shall discuss some theoretical aspects of translation and translation quality assessment based on our exemplary analysis of the eight textual pairs. We shall deal with: A. Translation and Text Typology; B. Some Suggestions for a Translation Typology; C. Refinement of the Model; and D. Generalizability of the Findings.

A. Translation and Text Typology

The preliminary division of the texts into the two broad functional categories <u>interpersonal</u> and <u>ideational</u>, while useful as a working hypothesis, needs to be refined given the completed analyses of the textual pairs: we have seen that all those texts that were preliminarily classified as having a dominant ideational functional component also possessed a well-marked interpersonal component, and we were able to show that for achieving translation equivalence, it is necessary to preserve this component as well. We would thus support Newmark's statement that "the common assumption that scientific and technical writing is concerned only with facts... is misplaced" (1969:80). As we have demonstrated in the analyses of the Scientific Text, the Commercial Text, and the Journalistic Article (cf. above, pp. 70-113), such texts may well contain interpersonal devices, e.g., specific didactic recommendations and addressee-oriented filterings of the "facts". Our analyses and comparisons of texts have revealed that seemingly "straightforward" ideational texts may contain subtle presuppositions and deliberate interpretations of facts which it is necessary to recognize and preserve in translation, or to alter in the case of established differences in the cultural heritage of the two language communities (as in the case of the Tourist Information Booklet, see above, pp. 123-24), where certain factual information had to be modified in the translation).

In order to assess the strength and particular nature of the two functional components which we suggest are clearly always co-present in a text, a detailed analysis of the individual text is unavoidable. Operating with notions of textual type based on a dominant functional component which alone is to be invariant in translation (as has been suggested by Reiss, 1971, see above, p. 23) is clearly an incomplete procedure. We have demonstrated in our test cases the insightfulness of using in-depth textual analysis with a multi-dimensional frame, and therefore incidentally demonstrated that the kind of text typology presupposed by Neubert's (1972a, b) suggestion of a "dictionary" for establishing translation equivalence relationships between lexical items and phrases of any two languages is too grossly conceived. Neubert's text types are roughly comparable to the entries on the dimension Province, i. e., he differentiates scientific, official, journalistic, etc., textual types which may be further subclassified, and which are further modified by the "style level" (roughly comparable to the Social Attitude dimension in our model), and goes on to suggest that an indexing for textual types could take the form of the traditional style markers, viz. "scientific, literary, everyday, stilted, slang, vulgar", etc. However, scientific texts may vary amongst themselves through the way each of the eight situational dimensions of our model operates in an individual text. Therefore, the entries in a textual-type dictionary may well vary according to these dimensional variations. Thus, a scientist will considerably vary his choice of lexical items, grammatical structures, and even of cohesion devices depending on whether he talks to students in his seminar, gives a presentation to his colleagues, or a talk at a conference, writes an abstract for a journal in his field, or chats with his adolescent son who happens to be interested in his subject. These interpersonal relationships cannot be captured by simplistic entries of the kind suggested by Neubert. We claim that an approach to listing translation equivalences which fails to take into account pragmatic-situational relationships revealed by the suggested situational dimensions is not adequate.

B. Some Suggestions for a Translation Typology

We have suggested above that attempts at setting up a text typology as a means of gaining insight into, and accounting for, different types of translation equivalence relationships are not fruitful. It seems to us that underlying such an approach is the presupposition that translation quality is somehow determined by the nature of the source text while the process of translation is itself a constant. Hence it has been presupposed that if one can classify texts successfully, then one shall have successfully accounted for differences in translations, and the theoretical problems surrounding the assessment of translation quality. However, in the light of our case studies, a reverse procedure seems likely to prove more insightful, namely to set up a translation typology whereby different texts which have been analyzed in detail according to the model we set up in Chapters III and IV above, are treated in different ways. In other words, our basic question in the following section is not, what different kinds of source texts are we here handling?, but, what different kinds of translation types have our analyses revealed?. There is, however, clearly some relation between source text type and appropriate translation type.

We suggest a basic division into two major translation types: overt translations and covert translations. We shall deal with the two types in turn:

1. An _overt_ translation is one in which the TT addressees are quite "overtly" not being directly addressed; thus an overt translation is one which must overtly be a translation, not, as it were, a "second original". In an overt translation, the ST is tied in a specific way to the source language community and culture; the ST is specifically directed at source language addressees but is also pointing beyond the source language community because ST--independent of its source language origin--is also of potential general human interest. STs that call for an overt translation have an established worth or value in the source language community and potentially in other communities. Such STs may be divided into two subgroups:

a) _overt, historically-linked_ STs, i. e., those tied to a specific occasion in which a precisely specified source language audience is/was being addressed; this case is clearly exemplified by the _Political Speech_ and the _Religious Sermon_ in our sample texts;

b) _overt, timeless_ STs, i. e., those transcending--as works of art and aesthetic creations--a distinct historical meaning while, of course, always necessarily displaying period (and culture) specificity because of the status of the addresser who is a product of his time and culture. In our corpus of texts, this type is represented by the _Moral Anecdote_ and the _Comedy Dialogue_, both of which--although timeless and transmitting a general human message--are culture-specific because of their being marked on the language user dimensions (presence of a particular état de langue and geographical dialect respectively) and because of their having independent status in the language community through belonging to the community's cultural products. Both texts are "literary" texts having the feature [+fictional], i. e., the texts are situationally abstract in that they do not immediately refer to a unique historic situation, in which both addresser and addressees find themselves. Fictional texts describe a kind of "fictive reality" which is, in every reception by an individual addressee, newly related to the specific historic reality in the concrete situation in which the addressee finds himself (cf. Werlich, 1975:20). The message in a fictional text is text-contained, which gives the text its independent value; the message "presupposes no wider context so that everything necessary for its interpretation is to be found within the message itself" (Widdowson, 1974c:203).

Both groups of STs, then, overt historically linked and overt timeless ones, necessitate overt translations. The requirements for this type of translation which lead to important modifications of our model as set up above are the following: a direct match of the original function of ST is not possible either because of ST's being tied to a specific (non-repeatable) historic event in the source language community or because of the unique status (as a fictional text) that a given ST has in the source culture.

In the case of texts that are bound to a specific historic occasion (e. g., the Political Speech and the Religious Sermon), the translator quite clearly cannot set out to match the original function that ST had for the original addressees but he must try to match a second level function: the one holding not only for the contemporary, educated middle class native speakers of the target culture but also for their potential counterparts in the source culture who are also not the original addressees. Similarly, in timeless overt translations a second level function must be met. In the case of the Moral Anecdote, for instance, we have a basically comparable case in that this text, although as a piece of fiction timeless and of general human interest, is tied on a language user dimension to a specific (bygone) period of time in the source culture. The translator has to again operate with the level of function which this work has for contemporary, educated middle class speakers of German, for whom the text would be marked [+archaic] when it was clearly not marked in this manner for the original addressees, who lived in the particular period of time in which the author produced the text.

In the case of the Comedy Dialogue, it is the text's being marked for a culture-unique geographical dialect on a language user dimension which necessitates a "topicalization" of the function. The text has to be transposed from one cultural area to another. The function that ST has for a contemporary educated middle class standard English speaker cannot be equivalent in TT because of the uniqueness of the intralinguistic variations in any particular culture.

In the two above mentioned examples of overt-timeless translations, the ST as a piece of work with a certain status in the source language community, i. e., the status of the addresser or of the work of art, has to remain as intact as possible given the process of transference into another language. On the other hand, cases of overt translation present difficulties precisely because the nature of their function in the socio-cultural context of the source language community, which must be topicalized in the target culture, frequently necessitates major changes. It is this dialectical relationship between preservation and alteration which makes the finding of translation equivalence difficult in cases of overt translation. The two examples from our corpus of texts illustrate this difficulty: in the case of the Comedy Dialogue, the translator completely failed to topicalize the textual function, which, in our view of an overt-timeless translation, would have been necessary. He might have achieved a second-level functional equivalence by selecting an "equivalent" target language geographical dialect, i. e., a dialect equivalent in "human or social geography" (cf. Catford, 1965:88). Taking standard English speakers as the potential addressees of the Comedy Dialogue text, and regarding Hiberno-English as a rather heavily marked dialect, (especially on the grammatical level), whose speakers are characterized by a marked striving for provincial, or national, independence and distinctiveness, which has its reflection in a strong folk tradition, the translator would have to search for an approximately comparable German dialect, e.g. Bavarian. Many speakers of this dialect share the separatist intentions and the "rootedness" in folk tradition with the Hiberno-English speakers. However, it must be stressed that such markedness on the dimension Geographical Origin clearly presents often insoluble equivalence problems, and always entails a second level function.

As we have seen in the Moral Anecdote, the presence of a marked temporal dialect or état de langue also presents considerable equivalence problems. Again, the principle of a second level or topicalized function necessitates a selection of approximately comparable [+archaic] items in TT to ensure an overt translation of ST. An employment of markers of a "comparably archaic" état de langue will create "to some extent a translation equivalent of the source language état de langue" (Catford, 1965:89). Catford's phrase "to some extent" clearly points to the impossibility of achieving a perfect match because of the uniqueness of cultural-historical context, and their non-transferability from the source language to the target language.

The two texts in our corpus which were linked to a specific historic occasion in the source language community, did not present such topicalization problems, but--given this type of ST--they may easily have done so.[1] However, in view of the fact that the overt-historically linked texts have the status of a document of a historical event in the source culture, where the culture specificity and uniqueness is more strongly marked than in the timeless [+fictional] texts, it seems for us to be more appropriate in these cases to abstain from finding approximate equivalents for culture-specific geographical, temporal, or social class markedness on the language user dimensions but to provide explanatory notes to the members of the target culture who are exposed to TT.

2. A <u>covert</u> translation is a translation which enjoys or enjoyed the status of an original ST in the target culture. The translation is covert because it is <u>not</u> marked pragmatically as a TT of an ST but may, conceivably, have been created in its own right. A covert translation is thus a translation whose ST is not specifically addressed to a target culture audience, i. e., not particularly tied to the source language community and culture. An ST and its covert TT are pragmatically of equal concern for source and target language addressees. Both are, as it were, equally directly addressed. An ST and its covert TT have

---

[1]Consider, for instance, the possibility that Churchill had spoken a regional dialect of English and, of course, this fact was evidenced in the ST, or consider the case of the speeches of Edmund Burke which are now temporally marked.

equivalent purposes: they are based on contemporary, equivalent needs of a comparable audience in the source and target language communities. In the case of covert TTs, it is thus both possible and desirable to keep the function of ST equivalent in TT.

The Commercial Text, the Scientific Text, the Journalistic Article, and the Tourist Information Booklet in our sample texts all fall within this category of STs necessitating a covert translation. All of these TTs have direct target language addressees, for whom this TT is as immediately and "originally" relevant as ST is for the source language addressees.

In the case of the Commercial Text, both source and target language addressees are shareholders of I. O. S., i. e., they differ "only" accidentally in their respective mother tongues. Similarly, in the cases of the Scientific Text, the Journalistic Article, and the Tourist Information Booklet, ST and TT are of the same potential value and immediate importance for both ST and TT addressees (who are here not as clearly specified as in the case of the commercial circular letter) precisely because ST is not source culture specific. Thus, the Scientific Text is clearly of equal (potential) concern for German speaking and English speaking science students; the Journalistic Article is of potential equal interest to German readers of the UNESCO Kurier who are interested in archaeology, and to the English readers of the UNESCO Courier who share this interest; the Tourist Information

Booklet is just as much directed at German speaking (potential) visitors of Nürnberg as it is directed at English speaking ones.

While it is thus clear that such texts are not source culture-specific, it is the covert type of translation that such texts require, which presents more difficult, and more subtle, cultural translation problems than those we encountered in the case of the overt translation type, where the particular source culture specificity had to be either left intact and presented as a culturally and historically linked monument, or overtly matched in the target culture setting. If ST and TT are to have truly equivalent functions, which is necessary in a covert translation, then the translator--in order to meet the needs of the target language addressees in their cultural setting, and in order to achieve an effect equivalent to TT's--has to take different cultural presuppositions[1] in the two language communities into account. In a covert translation, the translator has to place a cultural filter between ST and TT; he has to, as it were, view ST through the glasses of a

---

[1]By culture we here mean the anthropological concept of the overall way of life of a community, i. e., all those traditional, explicit, and implicit designs for living which act as potential guides for the behaviour of members of the culture. This concept of culture is to be differentiated from the humanistic conception of the "cultural heritage" as a model of refinement, an exclusive collection of a community's masterpieces in literature, fine arts, music, etc. Culture in the anthropological sense of a group's dominant and learned sets of habits, as the totality of its non-biological inheritance involves presuppositions, values, and preferences. These are, of course, hardly accessible.

target culture member.

A glance at the rich anecdotal literature on translation (cf. e.g., Störig, 1963, for an overview) may lead one to believe that there are, indeed, many crucial intercultural differences complicating any translation process. However, on closer examination, most of the impressive examples of differences are drawn from comparisons of a European language and languages of South East Asia, or American Indian languages, etc., where the socio-cultural differences are obviously remarkable. Thus, Catford (1965:90-91) illustrates the importance in translation of considering cultural "undercurrents" by describing how an oriental youth may use honorific forms when talking (at a specific occasion and on a specific matter) to his father, and how an English youth would, in the "same" situation, use only casual style.

We hypothesize that in the case of the contemporary English and German speaking communities, the differences in the socio-cultural norms between the two cultures are just as great as they are <u>within</u> the two language communities. To our knowledge there do not exist complete socio-cultural descriptions of the Germanophone and Anglophone cultural communities, let alone comparative descriptions. Thus, our rather simplistic hypothesis (put forward above, p.58) that the socio-cultural norms are <u>basically</u> comparable in the two language communities at the present time, cannot easily be verified or falsified. Clearly, the term <u>basically</u> leaves room for actually existing _and_ verified differences of the socio-cultural norms and presuppositions of cultural knowledge, which in our model of translation quality assessment will be established through applying a cultural filter. However, it seems reasonable to assume that the contemporary Anglophone and Germanophone educated middle class speakers of the respective standard languages, closely related through socio-political and economic ties, do not differ in relevant ways concerning, for instance, their reception of a scientific text, a journalistic article, or a commercial circular letter. Unless presuppositions concerning cultural differences are substantiated by ethnological and sociological research, it seems to us to be more reasonable in translation to follow our assumption of basic comparability for such closely related cultures as the ones we are dealing with here, than to take the liberty in translation of changing the ST on the assumption of cultural difference. Of course, we do not claim that differences in values and habits, in understating or emphasizing certain emotions, etc., do not exist between any two, however closely related, cultures. However, given the goal of achieving functional equivalence in a covert translation, assumptions of cultural difference should be carefully examined before any change in ST is undertaken. We therefore feel justified in the above analyses of the _Commercial Text_ and the _Journalistic Article_ (pp.82-113) in having classified as errors the possibly deliberate mismatches in TT resulting from an assumption of cultural difference. In other words, the translator may, in these cases, have applied a cultural filter whose application is not justified.

In the Commercial Text, the observed changes on the dimension Social Role Relationship form a consistent pattern such that the careful, hedging, and distantly polite tone (as evidenced in various linguistic devices described above in detail, cf. pp. 92-5) is changed into a much more direct, blunt, and undiplomatic tone which clearly acts against the textual function which we established through our analysis of ST. We claim that an assumption of a German audience's different expectations in this context (which may have caused the translator's alterations) is unwarranted since it is not substantiated by facts and only acts to perpetuate cliché assumptions of German audiences preferring such manifestations of a social role relationship.

In the case of the Journalistic Article, we observed changes on the dimensions Social Role Relationship, Province, and, consequently, all other language usage dimensions. We also hypothesize--because of the existence of a whole pattern of mismatches--that the translator entertained presuppositions about different social role relationships between the addresser and the addressees in the target language community, in this case between a professor of anthropology and the interested lay public. The TT which results is markedly different in that the slightly condescending, lightly entertaining and informal tone in ST is converted into a more serious, scientifically more accurate and certainly less entertaining TT. Again, the presupposition that a German audience prefers this kind of a textual profile in a TT of this Province is not culturally justified.

We may draw the following conclusions from this analysis of culturally conditioned mismatches: if a covert translation accommodates, unwarrantedly and in a patterned way, for the target culture group's different presuppositions about the Social Role Relationship, Social Attitude, and Participation of addressees vis à vis the addresser in a particular Province, then such a translation is no longer a translation but will be defined as a covert version. A covert version is by definition an inadequate translation in that the application of the cultural filter is unjustified.

Thus, TTs of the Journalistic Article and the Commercial Text are both covert versions because the translators--in order to preserve the function of ST--applied the cultural filter non-objectively and undertook changes on the dimensions. Since these changes are, however, not substantiated by facts, they created a covert version of the STs.

Covert versions must be clearly differentiated from overt versions which we have already mentioned in Chapter IV above (p. 59), and which are produced whenever a special function is (overtly) added to TT.[1]

A different situation occurs in the case of the Tourist Information Booklet where the translator rightly assumed that the TT addressees do not necessarily share the knowledge of the source culture's inventory of cultural phenomena such as nationally well-known artists or works of art. In this case, the supply of added information is justified, as it seems to be clearly distinct from the type of assumptions of different expectations on the part of the target culture addressees discussed above in connection with the Commercial and the Journalistic Texts. The change on the Social Role Relationship dimension through the addition of information for the benefit of the target culture addressees, will not be regarded as an error but will be explained through the necessity of the application of a cultural filter to ST which accounts for the changes undertaken.

In discussing different types of translation, and in distinguish-

---

[1]There are two cases of such overt functional change: a) TT is to reach a special audience. Examples are special editions for a youthful audience with the resultant omissions, simplifications, different accentuation of certain features of ST, etc., or popularizations of specialist works designed for the lay public; b) TT is given a special added purpose. Examples are interlingual versions or "linguistic translations" (cf. Casagrande, 1954:337) in which structural differences between the source and target languages are to be elucidated, or resumés and abstracts where it is the special purpose of the version producer to pass on only the most essential facts.

Overt versions may, of course, also occur within the source language. In this case we derive an intralingual overt version.

ing between a translation and a version of an ST, we have pointed to features of the eight textual pairs analyzed in Chapter V above which make a covert as opposed to an overt translation requisite for a particular text. In other words, we have assumed that a particular text may be adequately translated in only one of the ways we have specified. This assumption has resulted in our distinguishing in the eight STs different characteristics which divide them into texts for which an overt translation is required and those for which a covert translation is required. Our results may be displayed diagrammatically as shown on the following page.

The assumption that a particular text necessitates either a covert or an overt translation--while holding, we believe, in the detailed instances brought forward above--may, however, not hold in every case. Thus, any text may, for specific purposes, require an overt translation, i. e., it may be viewed as a document which "has independent status" and exists in its own right; e. g., our Commercial Text might be cited as evidence in a non-English speaking court of law, or its author may, in the course of time, prove to be a distinguished political or literary figure. In these two instances, the texts to be translated would clearly not have an equivalent function in translation, i. e., in both cases an overt translation would be appropriate. Further, there may well be STs for which the choice overt-or-covert translation is a subjective one, e. g., fairy tales may be viewed as

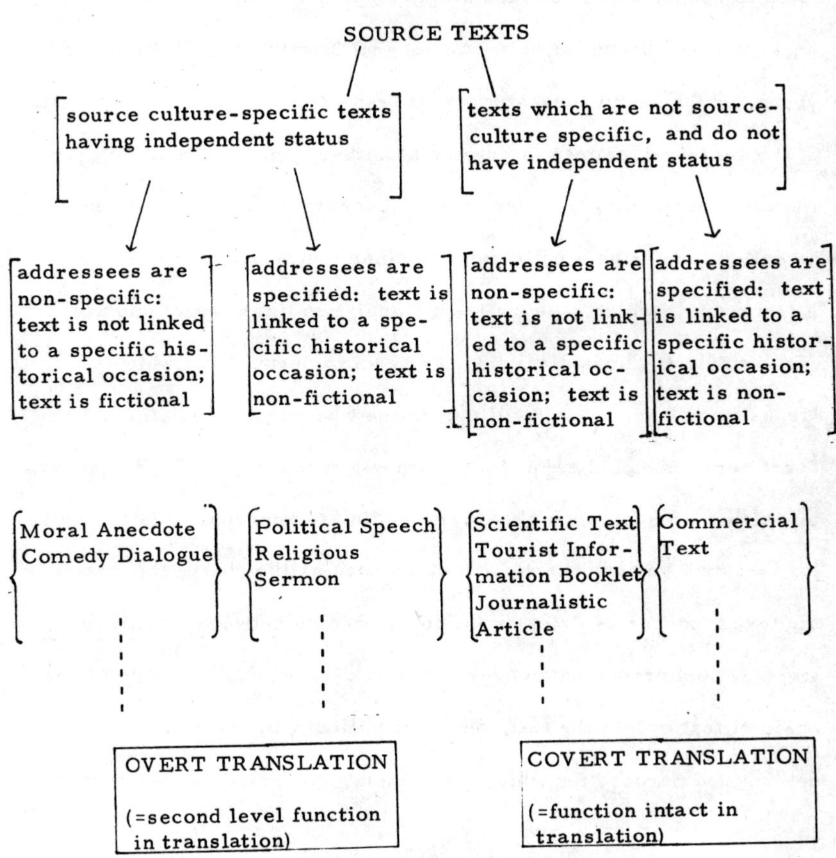
SOURCE TEXTS
source culture-specific texts having independent status
texts which are not source-culture specific, and do not have independent status
addressees are non-specific: text is not linked to a specific historical occasion; text is fictional
addressees are specified: text is linked to a specific historical occasion; text is non-fictional
addressees are non-specific: text is not linked to a specific historical occasion; text is non-fictional
addressees are specified: text is linked to a specific historical occasion; text is non-fictional
Moral Anecdote
Comedy Dialogue
Political Speech
Religious Sermon
Scientific Text
Tourist Information Booklet
Journalistic Article
Commercial Text
OVERT TRANSLATION
(=second level function in translation)
COVERT TRANSLATION
(=function intact in translation)

folk products of a particular culture, which would predispose a translator to opt for an overt translation, or as non-culture specific texts, anonymously produced, with the general function of entertaining the young, which would suggest a covert translation; or consider the case of the Bible, which may be treated as either a collection of historical literary documents, in which case an overt translation would seem to be called for, or as a collection of human truths directly relevant to Everyman, in which case a covert translation might seem appropriate.

Further, it is clear that the specific purpose for which a "translation" is required will determine whether a translation or an overt version should be made. In other words, just as the decision as to whether an overt or a covert translation is appropriate for a particular text may be conditioned by factors such as the changeable status of the text producer, so clearly the initial choice between translating a given ST and producing an overt version of it, cannot be made on the basis of features of the text, but is conditioned by the arbitrarily determined purpose for which the translation/version is required.

C. Refinement of the Model

The principle stated above (p.30) that a TT, in order to be adequate, should have a function equivalent to the function of its ST must now be refined: it is only in cases of covert translations that it is in fact possible to achieve functional equivalence. This functional equivalence is, however, difficult to achieve because differences of the socio-cultural norms have to be taken into account. As we have seen in our sample of texts, this is crucial whenever ST has a well-marked interpersonal component of the textual function. It is the interpersonal component which presents the most difficult problems of translation equivalence. In the case of the Scientific Text, the problems were relatively reduced precisely because the interpersonal component of this text's function was not strongly marked. In the case of the three other texts calling for a covert translation, however, the matching of the interpersonal component of the textual function (especially on the Social Role Relationship dimension) clearly presented the most subtle problems for the translator who had to apply a cultural filter before undertaking the match. From the viewpoint of the translation evaluator, the lack of objective knowledge about differences in the socio-cultural norms makes it difficult to assess the justifiability of any changes made as a result of the application of the filter.

In the case of overt translations, the achievement of strict functional equivalence is, in fact, impossible; a second level function must then be aimed at in translation. Since in an overt translation where the ST is, in a way, "sacrosanct" due to its status (as a work of art, or a historical record), the translator cannot strive for functional equivalence in the target culture, which would involve the undertaking of adjustments of cultural presuppositions, he has to restrict himself to simply transposing the ST from the source culture to the target culture. Overt translations are more "straightforward" since their STs are taken over unaltered, i. e., STs are merely transplanted into a new environment with no provisions being made for the TT addressees' (potentially different) norms of expectation. This can be demonstrated by the fact that in the Religious Sermon, the two references to local source culture phenomena are best translated by the exact source language terms Fasnacht and Mustermesse (cf. above, p. 139) to be explained, outside the body of the text, in a footnote. The source-culture orientation is clearly brought out through this procedure.

The difficulty of evaluation is also reduced in cases of overt translation since the entire stage of applying a cultural filter can be omitted. The major difficulty in translating overtly is, of course, the finding of linguistic-cultural "equivalents" on the language user dimensions. However, here we deal with overt manifestations of cultural phenomena which must be transferred only because they happen to be manifest linguistically in ST. A judgement whether a "translation" of culture-specific user characteristics is adequate in an overt TT cannot be objectively given, i. e., the degree of correspondence in terms of social status between dialects in two different cultures cannot be measured at the present time since no completed cultural-comparative study exists. Such an evaluation, therefore, must necessarily remain a subjective matter. However, as opposed to the difficulty of dealing with assumed differences of cultural presuppositions with respect to Social Role Relationship, Social Attitude, etc., in a particular Province, which characterizes the evaluation of covert translations, the explicit overt transference necessary in an overt translation is still easier to pin down and diagnose.

To sum up, the principle of functional equivalence which we proposed as the overriding criterion for translation quality must be relativized in the following way: in the case of an overt translation of a source-culture linked ST, an adequate TT will have a similar, topicalized (second-level) function in the target culture; in the case of a covert translation of a non-source culture linked ST, an adequate TT will have an equivalent function. The difficulties in both translating and evaluating are of a different nature in the two cases, with the covert translation presenting more subtle cultural evaluation problems. The addition of a special secondary function to a TT leads to what we defined as an overt version of the corresponding ST; the unjustified application of the cultural filter to an ST calling for a covert translation leads to the production of a covert version. A covert version is thus by definition an inadequate translation.

D. Generalizability of the Findings

As regards the evaluation of different translations of the same ST, our model facilitates an evaluative statement only to the extent that the relative importance of the individual dimensions has been demonstrated in the analysis. In that two TTs may show mismatches on the same parameter(s), their relative adequacy is clearly a function of the relative degree of mismatch on the particular parameter(s). In the case that two TTs have mismatches on different parameters, clearly this simple quantitative comparison is inadequate. We may say, however, that the degree to which a particular parameter is marked in an ST, is the degree to which it contributes towards that ST's function, i.e., for an individual text, a relative hierarchy in terms of parameters is feasible. Therefore, mismatches on parameter A in TT_1 may be seen as contributing to a greater or lesser extent to a functional mismatch between ST and TT_1 than the extent to which mismatches on parameter B in TT_2 contribute to a functional mismatch between ST and TT_2, given that the relative importance of parameters A and B is established by the ST analysis.

Further, let us consider the theoretical case in which TT_1 shows very few dimensional mismatches but contains many overtly erroneous errors, while TT_2 has several dimensional mismatches but no overtly erroneous errors. It seems to us that a comparative evaluation of these two TTs can only be arrived at from a consideration of the individual texts and the individual translations themselves. We may, however, hypothesize (as we did above, p. 57) that the subgroup of overtly erroneous errors which we called "mismatches of the denotative meaning" will be marked as a more serious detraction from the quality of a TT than dimensional mismatches whenever the text has a strongly marked ideational functional component, e.g., mismatches of the denotative meaning of items in a science text are likely to be rated higher than a mismatch on Social Attitude.

A detailed hierarchy of errors for any individual case can, however, only be given for a particular comparison of two or more texts depending in any particular case on the objectives of the evaluation, or, in the case of translations in the context of foreign language teaching, on the objectives set by the teacher in a unique teaching situation.

As already stated above (p.66), we have chosen our corpus of texts such that the texts represent a wide range of different Provinces excluding, however, pure poetic-aesthetic texts because of their basic untranslatability. Given the range of text "genres" and subject matters, we believe that we have successfully demonstrated the practicability of the suggested model, and that we have made some valid generalizations concerning the establishment and nature of translation equivalence being closely tied to the two basic translation types. We believe that these results are valid for our particular corpus of texts but also for other STs and TTs that can, on account of the criteria listed above (p. 203) be placed into either of the two types of texts calling for an overt or a covert translation including, of course, a clarification of the issues involved in the case of an "ambiguous" text.

Our study, we would claim, has a wider application than direct imitation for similar ST/TT pairs. We have already briefly discussed the extent to which our model may make the comparative assessment of different TTs of the same ST feasible. Further, we have, in distinguishing a version from a translation, and distinguishing covert from overt versions and translations, clarified what we believe to be some of the basic sources of confusion in the field. Our model may also be applied to the assessment of an overt version's adequacy. Given that the ways in which the addressees of the version differ from the addressees of ST, or the way the special function of the version differs from ST's function, can be precisely specified, these functional changes may be superimposed onto the textual profile of ST which results from our analysis. The resultant amended (or filtered) profile is then the yardstick against which the adequacy of the new version of the text is to be measured.

We have conceded that a particular ST does not necessarily require either a covert or an overt translation, given the different ways of viewing a text and different special purposes for which the translation may be required (see above, p. 202). However, we believe that in clarifying the distinction overt-covert, and detailing the consequences in translation practice and evaluation which are subsequent to choosing a particular translation type, we have shed some light on a theoretically problematical area of translation.

An important by-product of the development and demonstration of our model is its usefulness for improving the employment of translation in foreign language teaching. The application of our model to foreign language teaching is the topic of the next chapter.

CHAPTER VII

IMPLICATIONS FOR FOREIGN LANGUAGE TEACHING

The main purpose of this study has been the development of a model for translation quality assessment. To give a detailed account of the role which translation has played in foreign language teaching, and to fully explore the implications of our model for foreign language teaching would go beyond the framework of this study. In the following we shall, therefore, limit ourselves to an indication of some major trends in the role of translation in foreign language teaching, followed by an outline of what we envisage to be the implications of our model for alternative uses of translation in foreign language teaching.

A. Some Trends in the Role of Translation in Foreign Language Teaching

Translation as a crosslingual technique in foreign language teaching has a long tradition. Translation from the foreign language was probably first used in the third century by elementary school teachers of Latin in the Greek communities of the Roman Empire (cf. Kelly, 1969:172). During the early middle ages when Latin was still a "living language" and the only medium of instruction in the schools, translation is hardly mentioned as a teaching technique. However, translation began to gain importance once the vernaculars were being taught in the classrooms and vernacular translations of the classics gained in popularity. During the late middle ages, the technique of "construing" was combined with translating into the classical languages: the dissection of sentences and words according to their grammatical functions was followed by an establishment of vernacular equivalents for the individual analytical parts, and the resulting "literal" translation was gradually changed into an acceptable vernacular sentence. This procedure became a keystone of classical language instruction. During the Renaissance, "simple translation" into a foreign language, which was used as a device to develop a sense of style in the foreign language (complementing composition), was frequently complemented by "double translation", a combination of translation from and into the foreign language and intensive reading.

At the end of the eighteenth century, the teaching of Latin had turned into a formalized ritual--supposedly disciplining students' minds--which centred on grammatical rules and their application. This method of instruction of Latin was then naturally transferred onto those few modern languages that were beginning to be taught in the schools. (There is little information on translation in the teaching of modern languages up to the end of the eighteenth century, since modern languages were usually acquired privately by direct contact with a native speaker and with the objective of speaking the language only, an objective for which translation was not considered to be useful.)

Translation from the foreign language constituted the major form of exercise up to the last quarter of the eighteenth century; translation into the foreign language gained major importance largely through the influence of Meidinger (quoted in Mackey, 1965: 142) who first recommended translation into the foreign language through the application of grammatical rules: the basis of the "grammar-translation method" had been laid.

In the textbooks of nineteenth century authors like Seidenstücker, Plötz, Ahn, and Ollendorf (see Mackey, 1965: 143) translation became the single dominant feature of language learning exercises. Grammatical rules and paradigms were to be learned through their application in the translation of disconnected, artificially constructed sentences--a practice that clearly did gross injustice to language as a living, functioning entity. In the latter half of the nineteenth century, this practise, therefore, not surprisingly, provoked opposition by a number of methodologists, among them Marcel, Sauveur, Gouin, and Viëtor, who, basing themselves on the newly emerging sciences of linguistics and psychology, advocated a less formalized, more "natural" approach to language teaching. They stressed the importance of the spoken mode of the foreign language, and the essential similarity between mother tongue acquisition and foreign language learning, and they took a decided stand against the dominating role of translation in foreign language teaching. The attempts to reform foreign language teaching gave rise to the "direct method movement",[1] whose most extreme proponents made the exclusive use of the foreign language, i. e., the abolition of any form of translation to become one of its trademarks.[2] Later, when the application of the "direct method" in the schools demanded compromises, translation was again tolerated particularly at an advanced level.

At the beginning of the twentieth century, theorists like Sweet, Jespersen, and Palmer were taking a more balanced view of the nature of language teaching and learning, refraining from an a priori condemnation of translation. Sweet (1964:197-205) argued against the claim by direct methodologists that it is mainly translation which prevents a direct association of foreign language items with their extralinguistic referents. Sweet recommended the judicious use of translation: translation from the foreign language might be profitably used from the beginning to "make knowledge more exact" (1964:200);

---

[1]The label "direct" derives from the movement's emphasis on a "direct command" of the foreign language, i. e., one in which foreign language items are linked "directly" to their referents without the intermediary of the native language.

[2]Thus Palmer defines "direct method" as a "somewhat vague term loosely denoting a system of language teaching largely based on the doctrine that translation should be excluded in the greatest possible measure" (1968:225).

translation _into_ the foreign language should be undertaken only if and when a thorough knowledge of the foreign language is already guaranteed, translating into a partially known language being an "impossible task... [that] can be accomplished only under restrictions which make it either an evasion or a failure" (1964:203).

Jespersen (1967: especially 40-86) was more strongly opposed to translation, especially translation as an _aim_ in foreign language teaching: translation into the foreign language hinders the practical command of the foreign language, and translation into the native language tends to corrupt the command of the native language due to the restraining and confusing co-presence of foreign language items in the mind. Jespersen did concede that "translation might still be a useful and indispensable _means_ in the service of language instruction" (1967: 56)--translation from the foreign language as a means of economically interpreting foreign language items and testing comprehension, and translation into the foreign language as a means of giving students some practice in the production of foreign language items as well as of testing such production. However, Jespersen kept stressing the point that translation from the foreign language is by no means the _best_ means of getting at the meaning of foreign language items, and he presented a whole range of more advisable techniques (1967:58-79). _Occasional_ translation exercises might be advisable, i. e., translation not as the "daily bread of language instruction", but as an interesting change in a predominantly monolingual instruction.

Palmer (1968) advocated the use of translation from the foreign language as a legitimate way of "semanticizing", i. e., conveying the meaning of foreign language items, the total exclusion of translation being "an uneconomical and unnatural principle" (1968:90). In criticizing the "grammar-translation method's" use of translation of isolated items, Palmer stressed the danger of trying to find equivalences between contextless units in the foreign and native languages. A sensible use of translation should involve larger, connected linguistic units.

The influence of the direct method movement, and of theorists like Sweet, Jespersen, and Palmer on the practice of language teaching in Europe was considerable but, in spite of heated discussions, did not lead to a complete banning of translation from the repertoire of language teaching techniques. In Britain, a compromise method (I. A. A. M., 1949) evolved after much debate, in which translation into the foreign language called "prose composition" played a prominent part in advanced language instruction. In the higher educational field, translation has kept its key role in foreign language instruction even up to the present day. In the foreign language departments of European and North American universities, translation of (mostly) literary passages <u>into</u> the foreign language (prose composition, thème, Hinübersetzung), and from the foreign language often referred to as "unseen translation" (version, Herübersetzung), had and has always been widely used as a teaching technique and for examination purposes.[1]

In North America, the direct method movement had never had much official influence.[2] At the beginning of the twentieth century, the Report of the Committee of Twelve (Thomas, 1901) staunchly supported a type of grammar-translation methodology, the main purpose of foreign language teaching being described as the learner's ability to translate at sight, and the ultimate objective being the ability to read the foreign language. The "reading method"--like the "grammar-translation method" based on a formal (as opposed to a functional) approach to language learning--gained prominence in North American education during the interwar years. Primary attention was given to the decoding of written texts which were based on a controlled vocabulary; translation was used to teach the meaning of vocabulary items.

During the Second World War, the need to quickly bring large

---

[1]However, especially the traditional prose composition exercise has been severely criticized in recent decades (see e. g., Thomas 1963), for being an essentially literary device, which does not train students in the natural and creative use of the foreign language. Alternative uses of "the prose", suggested, for instance, by Lockwood (1955) and Thomas (quoted in Healey, 1967:48) give priority not to translation proper but to an in-depth linguistic-stylistic study of the foreign language text accompanied by occasional comparisons of native and foreign language elements. As a later (and minor) step, students translate a few sentences into the foreign language or compose a short passage in the foreign language on the basis of the prepared text.

[2]There were, however, private language schools using the "Berlitz-method", a "direct method" that places great emphasis on aural understanding and speaking, and tolerates no translation.

numbers of American government personnel to a fluent speaking knowledge of a foreign language led to the establishment of a program known as the "Army Specialized Training Program". The method underlying this program which, because of the active part played by linguists like Bloomfield in constructing it--was sometimes called the "Structural Linguists' Method" (cf. Hammerly, 1971:501), was mainly based on the assumption that language is primarily oral, and that communication is the main purpose of language learning. Oral skills were therefore stressed throughout a language course, and the native language was used as little as possible. Translation from the foreign language was, however, used for explanation, and for making students find sentence (never word-for-word) equivalences in the native language.

During the late 1950's, when the influence of behaviourist learning theory and structural linguistics was strong, a similar method became prominent which was later referred to as the "audio-lingual method". Mimicry, memorization, and pattern drill were the trademarks of this method; translation was relegated into the background but never completely banned from the foreign language classroom: audio-lingual courses usually included translations of the early foreign language dialogues; translation drills were part of most audio-lingual exercise batteries, and even translations of continuous passages into the foreign language were included in some audio-lingual courses --as a very advanced exercise. There were, however, audio-lingual theorists (e.g., Brooks, 1964) who stigmatized translation as a harmful exercise claiming that the exclusive use of the foreign language would minimize interference and thus improve the process of learning a foreign language. The opposition against translation as a teaching technique on the grounds that it stifled the ability to "think in the new language" (which had already motivated the direct methodists' attacks against translation) was now revived in a more modern guise: translation was blamed for failing to produce the right kind of bilingualism, i.e., <u>coordinate</u> (as opposed to <u>compound</u>) bilingualism.[1] Ervin and Osgood (1965:140) stated that it is mainly by immersing onself in the foreign language and by relying as little as possible on translation that one reaches coordinate bilingualism, a prerequisite for the desired ability to think in the foreign language. If one avoided translation, there would be no interposition of an intermediate process between a concept and the way it is expressed in the foreign language. Translation was also considered dangerous because it distracts the learner from establishing a relationship between a sentence and the situation in which the sentence is uttered by forcing the learner to relate a sentence in the foreign language to a sentence in the native language (and

---

[1]According to Ervin and Osgood (1965) <u>compound</u> bilinguals are those who operate with a single set of representational mediation processes for the two languages. <u>Coordinate</u> bilinguals possess two distinct semantic systems, i.e., a separate set of representational mediation processes for the two languages.

vice versa). An undesirable "merged code" or compound bilingualism is the result. However, there may be no theoretical justification for such a conceptual artifact as the coordinate-compound dichotomy (see, for instance, Macnamara (1970) for a severe challenge of the coordinate-compound distinction). But even if one accepts the theoretical construct of coordinate and compound commands of a foreign language, there is no clear evidence that avoidance of translation is linked to a coordinate command of a foreign language and translation to a compound one.

In the mid-sixties, Carroll's (1966b) proposal of a distinction between the "Audio-Lingual Habit Theory" and the "Cognitive Code Learning Theory" started a series of polarized methodological discussions about the advantages or disadvantages of audio-lingual and cognitive procedures, among the latter translation. Despite the fact that Carroll (1971) himself tried to reconcile the views by suggesting a "Cognitive Habit Formation Theory", much of the dichotomized thinking still prevails up to the present day. Experimental studies (e.g., Scherer and Wertheimer, 1964; Smith, 1970) could not resolve the methodological issues. However, in a recent overview of "global" experiments designed to assess the relative merit of audio-lingual and cognitive procedures, Cooke (1974) has shown that there is some evidence in favour of cognitive procedures--among them translation. In a smaller study with specific relevance to translation, Schiffler (1970) has proved the superiority in written comprehension of a beginning class in French that had used translation exercises (into the native language only) over a class that had had no translation exercises, and Parent and Belasco (1970) have found that for achieving the objective of reading comprehension, the use of bilingual texts can be recommended. However, as Carroll (1971:113) has stressed, it is difficult to resolve this methodological issue experimentally since a large degree of the variance in the results is due to the teacher and his ability to manage learning behaviour and learning procedures in the students--a largely unexplored variable in educational research.

In the recent "cognitive trend" in language teaching, which draws its rationale from Gestaltist and cognitive psychology and from transformational-generative grammar, conscious understanding and control of the structures of the foreign language through study and analysis are emphasized, as well as the necessity of actively using and "creating" linguistic structures rather than passively responding to them. It is mainly a renewed emphasis on the rules of grammar and explanation in language teaching, but not a concern with the role of translation which characterizes the post-Chomskyan period in language teaching.

However, there are a few trends in which the new ideas of stressing the importance of the learner's conscious recognition and control of the critical features of the foreign language system , e.g., those that differ from, or are similar to, his native language, have been used in arguments in favour of translation. It is thus the crucial role which the native language plays in providing cognitive support which is now most frequently stressed by those who argued for giving translation a more important place in language teaching. Dodson (1967) advocating a "bilingual method" of language teaching which includes the systematic use of the native language both in the process of conveying meanings and in practising, suggests that translation might be profitably used to assist the students' understanding of lexical and structural differences between the native and foreign languages. Dodson also makes a plea for something like "compound bilingualism" as an objective in foreign language teaching: "The sign of true bilingualism is not merely the possession of two languages but also the ability to jump easily from one to the other"(1967:90). Following Dodson, Butzkamm (1973) advocates what he calls "Aufgeklärte Einsprachigkeit" ("Enlightened monolingualism") giving a number of suggestions as to the employment of carefully selected and sequenced translation exercises. In a similar vein, Sepp (1973) presents a detailed schema of the use of translation exercises with reference to different phases of instruction (e.g., presentation, repetition, or control) and to different levels of language.

Stern (forthcoming) also makes a point of stressing the potential usefulness of the existence of the students' native language. Given the universal characteristics in any language, there may well be an advantage in using the students' knowledge of the native language as a building stone for the acquisition of the foreign language. It is unwise to ignore the learner's deeply anchored verbal behaviour system; on the contrary, it may be best to deliberately make use of it, for instance through several crosslingual techniques, including translation.

In several pleas for the employment of translation in language teaching, contrastive analysis has been used to provide a theoretical foundation for claims of the usefulness of translation exercises. Thus Kirkwood (1966) suggests that translation might well be used as a basis for contrastive analysis which, he argues, has a high explanatory value especially for advanced students. Kirkwood maintains that

> contrastive analysis through translation--translation as a means and not as an end in itself, and in small but intensive doses--is a way of bringing to the students' attention points of differences and conflict on a semantic and syntactic level, of coming to grips with these differences and conflicts and to some extent of resolving them (Kirkwood, 1966:178).

Similarly, Rivers (1972) suggests that translation as "the contrastive technique *par excellence* in foreign language teaching" (1972: 43) might profitably be used with advanced students in order to develop in the students a linguistic awareness of contrasts between native and foreign language items and structures. Students should analyze source language texts as well as their own tentative translations of these texts in order to uncover equivalence relationships. The exploration of the full range of similarity and contrast between the lexical items and structures of the two languages would demand a comparison of a number of alternative translation equivalents.

Wilss (1973) also adopts a contrastive approach to translation. He advocates the use of grammatical translation exercises in which source language sentences are first analyzed into their immediate constituents, and then step-by-step translated so that a conscious comparison of various structural similarities and divergencies is facilitated. Muskat-Tabakowska (1973) points to the usefulness of translation in making students not only aware of the peculiarities of the foreign language but also of their native language.

In listing the above suggestions by theorists who recently argued in favour of translation as a teaching technique, we should, however, not forget that there has always existed a strong "camp" of opponents to the use of translation in the foreign language classroom who refer to translation as an unnatural activity or a highly specialized art which is either not at all or (worse still) negatively related to how students operate in a genuine foreign language environment, and which is of very limited applicability to the desired development of the four skills. Thus, Söll (1966) points to the ever-present limits of translatability--especially in "literary texts"--and claims that, for this reason, translation can never be an appropriate exercise even for advanced learners.[1] Friedrich (1967) maintains that, in the beginning stages of foreign language learning, translation should be completely banned from the syllabus: translation is to be regarded as an independent fifth skill which has no relation to the acquisition of the four basic skills of listening, speaking, reading, and writing. Göller (1967) claims that, particularly in using translations from the foreign language, it is only passive knowledge of the foreign language which is being taught to the students, and which, in turn, will only negatively influence any active use of the foreign language. Hausmann (1975) maintains that translation can only be sensibly used for achieving competence in the (subsidiary) skill of writing in the foreign language.

The controversy about the use of translation is far from settled today. The two most important reasons for this continuing debate seem to us to be the following:

1) the fact that the nature of translation is still little understood by those who plead for or against the use of translation in language teaching. Any sensible discussion about the extent to which translation can be used in language teaching, and the ways in which it can be employed most fruitfully should, however, be done on the basis of some theoretical understanding of the nature of translation, the different types of translation, and ways of assessing the quality of translations. It has

---

[1]This argument had already been used by Jespersen (1967: 54-55).

been the purpose of this study to provide some such understanding which might form the basis for further investigations into the role of translation as a pedagogical device;

2) the fact that translation has hitherto most frequently been used (and recommended) to achieve the objective of linguistic competence only, and those supporting the use of translation in foreign language teaching have, in general, not progressed beyond making programmatic statements, i. e., they largely failed to propose concrete and detailed alternatives.[1] Hitherto translation has been mainly employed as a device to:

a. illustrate and explain grammatical points and drill certain constructions specially "made up" for this purpose,

b. help the teacher in controlling whether the students "understand properly" often contextless linguistic units,

c. provide the teacher with a handy means of large-scale testing of a variety of (largely unspecified) types of knowledge and skills. In evaluating translations for this purpose, it has been mainly "linguistic correctness" which has been measured, i. e., overtly erroneous errors have been given most attention.

---

[1]One notable exception is Rivers (1975) and Rivers et al.(1975) which are part of a series of practical guides for teaching foreign languages. In a section on translation, the authors give both concrete and detailed suggestions of various types of translation exercises.

Such uses of translation fail to exploit the real pedagogical usefulness of this complex crosslingual activity. It is the strong pragmatic component in translation which makes it so potentially useful in the teaching of foreign languages. In translation exercises, one should not --and this has been the crucial flaw of most uses of translation in the classroom--draw the learner's attention to the formal properties of the source and translation sentences alone, but stress the importance of situational meanings.[1]

In the following, we shall propose some methods of using translation in this way i. e., we are here concerned with translation as a technique, not as an objective in foreign language teaching.

B. Alternatives to Current Uses of Translation in Foreign Language Teaching

We believe that, if translation is carried out as an exercise in establishing pragmatic equivalences by relating linguistic forms to their communicative functions as utterances, it may fulfill a useful, contributory role in achieving the objective of communicative compe-

---

[1]Proposals of exercises along these lines have been made by Gramer (1973) with reference to simultaneous translation (interpretation), and by La Forge (1971) who, following Curran (quoted in La Forge, 1971:61), experimented with a method called "Community Language Learning" which also involves interpretation.

tence.[1] We thus suggest that the use of translation in the foreign language classroom be extended to embrace a whole range of translation activities involving, for instance, the explicit comparison of cultural phenomena in the source and target language communities, the creative production of source and target language texts, the changing of individual situational dimensions in ST and/or TT, as well as a context-sensitive evaluation of translations and versions.

In our concept of translation activities, we would aim at improving both receptive and productive aspects of communicative competence. We would suggest that translation activities be conducted mainly with advanced students, whose communicative competence is already so developed that they have an overview of the equivalence relations between the two languages and cultures.

In the suggested translation activities, we would give priority to the communicative use of language. In any language activity which focusses on communication, language ceases to be an isolated subject,

---

[1]The concept of communicative competence was first introduced by Campbell and Wales (1970) and Hymes (1971) who tried to present an alternative to the Chomskyan competence-performance dichotomy (cf. Chomsky, 1965) by positing this more comprehensive type of competence defined as the ability to produce and understand utterances that are appropriate to a given purpose and to the linguistic and extralinguistic context in which they are made. The concept of communicative competence has been used with reference to language teaching by various theorists, e.g., Savignon (1972), Lütjen (1973), Rivers (1973), White (1974), Paulston (1974), Piepho (1974), and Littlewood (1975).

but appears to be interlocked with other subjects. Our translation activities would, therefore, involve an amalgamation of linguistic study of the foreign language and cultural study, as well as the practice of interdisciplinary study, i. e., the coordination of language activities with activities in the social sciences, history, natural science, English, etc. in order to facilitate the use of a wide range of Provinces for the texts necessary in developing a high degree of communicative competence.

In our view, translation activities can only be conducted at the level of text.[1] Only at this level can both linguistic and extralinguistic context be given full consideration, and only through using texts can the nature of equivalence relations in translation, and the overriding importance of establishing a dimensional profile before actually starting to translate and to evaluate, be fully recognized.

The predominant use of written texts in translation has, we claim, a great advantage: it may be valuable for advanced students as it provides a good counterbalance to the current emphasis on the use of spoken language varieties in earlier stages of language learning.

Current concern with using situationalized speech acts in the teaching of foreign languages (cf., e. g., Weber, 1973; v. Ziegesar

---

[1]See Jäger (1972) and King (1973) who express a similar view criticizing the frequent use of translations of isolated words and sentences.

1975) and with basing language courses on a "notional syllabus"[1] (cf. Wilkins, 1972, 1973; van Ek, 1975) might also be profitably complemented by using translation in a deliberate comparison of the pragmatic potentials of the source and target languages. The suggested use of translation activities with a view to achieving communicative competence does seem to fit well into recent proposals of "functional language teaching" made, for instance, by Widdowson (1974 a, b) and Allen and Widdowson (1975).[2] Widdowson (1974 a, b) even expressly supports the use of translation in teaching students how to read scientific English. In our view, the use of translation need not be restricted to the teaching of a foreign language for special purposes, but might also be extended to all kinds of advanced students for whom the foreign language is already a fairly adequate means of expressing what they know, and are able to formulate, in their native language. Allen and Widdowson's (1975) suggestion of a re-introduction of translation as a teaching technique on the basis of a functional approach to language teaching, which would involve the establishment of common basic

---

[1]A "notional syllabus" is based on a selection of semantico-grammatical categories (e.g., "time" or "quantity") and communicative-functional categories (e.g., "suasion" or "argument"), which are related both to anticipated situations in which they are likely to occur, and to linguistic forms suitable for encoding them in actual utterances.

[2]See also Allen and Widdowson (1974), the first in a series of textbooks entitled English in Focus, which exemplify a "functional approach" to the teaching of reading comprehension skills.

propositions that are merely expressed "differently" on the surface of the two languages, needs, we believe, to be supplemented by a consideration of pragmatic aspects of meaning of the kind outlined above in the suggested model of translation quality assessment.

In view of the complexity of any type of translation activity, we would suggest that any (native or foreign language) source text should be analyzed, discussed, translated, and evaluated either in the class plenum or in small groups so that all students derive the maximum benefit out of the reflections about linguistic/pragmatic choices and their relative adequacy at every step of the translation activities.[1]

Given the division of translation types into covert and overt translations, we would suggest that it is covert translation which can be more profitably used in foreign language teaching: STs which are "live" texts, directly addressed to two corresponding contemporary source and target language audiences will be more immediately interesting and motivating than the kind of source-culture bound, often literary works which, however timeless they may be, are frequently mere "dead" documents to the students. For example, STs calling for an overt translation have been only too typical in translation exercises in the past and have accounted for much of the boredom that has accompanied translation exercises in the classroom.

---

[1]Such an "open forum" treatment of translation activities had already been suggested by Jespersen (1967:83-4).

All texts chosen for translation activities should be totally contextualized [1] for the students, i. e., they must be relevant to the students' particular range of experiences and interests, and they must be presented as part of a "situation" which approaches authenticity to the greatest possible degree. Student-relevant "situational teaching", which has recently been propagated by many language teaching theorists and practitioners (cf. e.g., Piepho, 1973; and Krumm, 1974), can, we claim, be done on the basis of the type of translation activities we envisage. In the following, we shall give some concrete suggestions for translation activites according to the model developed above. In these suggestions, we shall not, as is customarily done in the field, differentiate between "translations into the foreign language" and "translations from the foreign language". These two "types of translation" are often said to differ in terms of difficulty: translation into the foreign language is considered to be more difficult presupposing a thorough knowledge of the foreign language, whereas translation from the foreign language is often thought to require much less expertise in the foreign language. In our concept of translation activities, the kind

---

[1] With this suggestion, we follow Müller (1973) who proposed that any text used in a foreign language classroom should pass the "Kontextualisierbarkeitsprobe" ("contextualization test") for the particular students exposed to the text. See also Kleineidam (1974) who also stresses the importance of carefully selecting texts according to the particular needs and interests of the students.

of ST (either in the native or the foreign language) and TT treatment suggested in the above model, demands an advanced level for both translation directions. Therefore, no explicit distinction between the two directions will be made in the following suggestions of translation activities. However, it is obviously clear that STs in the foreign language will require more preparatory work with the students (i. e., a more detailed analysis and explanation of the linguistic peculiarities of the texts) than native language STs.

No claim is made that the kind of activities we suggest here are novel, nor is it claimed that they provide the final answer to the issue of how translation should be used in foreign language teaching. More effective translation activities may easily be conceived, and many useful translation exercises stressing the functioning of language in authentic situations have been carried out by imaginative language teachers --in an informal way--at all times. However, we believe that the following suggestions for translation activities may provide some stimulating ideas of how translation might be employed along the lines of the proposed model of translation quality assessment.

1. Translation Activities Involving Ready-Made STs. a) The teacher selects a variety of authentic textual pairs (STs and TTs) as realizations of particular functions in concrete situations, and conducts a simplified version of the kind of analysis, comparison, and evaluation suggested in this study. We believe that such a contrastive activity is

useful for sensitizing students to the different catalogue of linguistic means by which a particular function can be realized in the students' mother tongue and the foreign language. A comparison of ST and TT along the lines suggested in the model (cf. above, Chapters III and IV) may facilitate a conscious recognition of the different workings of the two languages in use for a particular purpose. This type of translation activity is thus useful in developing the "cognitive domain" of communicative competence. In a classroom, a foreign language is usually learned on the basis of previous knowledge of the native language; consequently, students tend to contrast the use of their native language for a particular purpose with that of the foreign language. Students are also likely to compare cultural features of the two language communities in order to discover similarities and divergencies. Such a linguistic-cultural comparison of native and foreign language utterances is a natural and ineradicable activity in any learner of a foreign language. Translation used to compare explicitly and directedly--in the manner suggested above--merely makes a virtue out of what has often been considered a vice.

The discussion of mismatches established in the course of the comparison of a specific ST and its (covert) TT may involve (as we have demonstrated above, pp.197 -200) a discussion of presuppositions of cultural differences, national stereotypes, etc. Translation activities may thus facilitate the joint teaching of linguistic and cultural aspects.

Further, our model of analyzing and comparing will enable the students, especially in the case of seemingly straightforward "ideational" texts, to recognize a wealth of latent information, of subtle linguistic attempts at manipulating the addressees (as was, for instance, the case in the Commercial Text, cf. pp. 82-98), emphasizing and underplaying facts, etc.

b) The teacher selects a variety of authentic source language or target language texts which match the students' level of communicative competence, analyzes the texts with the students in the manner described in our model, and asks the students to translate the texts. In a translation activity of this kind, it is important to fully situationalize the texts, i.e., to provide the students with a complete, motivating account of the origin of the text, and to make the task they are to perform as close as possible to fulfilling a real communicative need. Along the same lines, Rivers (1973) has pointed to the possibility of having students simulate a situation in which they pretend to relay information to a monolingual visitor in their midst. This idea can be concretely illustrated by the following two examples:

Situation 1:

A neighbour, who does not speak German, has just received a letter from a German girl written in German. She has noticed in the letter that frequent reference is being made to the name of her son who is working for the Canadian forces in the Black Forest in Germany. The neighbour is anxious to understand the letter as she is afraid it will be bad news. Now she has asked you--a student of German-- to give her both a quick summary of the contents in English and to write a translation of it for future reference, i.e., the students will be asked to produce an oral version (a resumé) of the ST as well as a written translation. We believe that giving a genuine oral version would exceed the students' competence; therefore, the oral version may well be done in writing in this context of learning a foreign language. Differences between the spoken and written modes and between a summarizing version and a translation may be discussed with the students.

Situation 2:

During your summer holidays, you are working on a building site. Your supervisor has just received a maintenance manual for the new fork-lift truck. Unfortunately, the manual is written in German. He knows that you know some German and asks you to translate the manual for him, and also to give the other workers an idea of its main points, i.e., as in situation 1 above, the students will be asked to produce both a written translation and an oral summarizing version.

Along those lines, the teacher may construct a whole range of situations which are likely to motivate the students because a communicative need is being simulated. Important in this connection is also the selection of a wide variety of Provinces and of the entire textual profile as conditioned by the other situational dimensions, in order to keep up the students' interest and at the same time broaden their repertoire of language varieties.

The TTs are evaluated, corrected, and discussed in class according to dimensional mismatches and overtly erroneous errors. Relative evaluation standards will be set by the teacher according to his particular teaching objective and the particular importance he assigns to any one parameter in his analysis. Mismatches on this parameter will then be rated higher than mismatches on others. The relative importance of certain types of overtly erroneous errors will depend, as outlined above (p. 209) on the relative strength of the ideational component of the textual function and, of course, on the teacher's particular rating standards and objectives. This differentiated assessment of students' TTs which always involves a detailed discussion in class of the exact reasons and consequences for a mismatch, seems to be a most important implication of our suggested contextualized use of translation in foreign language teaching. Whether translation quality assessment along the lines indicated here is a feasible procedure in regular teaching remains, however, an open question.

c) A more complicated variation of b) above: following the analysis and translation of a given (mother-tongue) ST in the suggested way, the students are asked to change ST's function, e.g., convert a specialist scientific text into a scientific text directed at a lay audience (i. e., a case of intralingual overt version production). Various parameter changes will be undertaken using the imagination of the students, and on the basis of these, the original ST will be rewritten. Following this production of a new ST (a version of the original ST) in the students' mother tongue, the students translate this new ST. Changes along the entire textual profile will be discussed in class with reference to both original and modified STs and TTs.

2. Translation Activities Involving the Production of Original STs. The following activities make use of the students' creative imagination and build on simulated close-to-reality communicative needs in the students. In these activities, the students start from the function of a text and construct the text in accordance with this function, and some other dimensional data contributing to this function as well as an outline of the content supplied to them.

a) The teacher gives the students the following assignment: Write a letter to a boy(girl) in Vancouver. The address of this boy (girl) has been given to you by a pen-friend association. He (she) is of your age and attends a comparable educational institution. In your letter to this boy (girl), you shall try to win him (her) over to be your pen-friend. It is your task to make your letter as polite, entertaining, and attractive as possible. You will have to demonstrate your interest in your potential pen-friend's personal habits, school environment, the attractions of his home town, etc.

Following this first task, the teacher and the students analyze the mother-tongue letter according to our suggested model. Then the teacher gives the students the second assignment: Translate this letter (covertly) into German, i.e., write the "same" letter to a potential pen-friend in Berlin, making all the necessary changes as to places you want to see and as to your potential pen-friend's home and school environment, interests, etc. An assessment of the students' covert translations will then again be done along the lines suggested in our model.

Taking the above example of the letters to an English-speaking and a German-speaking pen-friend as a model, the teacher may vary the <u>Province</u> and any other dimension thus training the students in a wide range of communication situations. For instance, he may ask the students to write to a major steel plant in Ontario and request information about the size of the plant, its capacity, the nature of various technical processes, production figures, etc. For this task, some assistance from the science and technical departments will obviously be necessary. Having written the letter, the students analyze it along the situational dimensions and then (covertly) translate the letter, i.e., write an equivalent letter to a well-known steel plant in Germany. If such a task can be <u>really</u> situationalized, and the letters actually sent because of a genuine need on the part of the class, so much the better.

b) Another interesting translation activity involving the creation of a mother tongue text, is the construction of advertisements: the foreign language teacher may coordinate his work with the English and social science departments, such that there will be cooperation in the collation of a corpus of advertisements, the discussion of the assumptions underlying the production of advertisements as well as their grammatical, lexical, and textual peculiarities. Following this introduction, the students will then first produce advertisements in their native language--preferably advertisements for products that are of interest to them as a group of consumers--and then covertly translate these advertisements into the foreign language making due allowance for differences in the two language communities' geography, climate, history, etc., as well as more subtle cultural phenomena. A discussion of stereotypes or national characters will form a natural part of this translation activity.

c) Foreign language learners might be exposed to practice in distinguishing overt from covert translations, and they might be sensitized to the cultural transposition which may be necessitated by the latter; students might be given a task in which an overt translation is commented upon, such that the TT reader is enabled to have a response to TT which is parallel to the response evoked by ST in the direct addressees or second-level addressees. For example, the students are asked to write a letter to a pen-friend in Germany and describe an amusing incident which centres on an English text which is to be translated as part of the letter he writes. Consider the following three examples of such texts:

1. A student forges a letter allegedly coming from his parents and accounting for his absence from school. In the body of the letter, he clearly, but unintentionally, reveals that it was written by himself, e.g., by having chosen a wrong form of address, or by making an incorrect pronominal reference to himself.

2. In an English lesson, a student writes an essay on "My Best Friend" describing an old sheepdog named "Blinker", which is the boy's nickname for the English teacher.

3. A notice appears on a board in school with some ambiguity, e.g., "The recreation room is to be closed for redecoration next week. Board games should be returned to Mr. Jones and balls to Mr. Smith."

In translating these texts, the students must translate overtly, but as the purpose of the overall translation of the letter to the penfriend is to amuse, he must seek to explain in the frame-letter how and why the original texts in their particular settings were amusing. (The use of culture-specific school terms, such as <u>taking attendance</u> is, of course, desirable.)

In all these activities, the teacher might also consider cooperation with teachers of other foreign languages that the students are learning. Translation activities involving several target languages might be especially useful for demonstrating linguistic and cultural differences between the various language communities.

It seems important to us that (advanced) students of a foreign language learn to perform motivated communicative acts in the foreign language, and to use the language creatively; that they learn to understand how others use the foreign language and why another's or their own use has gone wrong. Students will already have acquired all these skills in their mother tongue. One way of acquiring them in the foreign language may be through deliberate juxtaposition of the learner's verbal actions in the mother tongue and the foreign language in the kind of translation activities outlined above, which all included a detailed analysis and criticism of students' verbal actions by means of the model suggested in this thesis. The point of the examples of translation activities is, as was pointed out previously, not the novelty of the teaching techniques as such. Rather, it is the application of a particular translation model to language teaching.

CHAPTER VIII

CONCLUSION

In this chapter, we shall first give a summary of the proposed model for translation quality assessment, its theoretical consequences, and its pedagogical implications; second, we shall present a few suggestions for follow-up research to the present study.

A. Summary of the Proposed Model, its Theoretical Consequences, and Pedagogical Implications

This study attempted to develop a model for characterizing the linguistic-situational peculiarities of a given ST, comparing ST and TT, and making argued statements about the match of the two texts. The model was set up on the basis of pragmatic theories of language use, specifically speech act theory, functional and contextual views of language, and textual considerations.

The suggested basic requirement for equivalence of a given textual pair (ST and TT) is that TT should have a function--consisting of two functional components, the ideational and the interpersonal--which is equivalent to ST's function, and that TT should employ equivalent pragmatic means for achieving that function. The model's method of operation consists of the following steps: a given ST is first analyzed according to a set of eight dimensions, three language user dimensions (_Geographical Origin_, _Social Class_, _Time_), and five language use dimensions (_Medium_, _Participation_, _Social Role Relationship_, _Social Attitude_, _Province_), for which linguistic (syntactic, lexical, and textual) correlates are established. ST's resultant textual profile which characterizes its function such that each situational dimension contributes in a particular way to the two functional components is then taken as the yardstick against which TT is measured. Thus, TT's textual profile and function resulting from the same type of situational-linguistic analysis as that conducted with ST, is compared with ST's textual profile and function. The degree to which TT's profile and function match or do not match ST's, is the degree to which TT is more or less adequate in quality.

In evaluating the relative match between ST and TT, a distinction has been made between dimensional mismatches or _covertly erroneous errors_, and non-dimensional mismatches or _overtly erroneous errors_, the latter type of error comprising both mismatches of the denotative meanings of ST and TT elements and breaches of the target language system.

The final qualitative judgement of TT consists of a listing of both covertly and overtly erroneous errors, and of a statement of the resulting mismatches of each of the two functional components.

In order to demonstrate the model's practicability, it has been implemented with a corpus of eight German and English textual pairs (STs and TTs), four textual pairs being tentatively classified as belonging to the ideational functional category, four as belonging to the interpersonal functional category. The texts were selected so as to cover a wide range of different Provinces and they were matched in respect of the two languages.

On the basis of the results of these test cases, a "translation typology" has been suggested, i. e., a distinction between two basic types of translation: overt translation and covert translation. An overt translation is called for whenever an ST is source-culture linked and has independent status in the source language community. A covert translation is called for whenever an ST is not source-culture linked, and does not have independent status in the source language community; a covert translation is not marked pragmatically as a TT of an ST, but might equally well have been created in its own right.

The discovery of these two types of translation leads to an important modification of the provisional model as outlined above: the principle of functional equivalence which was proposed as the overriding criterion for translation quality has to be relativized in the following manner: it is only in cases of covert translation of non-source culture linked STs that it is possible to achieve functional equivalence. In cases of overt translation, the achievement of strict functional equivalence is impossible and a similar second level function is to be posited as a criterion for an adequate translation.

The difficulties in both translating and evaluating are of a different nature in the two cases, with covert translations presenting more subtle cultural transference and evaluation problems. Functional equivalence is difficult to achieve whenever a well-marked interpersonal component is discovered in the analysis of an ST calling for a covert translation. Differences in the cultural presuppositions in the source and target language communities may then necessitate the application of a cultural filter. The decision of whether the application of a cultural filter is necessary and justified involves, at the present time, in the absence of adequate ethnological research, a subjective judgement on the part of both translator and evaluator. The unjustified application of a cultural filter leads to the production of a covert version.

Cases of overt translation are generally more "straightforward": the overt transference leaving ST as intact as possible given the necessary linguistic recoding, presents less subtle cultural problems due to the omission of the stage of deciding whether a cultural filter ought to be applied. However, finding approximate linguistic-cultural equivalents on the language user dimensions may often be extremely difficult, and the evaluation of such "equivalents" involves--in the absence of completed linguistic-cultural contrastive analyses--a necessarily subjective element. The overt addition of a special secondary function to TT leads to an <u>overt version</u>.

Although we have been able to suggest the appropriateness of either a covert or an overt translation in the cases of the STs analyzed in detail in this study, it is, of course, true that--given the possibility of different subjective ways of viewing a text, and of specific arbitrarily determined purposes for a translation--<u>any</u> text may require an overt translation. The specific purpose for which a "translation" is required also determines whether a translation or an overt version should be produced.

The comparative assessment of different TTs of the same ST can be conducted on the basis of our model to the extent that the relative importance of the individual dimensions has been demonstrated in the analysis of ST. A relative weighting of covertly and overtly erroneous errors can, in the proposed model, only be achieved through a consideration of each individual textual pair. However, the subgroup of overtly erroneous errors referred to as "mismatches of the denotative meanings of ST and TT elements", will detract more seriously from the quality of a TT than dimensional mismatches, whenever the ST has a strongly marked ideational functional component. A detailed hierarchy of errors will depend in any given case on the particular objective(s) of the evaluation.

We believe that the suggested distinctions between a covert and an overt translation, and between a translation and a version, and the resultant consequences for the practice of translation and the assessment of translation quality, shed some light on a hitherto confused area of translation. The proposed model may also be used for assessing an overt version's adequacy: given a precise specification of the way the overt version's function differs from ST's function, the functional change may be "added" to ST's textual profile, and the amended profile is to be taken as the norm against which the overt version can be measured.

An important outcome of this study has been the demonstration of the potential usefulness of the model in the context of foreign language teaching. Thus, several alternative ways of using "translation activities" for the development of students' communicative competence have been suggested on the basis of the proposed model. These activities involve (1) ready-made STs used either for linguistic-cultural comparison, or for translation along the lines of the model, or for the production of different types of versions; (2) the production of STs on the basis of a given function and various dimensional data. It is suggested that covert translations are more likely to motivate students than overt ones, the latter having been (partially) responsible for the negative image of translation in foreign language teaching. Distinguishing between overt and covert translations, and a translation and a version, is also part of the envisaged range of translation activities.

The suggested translation activities are not necessarily novel;

however, they demonstrate how the suggested model of translation quality assessment may be applied to the use of translation in the foreign language classroom.

B. Some Suggestions for Future Research

From the present study which was mainly designed to develop a model for translation quality assessment, there seem to emerge three types of follow-up studies:

1. The first obvious follow-up to the present study would be a study in which the suggested model is applied directly to actual tasks of producing and evaluating translations in various institutional settings. Similarly, an investigation into the applicability of the model to the training of professional translators might be conducted. The purpose of both these studies would be to find out how the model works in realistic circumstances.

2. A second type of follow-up study would involve research undertaken on the basis of the model developed in the present study. Three possibilities suggest themselves: (a) a study might be conducted which would test the practicability of the model with a greater variety of texts using different language pairs than those that were used in the "test cases" of the present study; (b) a study designed to elicit informants' judgements on the basis of the model developed in the present study. Such a study might involve a number of bilingual or monolingual

judges, or both. The judges would be asked to rate selected sequences of translation sentences, and the questions put to the judges would be based on an analysis of the ST conducted along the lines of the proposed model. The claim put forward above (p.64) that there is no significant variation in intuitive judgements might be put to the test in such a study; (c) a study involving two culturally divergent languages such as Japanese and English, or an American Indian language and English. Interesting modifications and revisions of the present model might result from such an investigation.

3. Since the exploration of the model's implication for foreign language teaching has not been the central topic of the present study, a third important type of follow-up studies might involve future research on the pedagogical implications of the proposed model. The present study is only a beginning: it may be regarded as a first step to re-open the issue of the use of translation in foreign language teaching. In the light of the suggested model for translation quality assessment, an observational study might be designed to investigate the different ways in which translation is used in foreign language teaching, and the extent to which it is used. Further, an experimental study might be conducted which would attempt to apply the proposed model in an educational setting. It would be interesting to find out what the model would contribute to the use of translation in foreign language education and how it would work at different levels of language instruction, and

with different language pairs.

Although the present study did not treat, in full detail, the controversial issue of the role of translation in foreign language teaching, it suggests that the usefulness of translation as a pedagogical device in language teaching might well be re-considered. Such a re-examination of the role of translation in the foreign language classroom might benefit from the insights into the fascinating subject of translation and translation quality assessment which this study tried to provide.

BIBLIOGRAPHY

Abercrombie, D.

1965 "Conversation and Spoken Prose", in Studies in Phonetics and Linguistics. Ed. by D. Abercrombie. London: Oxford University Press. 1-9.

Admoni, W.

1973 Die Entwicklungstendenzen des deutschen Satzbaus von heute. München: Hueber.

Allen, J. P. B. and H. G. Widdowson

1974 English in Physical Science. London: Oxford University Press.

1975 "Grammar and Language Teaching", in Papers in Applied Linguistics. Ed. by J. P. B. Allen and S. P. Corder. London: Oxford University Press. 45-97.

Amos, F. R.

1920 Early Theories of Translation. Folcroft, Pa.: The Writer.

Austin, J. L.

1962 How to do Things with Words. London: Oxford University Press.

Bach, E.

1968 "Nouns and Noun Phrases", in Universals in Linguistic Theory. Ed. by E. Bach and R. T. Harms. New York: Holt, Rinehart and Winston. 90-122.

Bausch, K. -R.

1970 "Qualité en traduction et linguistique dite 'différentielle'", Babel 16:1. 13-20.

Bierwisch, M.

1970 "Semantics", in New Horizons in Linguistics. Ed. by J. Lyons Harmondsworth: Penguin. 166-84.

Blankenship, J.

1962 "A Linguistic Analysis of Oral and Written Style", The Quarterly Journal of Modern Speech 48. 419-22.

Brooks, N.

1964 Language and Language Learning. 2nd ed. New York: Harcourt, Brace and World.

Brown, R. and A. Gilman

1960 "The Pronouns of Power and Solidarity", in Style in Language. Ed. by T. A. Sebeok. Cambridge, Mass.: M.I.T. Press. 253-76.

Bühler, K.

1965 Sprachtheorie. 2nd ed. Stuttgart: Fischer. [First edition 1934].

Bullock, M.

1963 "Enquête", in Quality in Translation. Ed. by E. Cary and R. W. Jumpelt. New York: Macmillan.

Butzkamm, W.

1973 Aufgeklärte Einsprachigkeit. Heidelberg: Quelle-Meyer.

Campbell, R. and R. Wales

1970 "The Study of Language Acquisition", in New Horizons in Linguistics. Ed. by John Lyons. Harmondsworth: Penguin. 242-60.

Carroll, J. B.

1966a "An Experiment in Evaluating the Quality of Translations", Mechanical Translation 9. 55-66.

1966b "The Contributions of Psychological Theory and Educational Research to the Teaching of Foreign Languages", in Trends in Language Teaching. Ed. by A. Valdman. New York: McGraw-Hill. 93-106.

1971 "Current Issues in Psycholinguistics and Second Language Teaching", TESOL Quarterly, 5:2. 101-114.

Cary, E. and R. W. Jumpelt

1965 Quality in Translation. New York: Macmillan.

Casagrande, J. B.

1954 "The Ends of Translation", IJAL 20:4. 335-40.

Catford, J. C.

1965 A Linguistic Theory of Translation. London: Oxford University Press.

1966 "Rapport: les problèmes pédagogiques de la traduction", in Actes du Premier Colloque International de Linguistique Appliqueé, Octobre 1964. Nancy: Faculté des lettres et des sciences humaines de l'université de Nancy. 286-307.

Chiu, R. K.

1973 "Measuring Register Characteristics: Implications for TESOL Curriculum Development", IRAL 11:1. 51-68.

Chomsky, N.

1965 Aspects of the Theory of Syntax. Cambridge, Mass.: M.I.T. Press.

Coburn-Staege, U.

1973 Der Rollenbegriff. Heidelberg: Quelle-Meyer.

Cooke, D.

1974 "The Role of Explanation in Foreign Language Instruction", Unpublished Ph.D. Dissertation, University of Essex.

Corder, S. P.

1973 Introducing Applied Linguistics. Harmondsworth: Penguin.

Crystal, D. and D. Davy

1969 Investigating English Style. London: Longman.

Davidson, P. O. and C. G. Costello (eds.)

1969 N=1. Experimental Studies of Single Cases. An Enduring Problem in Psychology. New York: van Nostrand.

Dixon, R. M. W.

1964 "On Formal and Contextual Meaning", Acta Linguistica 14. 23-46.

Dodson, C. J.

1967 Language Teaching and the Bilingual Method. London: Pitman.

Dreitzel, H. P.

1972 Die gesellschaftlichen Leiden und das Leiden an der Gesellschaft. Stuttgart: Enke.

Dressler, W.

1972 Einführung in die Textlinguistik. Tübingen: Niemeyer.

Dye, Omar A.

1971 "The Effects of Translation on Readability", Language and Speech 14:4. 392-97.

Ek, J. A. van

1975 The Threshold Level in a European Unit/Credit System for Modern Language Learning by Adults. Strasbourg: Council for Cultural Cooperation of the Council of Europe.

Ellis, J. and J. N. Ure

1969 "Language Varieties: Register", in Encyclopedia of Linguistics, Information and Control. Ed. by A. R. Meetham and R. A. Hudson. London: Pergamon Press. 251-59.

Elsen, C.

1963 "Enquête", in Quality in Translation (cf. Cary and Jumpelt). 74-75.

Enkvist, N. E.

1973 Linguistic Stylistics. The Hague: Mouton.

Enkvist, N. E., J. W. Spencer and M. J. Gregory.

1964 Linguistics and Style. London: Oxford University Press.

Ervin, S. M. and C. E. Osgood

1965 "Second Language Learning and Bilingualism", in Psycholinguistics: A Survey of Theory and Research Problems. Ed. by C. E. Osgood and T. A. Sebeok. Bloomington, Indiana: Indiana University Press. 139-45. [First published in 1954.]

Feider, H.

1969 "A Comparative Syntactic Description of Spoken and Written English", Unpublished Ph. D. Dissertation, Indiana University.

Firbas, J.

1964 "On Defining the Theme in Functional Sentence Analysis", Travaux linguistiques de Prague 1. 267-80.

1966 "Non-thematic Subjects in Contemporary English", Travaux linguistiques de Prague 2. 239-56.

Flesch, R.

1948 "A New Readability Yardstick", Journal of Applied Psychology 32:3. 221-33.

Forster, L.

1958 "Introduction", in Aspects of Translation. Ed. by A. D. Booth. London: Secker and Warburg. 1-28.

Friederich. W.

1963 "Zwei Grundbegriffe zur Bestimmung der Übersetzungsqualität", in Quality in Translation (cf. Cary and Jumpelt). 349-50.

Friedrich, W.

1967 "Zehn Thesen zum Sprachenlernen und Übersetzen", Praxis des neusprachlichen Unterrichts 14. 44-49.

Gleason, H. A.

1968 "Contrastive Analysis in Discourse Structure", in Monograph Series on Languages and Linguistics. Ed. by J. E. Alatis, no. 21. Washington, D. C.: Georgetown University Press. 39-63.

Göller, A.

1967 "Gedanken zur Herübersetzung", Praxis des neusprachlichen Unterrichts 14. 271-77.

Gold, D. L.

1972 "On Quality in Translation", parts I and II, Babel 18:1. 10-12 and 18:4. 29-30.

Govaert, M.

1971 "Critères de la traduction", in Interlinguistica. Ed. by K.-R. Bausch and H. M. Gauger. Tübingen: Niemeyer. 425-37.

Gramer, R.

1973 "Die Simultanübersetzung-Sprachlaborarbeit in der Oberstufe", Praxis des neusprachlichen Unterrichts. 20:1. 69-75.

Gregory, M.

1967 "Aspects of Varieties Differentiation", Journal of Linguistics 3. 177-98.

Gülich, E. and W. Raible

1972 Textsorten. Differenzierungskriterien aus linguistischer Sicht. Frankfurt· Athenäum.

1975 "Textsorten-Probleme", in Linguistische Probleme der Textanalyse. Jahrbuch 1973 des Instituts für deutsche Sprache. Düsseldorf: Schwann. 144-97.

Halliday, M. A. K.

1970a "Language Structure and Language Function", in New Horizons in Linguistics. Ed. by John Lyons. Harmondsworth: Penguin. 140-65.

1970b "Functional Diversity in Language as seen from a Consideration of Modality and Mood in English", Foundations of Language 6. 322-61.

1971 "Linguistic Function and Literary Style", in Literary Style: A Symposium. Ed. by S. S. Chatman. London: Oxford University Press. 330-68.

1973 Explorations in the Functions of Lanugage. London: Arnold.

Halliday, M. A. K., A. McIntosh and P. Strevens

1964 The Linguistic Sciences and Language Teaching. London: Longman.

Hammerly, H.

1971 "Recent Methods and Trends in Second Language Teaching", Modern Language Journal 55:8. 499-505.

Hausmann, F. -J.

1975 "Übersetzen-und was weiter? Zur Praxis der Fremdsprachenausbildung in der Universität", Linguistische Berichte 35. 54-56.

Havránek, B.

1964 "The Functional Differentiation of the Standard Language", in A Prague School Reader on Aesthetics, Literary Structure and Style. Ed. and trans. by Paul L. Garvin. Washington, D. C.: Georgetown University Press. 3-16.

Hayakawa, S. I.

1972 Language in Thought and Action. 3rd ed. New York: Harcourt, Brace and Jovanovich.

Healey, F. G.

1967 Foreign Language Teaching in the Universities. Manchester: Manchester University Press.

Hill, T.

1958 "Institutional Linguistics", Orbis 7:1. 441-54.

Hymes, D.

1968 "The Ethnography of Speaking", in Readings in the Sociology of Language. Ed. by J. A. Fishman. The Hague: Mouton. 99-138.

1971 On Communicative Competence. Philadelphia: University of Pennsylvania Press.

I. A. A. M. (The Incorporated Association of Assistant Masters in Secondary Schools)

1949 The Teaching of Modern Languages. London: University of London Press.

Jäger, G.

1972 "Übersetzen und Übersetzung im Fremdsprachenunterricht", Deutsch als Fremdsprache 9. 257-64.

1973a "Invarianz und Transferierbarkeit", in Neue Beiträge zu Grundfragen der Übersetzungswissenschaft. Ed. by A. Neubert and O. Kade. Frankfurt: Athenäum. 47-59.

1973b "Konfrontation und Translation", Wissenschaftliche Zeitschrift der Humboldt Universität 22:3. 157-63.

1975 Translation und Translationslinguistik. Halle: VEB Niemeyer.

Jakobson, R.

1960 "Closing Statement: Linguistics and Poetics", in Style in Language. Ed. by T. A. Sebeok. Cambridge, Mass: M.I.T. Press. 350-77.

Jakobson, R.

1966 "On Linguistic Aspects of Translation", in On Translation. Ed. by R. A. Brower. New York: Oxford University Press. 232-39.

Jespersen, O.

1967 How to Teach a Foreign Language. London: Allen and Unwin [First published in 1904].

Joos, M.

1959 "The Isolation of Styles", in Monograph Series on Languages and Linguistics. Ed. by R. S. Harrell, no. 12. Washington, D. C.: Georgetown University Press. 107-13.

1961 The Five Clocks. New York: Harcourt, Brace and World.

Kade, O.

1964 "Qualitätsstufen der Übersetzung", Fremdsprachen 4. 250-60.

1968 Zufall und Gesetzmässigkeit in der Übersetzung. Leipzig: VEB Verlag Enzyklopädie.

Kelly, L. G.

1969 25 Centuries of Language Teaching. Rowley, Mass.: Newbury House.

Kern, P.

1969 "Bemerkungen zum Problem der Textklassifikation", in Forschungsberichte des Instituts für deutsche Sprache, vol. 3. Ed. by U. Engel and I. Vogel. Düsseldorf: Schwann. 3-23.

King, P. B.

1973 "Translation in the English Language Course", ELT 28:1. 53-59.

Kirkwood, H. W.

1966 "Translation as a Basis for Contrastive Linguistic Analysis", IRAL 4. 175-82.

Klare, G. R.

1963 The Measurement of Readability. Ames, Iowa: Iowa University Press.

Kleineidam, H.

1974 "Für und Wider das Übersetzen: Zur Rolle der Übersetzung in der Ausbildung zukünftiger Fremdsprachenlehrer", Linguistische Berichte 32. 80-92.

Koller, W.

1972 Grundprobleme der Übersetzungstheorie. Bern: Francke.

1974 "Anmerkungen zu Definitionen des Übersetzungs"vorgangs" und der Übersetzungskritik", Aspekte der Theoretischen, Sprachenpaarbezogenen und Angewandten Sprachwissenschaft. Ed. by W. Wilss and G. Thome. Heidelberg: Groos. 35-45.

Krumm, H. J.

1974 "Fremdsprachenunterricht: Der Unterrichtsprozess als Kommunikationssituation", Unterrichtswissenschaft 4. 30-39.

LaForge, P. G.

1971 "Community Language Learning: A Pilot Study", Language Learning 21:1. 45-61.

Leech, G.

1974 Semantics. Harmondsworth: Penguin.

Lerchner, G.

1972 "Sprachnorm als linguistische und soziologische Kategorie", Linguistische Arbeitsberichte 6. 26-36.

Lévy, J.

1967 "Translation as a Decision Process", in To Honor Roman Jakobson on the Occasion of his Seventieth Birthday. Vol. 2. The Hague: Mouton. 1171-82.

Littlewood, W. T.

1975 "The Acquisition of Communicative Competence in an Artificial Environment", Praxis des neusprachlichen Unterrichts 22:1. 13-21.

Lockwood, W. B.

1955 "An Alternative to Prose Composition", Modern Languages 36:3. 105-108.

Lütjen, H. P.

1973 "Zur Kommunikativen Kompetenz in der Fremdsprache", IRAL 11:1. 81-89.

Lyons, J.

1969 Introduction to Theoretical Linguistics. Cambridge: Cambridge University Press.

Macnamara, J.

1967 "The Bilingual's Linguistic Performance: A Psychological Overview", The Journal of Social Issues 23:2. 58-77.

1970 "Bilingualism and Thought", in Monograph Series on Languages and Linguistics. Ed. by J. E. Alatis , no. 23. Washington, D. C.: Georgetown University Press. 25-40.

Mackey, W. F.

1965 Language Teaching Analysis. London: Longmans, Green.

Mathesius, V.

1971 "Die funktionale Linguistik", in Stilistik und Soziolinguistik. Ed. by E. Beneš and J. Vachek. München: List. 1-18. [Translation of the Czech original which appeared in 1929.]

Metscher, T.

1968 Sean O'Caseys dramatischer Stil. Braunschweig: Westermann.

Miller, G. A. and J. A. Beebe-Center

1958 "Some Psychological Methods for Evaluating the Quality of Translations", Mechanical Translation 3. 73-80.

Müller, R. M.

1973 "Situation und Lehrbuchtexte: Die Kontextualisierbarkeitsprobe", in Lehrwerkkritik: ein Neuansatz. Ed. by H. Heuer and R. M. Müller. Dortmund: Lambert Lensing. 31-45.

Mukarovsky, J.

1964 "Standard Language and Poetic Language", in A Prague School Reader on Aesthetics, Literary Structure and Style. Ed. and trans. by Paul L. Garvin. Washington, D.C.: Georgetown University Press. 17-30.

Muskat-Tabakowska, E.

1973 "The Function of Translation in Foreign Language Teaching", in Papers and Studies in Contrastive Linguistics, vol. 1. Ed. by J. Fisiak. Washington, D. C.: Centre for Applied Linguistics. 131-39.

Neubert, A.

1968 "Pragmatische Aspekte der Übersetzung", in Grundfragen der Übersetzungs wissenschaft. Ed. by A. Neubert. Leipzig: VEB Verlag Enzyklopädie. 21-33.

1972a "Invariance and Textual Types in Translation", in Proceedings of the Third Congress of the A. I. L. A. Copenhagen 1972. vol. 3. Ed. by J. Qvistgaard et al. Heidelberg: Groos. 482-90.

1972b "Theorie und Praxis für die Übersetzungswissenschaft", in Proceedings of the Third Congress of the A. I. L. A.Copenhagen 1972. vol. 3. Ed. by J. Qvistgaard et al. Heidelberg: Groos. 38-60.

1973 "Invarianz und Pragmatik", in Neue Beiträge zu Grundfragen der Übersetzungswissenschaft. Ed. by A. Neubert and O. Kade. Frankfurt: Athenäum. 13-25.

Newmark, P.

1969 "Some Notes on Translation and Translations", The Incorporated Linguist 8:4. 79-85.

1974 "Further Propositions on Translation", part 2. The Incorporated Linguist 13:3. 62-72.

Nida, E. A.

1964 Toward a Science of Translating. Leiden: Brill.

1974 "Semantic Structure and Translating", in Aspekte der Theoretischen, Sprachenpaarbezogenen und Angewandten Übersetzungswissenschaft. vol. 2. Ed. by W. Wilss and G. Thome. Heidelberg: Groos. 33-63.

1975 "Translation as Communication", Paper delivered at the Fourth Congress of the A. I. L. A., Stuttgart, 1975.

Nida, E. A. and C. R. Taber

1969 The Theory and Practice of Translation. Leiden: Brill.

Ogden, C. K. and I. A. Richard

1946 The Meaning of Meaning. 8th ed. London: Routledge and Kegan Paul [First edition 1923]

Oomen, U.

1971 "Systemtheorie der Texte", Folia Linguistica 5. 12-34.

Palmer, H. E.

1968 The Scientific Study and Teaching of Languages. London: Oxford University Press [First published in 1917]

Parent, P. and S. Belasco

1970 "Parallel-Column Bilingual Reading Materials as a Pedagogical Device; An Experimental Evaluation", Modern Language Journal 54:7. 493-504.

Paulston, C. B.

1974 "Linguistic and Communicative Competence", TESOL Quarterly 8:4. 347-62.

Piepho, H. E.

1973 "Linguistische, soziolinguistische und didaktische Anmerkungen zum Begriff 'Situation' im modernen Fremdsprachenunterricht", Zielsprache Französisch 1. 12-20.

1974 Kommunikative Kompetenz als übergeordnetes Lernziel im Englischunterricht. Dornburg-Frickhofen: Frankonius.

Pike, K.

1967 Language in Relation to a Unified Theory of Human Behaviour. 2nd ed. The Hague: Mouton.

Pigors, P. and F. Pigors

1961 Case Method in Human Relations: The Incident Process. New York: McGraw-Hill.

Polenz, P. von

1972 "Sprachnorm, Sprachnormierung, Sprachnormenkritik", Linguistische Berichte 17. 76-84.

Politzer, R. L.

1956 "A Brief Classification of the Limits of Translatability", Modern Language Journal 40. 319-22.

Postgate, J. P.

1922 Translation and Translations. London: Bell.

Quirk, R. and S. Greenbaum

1973 A University Grammar of English. London: Longman.

Reid, T. B.

1956 "Linguistics, Structuralism and Philology", Archivum Linguisticum 8. 28-37.

Reiss, K.

1968 "Überlegungen zu einer Theorie der Übersetzungskritik", _Linguistica Antverpiensia_ 2. 369-83.

1971a "Die Bedeutung von Texttyp und Textfunktion für den Übersetzungsprozess", _Linguistica Antverpiensia_ 5. 137-48.

1971b _Möglichkeiten und Grenzen der Übersetzungskritik_. München: Hueber.

1973 "Der Texttyp als Ansatzpunkt für die Lösung von Übersetzungsproblemen", _Linguistica Antverpiensia_ 7. 111-27.

Riffaterre, M.

1959 "Criteria for Style Analysis", _Word_ 15. 154-74.

1961 "Vers la définition du style", _Word_ 17. 318-44.

Rivers, W. M.

1972 "Contrastive Linguistics in Textbook and Classroom", in _Speaking in Many Tongues. Essays in Foreign Language Teaching_. Rowley, Mass.: Newbury House. 36-44.

1973 "From Linguistic Competence to Communicative Competence", _TESOL Quarterly_ 7:1. 25-34.

1975 _A Practical Guide to the Teaching of French._ New York etc.: Oxford University Press.

Rivers, W. M. _et al._

1975 _A Practical Guide to the Teaching of German._ New York etc.: Oxford University Press.

Rülker, K.

1971 "Zur Rolle der Pragmatik in der zweisprachigen Kommunikation", in _Studien zur Übersetzungswissenschaft III/IV. Beihefte zur Zeitschrift Fremdsprachen_. Leipzig: VEB Verlag Enzyklopädie. 99-112.

Rülker, K.

1973 "Zur pragmatischen Invarianz bei der Translation", in Neue Beiträge zu Grundfragen der Übersetzungswissenschaft. Ed. by A. Neubert and O. Kade. Frankfurt: Athenäum. 29-36.

Sapir, E.

1921 Language. New York: Harcourt, Brace and World.

Savignon, S.

1972 Communicative competence: An Experiment in Foreign Language Teaching. Philadelphia: Center for Curriculum Development.

Savory, T.

1963 "Enquête", in Quality in Translation (cf. Cary and Jumpelt) 153-54.

1968 The Art of Translation. Boston: The Writer.

Scherer, G. A. C. and M. Wertheimer

1964 A Psycholinguistic Experiment in Foreign Language Teaching. New York: McGraw-Hill.

Schiffler, L.

1970 "Empirische Untersuchung zur Effektivität der Übersetzung in die Muttersprache im Fremdsprachenunterricht", Neusprachliche Mitteilungen 4. 241-44.

Schmidt, S. J.

1972 "Ist 'Fiktionalität' eine linguistische oder eine texttheoretische Kategorie?", in Textsorten (cf. Gülich and Raible) 59-71.

Searle, J. R.

1969 Speech Acts. An Essay in the Philosophy of Language. Cambridge: Cambridge University Press.

Sepp, B.

1973 "Überlegungen zur Funktionsbestimmung der Übersetzung im Fremdsprachenunterricht", in PAKS-Arbeitsbericht. no. 7. Berlin: Cornelsen. 167-86.

Smith, P. D.

1970 A Comparison of the Cognitive and Audio-Lingual Approaches to Foreign Language Instruction--The Pennsylvania Foreign Language Project. Philadelphia, Penn.: Centre for Curriculum Development.

Söll, L.

1966 "Zur Problematik des Übersetzens", Praxis des neusprachlichen Unterrichts 13:1. 9-16.

1971 "Traduisibilité et intraduisibilité", Meta 16:1/2. 25-31.

1974 Gesprochenes und Geschriebenes Französisch. Berlin: Schmidt.

Spitzer, L.

1948 Linguistics and Literary History; Essays in Stylistics. Princeton: Princeton University Press.

Stalnaker, R. C.

1972 "Pragmatics", in Semantics of Natural Language. Ed. by D. Davidson and G. Harman. Dordrecht: Reidel. 380-97.

Stern, H. H.

forthcoming Theory of Second Language Teaching. London: Oxford University Press.

Störig, H.-J.

1963 Das Problem des Übersetzens. Stuttgart: Goverts.

Strang, B. M. H.

1962 Modern English Structure. London: Arnold.

Strevens, P.

1965 "Varieties of English", in Papers in Language and Language Teaching. Ed. by P. Strevens. London: Oxford University Press. 74-86.

Sweet, H.

1964 The Practical Study of Languages. London: Oxford University Press [First published in 1899]

Thomas C. (ed.)

1901 Report of the Committee of Twelve of the Modern Language Association of America. Boston: Heath.

Thomas, R. H.

1963 "Prose Composition and the Teaching of Modern Foreign Languages", Modern Languages 44:2. 70-72.

Vinay, J. P. and J. Darbelnet

1967 Stylistique comparée du francais et de l'anglais. 2nd ed. Paris: Didier.

Weber, H.

1973 "Äusserungen als illokutive Handlungen", Praxis des neusprachlichen Unterrichts 20. 22-32.

Wellek, René

1969 The Literary Theory and Aesthetics of the Prague School. Ann Arbor, Mich.: Dept. of Slavic Languages and Literature, University of Michigan.

Werlich, E.

1975 Typologie der Texte. Heidelberg: Quelle-Meyer.

White, R. V.

1974 "Communicative Competence, Registers and Second Language Teaching", IRAL 12:2. 127-41.

Widdowson, H. G.

1973 "Directions in the Teaching of Discourse", in Theoretical Linguistic Models in Applied Linguistics. Ed. by S. P. Corder and E. Roulet. Paris: Didier. 65-76.

1974a "The Deep Structure of Discourse and the Use of Translation", in Linguistic Insights in Applied Linguistics. Ed. by S. P. Corder and E. Roulet. Paris: Didier.

1974b "An Approach to the Teaching of Scientific English Discourse", RELC Journal 5. 27-40.

1974c "Stylistics", in Techniques in Applied Linguistics. Ed. by J. P. B. Allen and S. P. Corder. London: Oxford University Press.

Wilkins, D. A.

1972 An Investigation into the Linguistic and Situational Content of the Common Core in a Unit/Credit System. Strasbourg: Council of Europe.

1973 "Grammatical, Situational, and Notional Syllabus", ELT Documents 6. 2-9.

Wilss, W.

1973 "Die Funktion der Übersetzung im Fremdsprachenunterricht", Neusprachliche Mitteilungen. 26:1. 16-24.

1974 "Probleme und Perspektiven der Übersetzungskritik", IRAL 12:1. 23-41.

Wunderlich, D.

1970 Tempus und Zeitreferenz im Deutschen. München: Hueber.

Zenner, E.

1971 "Der Äquivalenzbegriff in der übersetzungswissenschaftlichen Literatur der Gegenwart und seine Relevanz für die Beurteilung der Qualität von Übersetzungen", Unpublished Diploma Thesis, Saarbrücken University.

Ziegesar, D. von

1975 "Sprachfunktionen und Sprechakte im Fremdsprachenunterricht", Linguistische Berichte 36. 84-95.

Zilahy, S. P.

1963 "Quality in Translation", in Quality in Translation (cf. Cary and Jumpelt) 285-89.

APPENDIX

I. Scientific Text

1. ST: excerpt from Arnold Sommerfeld, Partielle Differentialgleichungen. Leipzig: Geest and Portig. 1947. 27-29.

Allgemeines über partielle Differentialgleichungen

7. Vorkommen der einfachsten partiellen Differentialgleichungen

I 1 Man kennt die Potentialgleichung

(1) $\Delta u = 0$ bzw. (1a) $\Delta u = -(4\pi)\varrho$

als Ausdruck des Feldwirkungsstandpunktes in der Gravitationstheorie, im Gegensatz zu dem Fernwirkungsstandpunkt Newtons. /

2 Die Bedeutung des Laplace-Operators ist bekanntlich

(2) $$\Delta = \frac{\partial^2}{\partial x^2} + \frac{\partial^2}{\partial y^2} + \frac{\partial^2}{\partial z^2} = \operatorname{div}\operatorname{grad}.$$

3 Dieselben Gl. (1) und (1a) liegen aber auch den statischen elektrischen und magnetischen Feldern zugrunde, (1) im leeren Raum, (1a) beim Vorhandensein von Quellen der Dichte ϱ; den Faktor 4π in (1a) haben wir eingeklammert, weil er durch rationelle Wahl der Masseneinheiten zum Fortfall gebracht werden kann.

II 1 Gl. (1) tritt auch in der Hydrodynamik der inkompressibeln und wirbelfreien Strömungen auf; u bedeutet hier das Geschwindigkeits potential. /

2 Wir erwähnen auch die zweidimensionale Potentialgleichung

(3) $$\frac{\partial^2 u}{\partial x^2} + \frac{\partial^2 u}{\partial y^2} = 0$$

als Grundlage der Riemannschen Funktionentheorie, die wir kurz
als "Feldtheorie" der analytischen Funktionen $f(x+iy)$ charak-
3 terisieren können. / Man kennt andererseits die Schwingungsglei-
chung

(4) $$\Delta u = \frac{1}{c^2} \frac{\partial^2 u}{\partial t^2}.$$

4 Sie beherrscht die Akustik (c=Schallgeschwindigkeit), die Elektro-
dynamik veränderlicher Felder (c=Lichtgeschwindigkeit), insbe-
5 sondere also die Optik. / Indem man in der speziellen Relativi-
tätstheorie zu den räumlichen Koordinaten x_1, x_2, x_3 als vierte
Koordinate einführt x_4 (oder x_o) $= ict$, kann man (4) als vierdi-
mensionale Potentialgleichung

(5) $$\Box u = 0 \quad \text{mit} \quad \Box = \sum_{k=1}^{4} \frac{\partial^2}{\partial x_k^2}$$

6 schreiben. / In zwei Dimensionen tritt (4) bei der schwingenden
Membran, in einer Dimension bei der schwingenden Saite auf. /
7 In letzterem Falle schreiben wir

(6) $$\frac{\partial^2 u}{\partial x^2} = \frac{1}{c^2} \frac{\partial^2 u}{\partial t^2} \quad \text{oder auch} \quad (6a) \quad \frac{\partial^2 u}{\partial x^2} - \frac{\partial^2 u}{\partial y^2} = 0,$$

8 indem wir vorübergehend $y = ct$ (nicht $y = ict$) setzen. / Beide,
Membran und Saite, besitzen keine Eigenelastizität; ihre Konstante

c berechnet sich aus der ihnen von aussen her aufgezwungenen Spannung und aus ihrer Dichte pro Flächen- bzw. Längeneinheit.

III 1 Als Sonderfall der allgemeinen Elastizitätstheorie entsteht die Differentialgleichung für die Transversalschwingungen einer dünnen Platte

$$\Delta\Delta u = -\frac{1}{c^2}\frac{\partial^2 u}{\partial t^2}, \quad \Delta\Delta = \frac{\partial^4}{\partial x^4} + 2\frac{\partial^4}{\partial x^2 \partial y^2} + \frac{\partial^4}{\partial y^4}; \tag{7}$$

c bedeutet hier aus dimensionellen Gründen natürlich nicht, wie in der Akustik, die Schallgeschwindigkeit des elastischen Materials, sondern berechnet sich aus Elastizität, Dichte und Dicke der

2 Platte. / Entsprechend ergibt sich als Differentialgleichung eines schwingenden elastischen Stabes

$$\frac{\partial^4 u}{\partial x^4} = -\frac{1}{c^2}\frac{\partial^2 u}{\partial t^2}. \tag{8}$$

3 Sie wird in Übungsaufgabe II. 1 abgeleitet werden, wobei die daraus folgenden Eigenschwingungen mit den akustischen Schwingungen einer offenen und einer gedeckten Pfeife zu vergleichen sein werden.

IV 1 Als dritten Typus stellen wir neben die Differentialgleichungen der Gleichgewichtszustände [Gl. (1) bis (3)] und der Schwingungsvorgänge [Gl. (4) bis (8)] die Differentialgleichung

2 der _Ausgleichsprozesse_. / Als ihren vornehmsten Repräsentanten betrachten wir hier die _Wärmeleitung_ (Ausgleich von Energie-

differenzen) etwas näher, bemerken aber sogleich, dass auch die Diffusion (Ausgleich von materiellen Dichtedifferenzen), die Flüssigkeitsreibung (Ausgleich von Impulsdifferenzen), sowie die Elektrizitätsleitung (Ausgleich von Spannungsdifferen) nach demselben Schema erfolgen.

V 1 Es sei G ein Vektor von der Grösse und Richtung des Wärme-
2 flusses./Den ins Auge gefassten Aufpunkt P umgeben wir mit einem
3 infinitesimalen Raumelement $d\tau$. / Dann bedeutet div G$d\tau$ den Aus-
4 fluss der Wärmeenergie aus $d\tau$ pro Zeiteinheit. / Ihm entspricht
eine Abnahme des Wärmeinhalts von $d\tau$, die wir, ebenfalls pro
5 Zeiteinheit gerechnet, mit $\partial Q/\partial t$, bezeichnen. / Wir haben dann

$$(9) \qquad \operatorname{div} \mathfrak{G}\, d\tau = -\frac{\partial Q}{\partial t}.$$

Unseren Wärmeleiter sehen wir dabei als starren Körper an, so
dass wir von Ausdehnung und Arbeitsleistung abstrahieren können;
6 Wärmeinhalt bedeutet dann soviel wie Energieinhalt. / Nun bewirkt
jede Wärmezufuhr dQ eine Temperaturerhöhung von $d\tau$, jede Wärme-
7 abfuhr -dQ eine Temperaturerniedrigung. / Bezeichnen wir die
Temperatur mit u, so gilt

$$(10) \qquad dQ = c\, dm\, du, \quad dm = \varrho\, d\tau.$$

c ist die spezifische Wärme (beim starren Körper braucht man

9 nicht zwischen c_v und c_p zu unterscheiden). / Der Faktor dm bei
c rührt daher, dass sich c auf die Masseneinheit bezieht.

10 Aus (9) und (10) ergibt sich

(11) $$\mathrm{div}\,\mathfrak{G} = -c\varrho\frac{\partial u}{\partial t}.$$

11 Hier tritt nun der Fouriersche Ansatz in Kraft, welcher den Zu-
12 sammenhang zwischen G und u festlegt. / Er besagt im isotropen
Medium

(12) $$\mathfrak{G} = -\varkappa\,\mathrm{grad}\,u.$$

13 Der Wärmefluss findet in Richtung des Temperaturgefälles statt
14 und ist proportional der Stärke dieses Gefälles. / Der Proportio-
15 nalitätsfaktor x heisst Wärmeleitfähigkeit. Mit (12) entsteht aus
(11) die Differentialgleichung der Wärmeleitung

(13) $$\Delta u = \frac{1}{k}\frac{\partial u}{\partial t}, \quad k = \frac{\varkappa}{c\varrho}.$$

2. TT: excerpt from Arnold Sommerfeld, Partial Differential Equations
in Physics. New York: Academic Press. 1949. 32-34.

Introduction to Partial Differential Equations

7. How the Simplest Partial Differential Equations Arise

I 1 The potential equation

(1) $\Delta u = 0$ or (1a) $\Delta u = -(4\pi)\varrho$

is known in the theory of gravitation as the expression of the
field-action approach, as opposed to the action-at-a-distance
2 approach of Newton. / The Laplace operator is defined as

(2) $$\Delta = \frac{\partial^2}{\partial x^2} + \frac{\partial^2}{\partial y^2} + \frac{\partial^2}{\partial z^2} = \text{div grad.}$$

3 The same equations (1) and (1a) are fundamental for eloctrostatic
and magnetic fields, (1) in empty space, (1a) in the presence of a
source of density ϱ ; the factor 4π in (1a) has been put in parentheses since it can be removed by a proper choice of units.

II 1 Equation (1) appears also in the hydrodynamics of incom-
pressible and irrotational fluids, u standing for the velocity
2 potential. / We also mention the two-dimensional potential equation

(3) $$\frac{\partial^2 u}{\partial x^2} + \frac{\partial^2 u}{\partial y^2} = 0$$

as the basis of Riemannian function theory, which we may characterize as the "field theory" of the analytic functions $f(x+iy)$.

3 Equally well known is the wave equation

$$(4) \qquad \Delta u = \frac{1}{c^2}\frac{\partial^2 u}{\partial t^2}.$$

4/5 It is fundamental in acoustics (c=velocity of sound). / It is also
fundamental in the electrodynamics of variable fields (c=velocity
6 of light), and therefore in optics. / In the special theory of relativity, one may write (4) as the four-dimensional potential equation

$$(5) \qquad \Box u = 0 \qquad \text{with} \qquad \Box = \sum_{k=1}^{4} \frac{\partial^2}{\partial x_k^2}$$

by introducing the fourth coordinate x_4 (or x_0) = ict in addition to
7 the three spatial coordinates x_1, x_2, x_3. / For an oscillating membrane, we have (4) with two spatial dimensions, for an oscillating
8 string we have one spatial dimension. / In the latter case we write

$$(6) \qquad \frac{\partial^2 u}{\partial x^2} = \frac{1}{c^2}\frac{\partial^2 u}{\partial t^2} \qquad \text{or sometimes (6a)} \qquad \frac{\partial^2 u}{\partial x^2} - \frac{\partial^2 u}{\partial y^2} = 0,$$

9 setting, for the time being, y=ct (not y=ict). / Neither membrane nor string has a proper elasticity; the constant c is computed from the tension imposed from outside and from the density per unit of area or of length.

III 1 In the general theory of elasticity one has, as a special case, the differential equation for the transverse vibrations of a thin disc

$$(7) \qquad \Delta\Delta u = -\frac{1}{c^2}\frac{\partial^2 u}{\partial t^2}, \qquad \Delta\Delta = \frac{\partial^4}{\partial x^4} + 2\frac{\partial^4}{\partial x^2 \partial y^2} + \frac{\partial^4}{\partial y^4};$$

for reasons of dimensionality c here does not stand for the velocity of sound in the elastic material, as it does in acoustics, but is computed from the elasticity, density, and thickness of the

2 disc. / Analogously, the differential equation of an oscillating elastic rod is

$$(8) \qquad \frac{\partial^4 u}{\partial x^4} = -\frac{1}{c^2}\frac{\partial^2 u}{\partial t^2}.$$

3 This will be derived in exercise II. 1, where the resulting characteristic frequencies will be compared with the acoustic frequencies of open and of covered pipes.

IV 1 As a third type we add to the differential equations of states of equilibrium [(1) to (3)], and of oscillating processes [(4) to (8)],

2 those of equalization processes. / As their chief representative we shall here consider heat conduction (equalization of energy

3 differences). / We remark, however, that diffusion (equalization of differences of material densities), fluid friction (equalization of impulse differences), and pure electric conduction (equalization of differences of potential), follow the same pattern.

V 1 Let G be a vector of the magnitude and direction of the heat flow and let the initial point P be surrounded by an element

2 of volume $d\tau$. / Then div G $d\tau$ is the outflow of heat energy from

3 $d\tau$ per unit of time. / A decrease per unit of time in the amount of heat in $d\tau$, which we shall denote by $-\partial Q/\partial t$, corresponds to

4 this. / We then have

$$(9) \qquad \operatorname{div} G \, d\tau = -\frac{\partial Q}{\partial t}.$$

5 Our heat conductor is here considered to be a rigid body so that we can neglect expansion; heat content is then the same as energy

6 content. / Now every increase dQ in heat causes an increase in the temperature of $d\tau$, every decrease -dQ in heat causes a de-

7 crease in temperature. / Denoting the temperature by u, we have

$$(10) \qquad dQ = c \, dm \, du, \qquad dm = \varrho \, d\tau.$$

c being the specific heat (for a rigid body we need not distinguish

8 between c_v and c_p). / The factor dm is due to the fact that c is related to the unit of mass.

9 From (9) and (10) we get

$$(11) \qquad \operatorname{div} G = -c \varrho \frac{\partial u}{\partial t}.$$

10 We now apply Fourier's law, which determines the relation be-

11 tween G and u. / It states that for an isotope medium

$$(12) \qquad G = -\varkappa \operatorname{grad} u:$$

the flow of heat is in the direction of decreasing temperature and

12 is proportional to the rate of this decrease. / The factor of proportionality x is called the heat conductivity.

13 Introducing (12) in (11) we get the differential equation of heat conduction

(13) $$\Delta u = \frac{1}{k}\frac{\partial u}{\partial t}, \qquad k = \frac{\varkappa}{c\,\varrho}.$$

II. <u>Commercial Text</u>

1. ST: M. F. Meissner, President, Investors Overseas Services,

<u>Letter to Shareholders</u>, dated 27. 12.1971.

December 27, 1971

I .1 Dear Shareholder,

II .1 The Board of Directors of I. O. S., Ltd. has declared a pro-
rata dividend payable on and after December 20, 1971, to all
shareholders of record as of the close of business on December
.2 17, 1971. / The dividend consists of shares of Value Capital Limited, a newly established Bahamian holding company, and will be
paid on the basis of one share of Value Capital Limited for each
3 whole ten shares held of I. O. S., Ltd. / Of course, each shareholder continues ownership of any share that he now holds of IOS.

III 1 In organizing Value Capital Limited, IOS contributed to it
certain companies including IVM (the Dutch insurance company),
IVM Invest Management Company Limited, ILI Luxembourg, ILI
Bermuda, IOS Real Estate Holdings, IPI Management Co., and
Resources Services Limited, together with certain other contrac-
.2 tual rights and assets. / In return for its contribution, IOS received 6. 2 million shares of Value Capital Limited (the total of
the issued and outstanding shares of that Company), and, in turn,
is distributing to its shareholders all of these shares.

IV .1 The total stockholders' equity of Value Capital Limited

2 is $1. 3 million. / Since future earnings of Value Capital Limited
will not be controlled by IOS, historical earnings performance
would not be indicative of expected future performance.

V 1 The dividend will be represented by bearer certificates
2 which, as you know, are negotiable instruments. / That is, they
3 may be traded by anyone in possession of the certificate. / In
order to avoid the possibility of accidental misdirection of your
certificates, and to expedite the distrubiton, your assistance is
4 required. / We have enclosed a "Dividend Instruction Form" for
your completion; this should be returned in the pre-addressed
envelope.

VI 1 As you will note, we have asked that you designate a bank
2 (or broker) to which your dividend certificates will be sent. / Your
bank (or broker) should indicate its confirmation of your signature by executing the bottom half of the "Dividend Instruction
Form" including its official signature and stamp (or seal).

VII 1 It is anticipated that your new Company will issue its first
report, covering its financial position at May 31, 1972, as soon
2 as possible following that date. / This report will include full details on the Company's organization, management and plans for
3 future development. / In the interim period, the 15,000 to 20,000
shareholders of Value Capital Limited can expect that public trad-
4 ing of their shares will develop. / It is the present intention

of Value Capital Limited to secure the listing of its shares on a
recognized exchange at the earliest possible time.

VIII 1 As a result of the dividend by IOS of its complete holdings
of Value Capital shares, there remains no equity ownership or
2 control of Value Capital in the hands of IOS. / Therefore the future market value of Value Capital shares should in no way be
related to, or depend upon, the future development of IOS.

IX 1 The principal reason for the establishment of Value Capital Limited, and the distribution of its ownership to the IOS shareholders, was to permit the continuation and expansion of essential communication with the hundreds of thousands of fund clients. /
2 Recent Swiss legislation precluded the maintenance of these operations from Switzerland as in the past.

X 1 Value Capital's client service functions will be conducted
from new facilities being established outside of Switzerland. /
2 The implementation of these client services should result in a
residual benefit to the business of the principal operating sub-
sidiaries, IOS Insurance Holdings and Transglobal Financial
Services, which are retained by IOS.

XI 1 Value Capital Limited additionally intends to establish an
international insurance operation based upon the three insurance
2 companies which IOS contributed to it. / Certain of the other
Value Capital operations were contributed by IOS in order to

provide an immediate income flow to the new Company and thus insure stability throughout its formative phase.

XII 1 It is expected that the IOS shareholders will realize a greater growth potential through their direct interest in the new Value Capital Limited operations than would have been possible had those operations remained within the IOS group.

XIII 1 Very truly yours,

Milton M. Meissner
President

2. TT: M. F. Meissner, President, Investors Overseas Services,
Brief an die Aktionäre, dated 27.12.1971.

27. Dezember 1971

I 1 Sehr geehrter Aktionär,

II 1 Der Verwaltungsrat der I. O. S. , Ltd. hat eine anteilige
Dividende beschlossen, die ab 20. Dezember 1971 an alle Aktionäre
zur Ausschüttung gelangt, die zum Geschäftsschluss am 17. Dezem-
2 ber 1971 registriert sind. / Die Dividende besteht aus Aktien der
Value Capital Limited, einer nach dem Recht der Bahamas neu-
3 gegründeten Gesellschaft. / Jeder Aktionär erhält auf je volle zehn
Aktien der I. O. S., Ltd. eine Aktie der Value Capital Limited. /
4 Er bleibt natürlich weiterhin Eigentümer aller seiner bisherigen
Aktien der I. O. S., Ltd.

III 1 Bei der Gründung der Value Capital Limited übertrug die
IOS auf diese Gesellschaft bestimmte Gesellschaften, einschliess-
lich der IVM (die niederländische Versicherungsgesellschaft), IVM
Invest Management Company Limited, ILI Luxembourg, ILI Bermuda, IOS Real Estate Holdings, IPI Management Co. und Resources Services Limited, sowie bestimmte vertragliche Rechte
2 und Aktiva. / Als Gegenleistung erhielt die IOS 6.2 Millionen
Aktien der Value Capital Limited (die gesamte Zahl der von dieser

Gesellschaft ausgegebenen und in Umlauf gesetzten Aktien), die
alle von der IOS an ihre Aktionäre verteilt werden.

IV 1 Das gesamte Eigenkapital der Value Capital Limited be-
2 tragt l. 3 Millionen Dollar. / Da die IOS keinen Einfluss auf die zu-
künftige Gewinnentwicklung der Value Capital Limited haben wird,
würde die bisherige Ertragsleistung keinen Aufschluss über die
Gewinnentwicklung geben.

V 1 Die Dividende wird durch Inhaberzertifikate verbrieft. /
2 Diese sind bekanntlich frei begebbare Urkunden, d. h., sie können
3 von jedem veräussert werden, der in ihren Besitz gelangt. / Um
zu vermeiden, dass Ihre Zertifikate versehentlich fehlgeleitet
werden und um die Zustellung zu beschleunigen, bitten wir Sie, das
beigefügte Dividenden-Zustellungsformular (Dividend Instruction
Form) auszufüllen und in dem ebenfalls beigelegten adressierten
Umschlag zurückzuschicken.

VI 1 Wie Sie feststellen werden, haben wir Sie gebeten, eine
Bank (oder einen Makler) zu benennen, an den die Aktienzertifikate
2 geschickt werden sollen. / Sie müssen die Bank (oder den Makler)
bitten, Ihre Unterschrift auf dem Dividenden-Zustellungsformular
3 zu bestätigen. / Hierfür ist auf dem unteren Teil des Formulars eine
Stelle vorgesehen, wo die Betreffenden unterzeichnen und ihren
Stempel anbringen.

VII 1 Den ersten Bericht über ihre Finanzlage zum 31. Mai 1972
wird die Value Capital Limited so bald wie möglich nach dem be-
2 sagten Datum veröffentlichen. / Der Bericht wird u. a. über den
Aufbau der Gesellschaft, ihre Verwaltung und Entwicklungspläne
3 volle Auskunft geben. / In der Zwischenzeit können die 15.000 bis
20.000 Aktionäre der Value Capital Limited erwarten, dass sich
4 der öffentliche Handel ihrer Aktien entwickeln wird. / Die Value
Capital Limited beabsichtigt z. Z., die Zulassung ihrer Aktien zum
Börsenhandel an einer anerkannten Börse möglichst bald zu erlan-
gen.

VIII 1 Durch die Dividendenausschüttung begibt sich die IOS aller
2 von ihr gehaltenen Aktien der Value Capital Limited. / Infolgedessen
verfügt sie in Zukunft weder über Anteile am Kapital der Value
Capital Limited noch über einen beherrschenden Einfluss auf diese
3 Gesellschaft. / Irgendein Zusammenhang zwischen der weiteren
Entwicklung der IOS und dem künftigen Kurs der Value Capital-
Aktien sollte deshalb ausgeschlossen sein.

IX 1 Die Aufrechterhaltung und weitere Entwicklung wesentlicher
Kommunikationen mit den Hunderttausenden von Kunden waren die
Hauptgründe für die Errichtung der Value Capital Limited und für
die direkte Beteiligung der IOS-Aktionäre an dieser Gesellschaft. /
2 Infolge neuer schweizerischer Gesetzesbestimmung war die

Fortführung des bisherigen Betriebes von der Schweiz aus unmög-
lich geworden.

X 1 Die Dienstleistungen der Value Capital Limited für die
Kunden werden von neuen Einrichtungen ausserhalb der Schweiz
2 erbracht. / Aus diesen Dienstleistungen dürften sich für das Ge-
schäft der wichtigsten im Besitz der IOS verbleibenden Tochterbe-
triebsgesellschaften, IOS Insurance Holdings und Transglobal Financial Services, restliche Gewinne ergeben.

XI 1 Ausgehend von den drei Versicherungsgesellschaften, welche die IOS auf die Value Capital Limited übertragen hat, beabsichtigt diese ausserdem ein internationales Versicherungsunternehmen
2 aufzubauen. / Gewisse andere Betriebe sind von der IOS auf die
Value Capital Limited übertragen worden, um zu gewährleisten,
dass die neue Gesellschaft über sofortige Einnahmen verfügt und
somit die Stabilität in der Errichtungsperiode gesichert ist.

XII 1 Durch ihre direkte Beteiligung an der neugegründeten
Value Capital Limited wird sich für die IOS-Aktionäre voraussichtlich ein grösseres Wachstumspotential ergeben, als ihnen die auf
die neue Gesellschaft übertragenen Unternehmen hätten bieten
können, wenn sie in der IOS-Gruppe verblieben waren.

XIII 1 Mit freundlichem Gruss

Milton F. Meissner
Präsident

III. Journalistic Article

1. ST: excerpt from William W. Howells, "Homo Sapiens: 20 million years in the making", in *The UNESCO Courier*. August-September 1972. 6-8.

I 1 It was out of *Dryopithecus* stock that man emerged, and,
in fact it was from among the fossils of *Dryopithecus* that our an-
2 cestor *Ramapithecus* became known. / G. E. Lewis of Yale in
1934 described the first upper jaw, found in India's Siwalik Hills,
and pointed to some man-like features.

II 1 Your own mouth will show you these things, where you
2 can feel them with your finger. / Your dental arch is short and
rounded in front, while that of apes has become increasingly
longer and broad across the front, with large canine teeth and
3 broad incisors. / Your molar teeth have the cusp and furrow pat-
4 tern of *Dryopithecus*, but are square; an ape's are longer. / This
length makes an ape's face projecting; yours is straighter.

III 1 Approaches to the human shape could be seen in the small frag-
ment of *Ramapithecus* as though he had just set his foot on a path
diverging from *Dryopithecus*, although unfortunately we have
2 not found the foot, only the jaw. / So Lewis thought *Ramapithecus* might belong in our ancestry.

IV 1 But the tide of scientific opinion--and such tides are apt
to influence, not facts, but the way we see facts--was against

Ramapithecus, and the fossil was put away in a drawer as sim-
2 ply one more kind of *Dryopithecus*. / After almost thirty years,
however, L. S. B. Leakey found a very similar fossil at Fort
Ternan in Kenya, which he could date as being 14 million years
old.

V 1 It happened that at the same time, Elwyn Simons at Yale
2 was looking once again at *Ramapithecus*. / He was impressed
with what Lewis had pointed to, and saw the same features in
Leakey's new specimen.

VI 1 Perhaps more important, Simons rescued other pieces of
2 *Ramapithecus* from burial in museum drawers. / He began examining old collections in various places from the U.S.A. to
India, and recognized a few more fragments with the same special features, fragments which had previously been misnamed
and ignored, but which he identified as fossils of *Ramapithecus*.

VII 1 This careful sorting out made it easier to see the slight
distinctions between *Ramapithecus* on one hand and *Dryopithecus*,
2 ancestor of the apes, on the other. / Thus we also see the be-
ginnings of the separating paths of human and ape evolution, or
between animals properly called pongids (apes) and those called
3 hominids (anything on the human side of the same group). / So
palaeontology is not all looking for fossils in old river banks.

VIII 1/2 What brought the split about?/ Evolution has "reasons"--

it follows lines of successful adaptation--but we know so little
about *Ramapithecus* having only his jaws and teeth, that we can-
3 not see the "reason". / We cannot simply say that it is better or
more successful to be "human", because that really means nothing, and *Ramapithecus* certainly resembled the ancestral apes
4 far more than he resembled man. / Like some chimpanzee popu-
lations he seems to have lived in an open wood and, again like
chimpanzees, it is probable that he was still a tree-user.

2. TT: excerpt from William W. Howells, "Zwanzig Millionen Jahre
unterwegs zum Menschen", in UNESCO Kurier. August-
September 1972. 5-7.

I 1 Der Mensch ist aus der Art des Dryopithecus hervor-
gegangen, und über die Dryopithecus-Fossilien wurde unser
2 Vorfahr, der Ramapithecus bekannt. / G. E. Lewis aus Yale
beschrieb 1934 den ersten Fund eines Oberkiefers im indischen
Siwalik-Gebirge und wies dabei auf einige menschenartige
Merkmale hin.

II 1 Wenn wir in unserem Mund mit dem Finger den Zahnboden
entlangfahren, stellen wir fest, dass er kurz ist und vorne
2 gebogen. / Derjenige des Affen ist lang und vorne breit, mit
3 grossen Eck- und scharfen Schneidezähnen. / Die Molaren des
Menschen haben dieselben Höcker und dasselbe Furchenmuster
4 wie die des Dryopithecus, sind aber quadratisch. / Jene der
5 Affen sind länger. / Die Länge der Molaren bedingt, dass das
Gesicht der Affen--im Vergleich zum menschlichen--anders ist.

III 1 Annäherungen an eine menschliche Gesichtsform
konnten aus kleineren Fragmenten vom Ramapithecus heraus-
2 gelesenwerden./ Es schien als ob er seinen Fuss in eine
vom Dryopithecus abweichende Richtung gesetzt habe--obschon
wir leider nicht seinen Fuss, sondern bloss seinen Kiefer
3 fanden. / Dies bewog Lewis, ihn in unsere Ahnenreihe

aufzunehmen

IV 1 Doch die Meinungen der Wissenschaft sind beeinflussbar
--nicht allein durch Tatsachen, sondern durch die Art und
2 Weise, wie die Tatsachen ausgelegt werden. / Damals war
3 man gegen den *Ramapithecus*. / Das Fossil, als eine weitere
Art von *Dryopithecus* abgetan, verschwand vorerst in einer
4 Schublade. / Fast dreissig Jahre später machte L. S. B. Leakey
in Fort Ternan, Kenia, einen ähnlichen Fund, dessen Alter
auf vierzehn Millionen Jahre geschätzt wird.

V 1 Der Zufall wollte es, dass sich Elwyn Simons in Yale
zur selben Zeit nochmals mit dem *Ramapithecus* beschäftigte. /
2 Lewis' Bemerkungen leuchteten ihm ein, und er erkannte an
Leakey's neuem Exemplar die gleichen Merkmale.

VI 1 Was vielleicht noch wichtiger war: Simons verhinderte
damit, dass weitere Funde vom *Ramapithecus* in Museen ver-
2 schwanden und vergessen wurden. / Von den Vereinigten Staaten
bis Indien schaute er sich zahlreiche alte Sammlungen an und
entdeckte einige weitere Fragmente mit denselben Merkmalen. /
3 Fragmente, die bis dahin falsch benannt oder ignoriert worden
waren, die er aber als Fossilien des *Ramapithecus* identifi-
zieren konnte.

VII 1 Dieses sorgfältige Aussortieren erleichterte das

Erkennen der feinen Unterschiede zwischen dem *Ramapithecus*
einerseits und dem *Dryopithecus,* dem Vorläufer der
2 Menschenaffen, andererseits. / An diesem Punkt der
Evolutionsgeschichte beginnt die Trennung von Menschenaffen
und Menschen oder, allgemeiner gefasst, von Pongiden
(Affen und Menschenaffen) und Hominiden (alle Arten mit
Ansätzen von menschenartigen Merkmalen).

VIII 1/2 Weshalb aber diese Trennung? / Die Evolution folgt
3 einem Plan. / Ziel ist eine möglichst vorteilhafte Adaptation. /
4 Wir wissen aber so wenig über den *Ramapithecus*--wir haben
ja nur seinen Kiefer und seine Zähne --dass wir hier keinen
5 Plan erkennen können. / Es wäre unsinnig, "menschlich" mit
6 "vorteilhafter" gleichsetzen zu wollen. / Bestimmt stand der
7 *Ramapithecus* dem Affen näher als dem Menschen. / Wie
gewisse Schimpansenarten, so vermutet man, lebte er in
lichten Wäldern, teils noch immer auf Bäumen.

IV. Tourist Information Booklet

1. ST: excerpt from Verkehrsverein Nürnberg, Nürnberg. Nürnberg: Sebald. 1975 (no pagination).

I 1 Die Blütezeit der Stadt Nürnberg im 15. und 16.
Jahrhundert war auch die Zeit des Meistergesanges, die Zeit
2 des Schuhmachers und Meistersingers Hans Sachs. / Über
4000 Lieder geistlichen und weltlichen Inhalts sind uns
bekannt, viele seiner Werke hielten sich bis auf den heutigen
3 Tag. / Richard Wagner widmete den Meistersingern von
4 Nürnberg ein Musikdrama. / Auch Hans Sachs hat zu seiner
Zeit ein Lobgedicht über seine Vaterstadt geschrieben. /
5 Textauszüge aus diesem Buch von 1554: "Ein Lobspruch-Der
Stadt Nürnberg" wurden als graphische Elemente in diese
6 Broschüre übernommen. / Ein Exemplar des Werkes befindet
sich im Besitz der Stadtbibliothek.

II 1 Nürnbergs Stadtantlitz ist von den Sonnenstrahlen und
Stürmen einer mehr als 900jährigen Geschichte gezeichnet. /
2 In ihm spiegeln sich Reichtum, Würde und Macht der Freien
Reichsstadt von einst ebenso wider wie Bürgerstolz, Fleiss
3 und Beharrlichkeit der Halbmillionenstadt von heute. / So
bietet Nürnberg eine Fülle reizvoller Kontraste zwischen
Mittelalter und Neuzeit, eindrucksvoller Spielarten von

Geschichte und Gegenwart.

III 1/2 Nürnbergs Herz schlägt in der Altstadt. / In seinen
Bauten sind Geist und Lebensstil vergangener Epochen leben-
3 dig. / Seine Mauern aber sind erfüllt vom pulsierenden
Leben der Gegenwart.

IV 1 Nürnberg steht im Spannungsfeld von Gestern und
2 Heute. / Die Stadt bewahrt ihr kostbares Erbe in den Bürger-
hausern eines Albrecht Dürer und in den Kunstschätzen eines
Veit Stoss, macht jedoch auch die Baugesinnung dieser Tage
in der Meistersingerhalle, im neuen Messezentrum und im
Hafen am Europakanal sichtbar.

V 1/2 Nürnberger Tand geht in alle Land. / Dieses geflügelte
Wort kündet von der Erfindungsgabe und der Geschicklichkeit
3 der Künstler und Handwerker in aller Welt. / Der erste
Globus und die erste Taschenuhr, das Männleinlaufen und
der Englische Gruss bieten nur einige bleibende Beispiele
dieser handwerklichen Fähigkeiten, die Nürnberg berühmt
gemacht haben.

VI 1 Nürnbergs alte Meister leben fort in ihren Werken. /
2 Die Kirchen und Museen der Stadt bergen Kunstwerke von
3 unschätzbarem Wert. / In Ateliers und Werkstätten,
Kunsthallen und Galerien ist dem zeitgenössischen Schaffen
nachzuspüren.

VII 1/2 Nürnberg verwöhnt seine Gäste. / Die weltoffenen
Bürger der Stadt setzen ihren ganzen Ehrgeiz darein, ihre
Gaste freundlich zu empfangen und ihren Aufenthalt zu einem
3 Vergnügen zu gestalten. / In der Gastfreundschaft wetteifern
Hotels and Restaurants, Gaststätten und Kneipen miteinander. /
4 Der "Mann auf der Strasse" will ihnen in nichts nachstehen.

VIII 1 Nürnberg deckt den Tisch mit lukullischen Köstlichkeiten. /
2 Bratwürste und Bier, Karpfen and Frankenwein haben hier
3 Geschichte und Geschichten gemacht. / Aber auch der Duft
4 der weiten Welt weht durch die Nürnberger Küchen. / Auf
eine Spezialität ist die Gastronomie besonders stolz: In keiner
anderen Grossstadt kann man so preiswert essen und trinken.

IX 1/2 Nürnberg lebt rund um die Uhr. / Historische Plätze
bieten eine malerische Kulisse für das Stelldichein von Jung
und Alt, geschichtsträchtige Innenhöfe laden zu Theater-und
Musikaufführungen ein, Ballsäle erwarten ein elegantes
Publikum, Theater entfalten einen bunten Fächer vom
3 Kammerspiel bis zur Oper. / Abend und Amusement sind für
Nürnberg ein passendes Wortpaar.

X 1/2 Nürnberg kennt keinen Zapfenstreich. / Vom frühen
Abend bis spät in die Nacht kann der Gast auf seine Rechnung
kommen, sei es beim Bier in der Kneipe oder beim Sekt in der
Bar, sei es beim Theater unter freiem Himmel oder beim

3 Konzert unter historischen Gewölben. / Zu jeder Stunde stehen andere Attraktionen auf dem Programm der Grossstadt.

2. TT: exerpt from Verkehrsverein Nürnberg, <u>Nürnberg.</u> Nürnberg:
Sebald. 1975 (no pagination).

I 1 Nuremberg's Golden Age in the 15th and 16th centuries was
also the age of the mastersingers and their best-known represen-
2 tative, the shoe-maker Hans Sachs. / We know of over 4,000 of
his songs, both spiritual and secular and many of his works are
3 still extant today. / The Mastersingers of Nuremberg inspired
4 Richard Wagner to write one of his operas about them. / Hans
Sachs was also inspired to write a poem in praise of his home
5 town. / This brochure is embellished with extracts from his
"Eulogy-The Town of Nuremberg" of 1554, an original copy of
which is owned by the Nuremberg City Library.

II 1 Nuremberg's features have been weathered by the sun-
2 shine and storms of over 900 years of history. / They reflect the
wealth, dignity and power of the former Free Imperial City but
also the tenacity and industriousness of modern Nuremberg with
its half-a-million inhabitants and the pride of these Nurember-
3 gers in their city. / Nuremberg is full of charming contrasts between its medieval and its modern self.

III 1/2 The Old City is still the city's heart. / The spirit and
life-style of by-gone times are alive in its ancient buildings but
the life of today also pulses within the old city walls.

IV 1 The city preserves its precious inheritance in its burgher

houses, like that of Albrecht Dürer, and the treasures of its
2 artists, for example Veit Stoss. / But a glance at the Meister-
singer Hall, the Trade Fair Centre or the harbour make it clear
that Nuremberg also keeps with the times.

V 1 "Nuremberg wares go all over the world"--this saying
bears witness to the inventiveness and skill of Nuremberg's
2 craftsmen and artists. / The first globe and the first pocket
watch, the moving figures on the ancient mechanical "Männleinlaufen" clock and the artistic skill of the carved Annunciation,
the famous "Engelsgruss", are just a few surviving examples of
the ingenious craftsmanship which made Nuremberg so famous.

VI 1/2 Nuremberg's Old Masters live on in their works. / The
city's churches and museums house priceless treasures from
by-gone times, whilst contemporary art is produced and displayed in its studios, workshops, and art galleries.

VII 1/2 Nuremberg's guests are spoilt. / Its citizens are men of
the world, eager to offer a friendly welcome to their visitors and
3 make their stay a pleasure. / Hotels and restaurants, inns and
pubs vie with each other and the "man in the street" is just as
welcoming.

VIII 1 Nuremberg's table is piled high with local delicacies--
2 grilled sausages and beer, carp and Franconian wine. / But the
scent of dishes from all over the world also wafts through Nur-

3 emberg's kitchens. / And in no other big city can one eat and
drink at such a reasonable price.

IX 1/2 Nuremberg is awake 24 hours of the day. / Historical
squares are a picturesque setting for the rendezvous of young
3 and old. / Ancient courtyards resound with the voices of actors
4 and the notes of musicians. / Ballrooms open their doors to their
elegant guests, the theatres offer a colourful range of performan-
5 ces from workshop theatre to grand opera. / In Nuremberg the
words evening and entertainment go hand in hand.

X 1 There are "no early closing hours" in Nuremberg. /
2 Far into the night visitors can enjoy a pint in the pub or cham-
pagne at the bar, open-air theatre or a concert beneath histori-
3 cal vaulting. / The city offers various attractions at every hour.

V. Religious Sermon

1. ST: excerpt from Karl Barth, Rufe Mich An! Neue Predigten aus der Strafanstalt Basel. Zürich: E. V. Z. Verlag. 1965. 28-31.

I 1 Rufe mich an in der Not, so will ich dich erretten und du sollst
mich preisen!
2 Liebe Brüder und Schwestern!
II 1/2 'Rufe mich an!' heisst es da. / Das könnte mich wohl daran
erinnern, wie es ist, wenn Einer mich 'anruft', am Telefon nämlich, unterbricht und stört mich bei meiner Arbeit oder mitten in
einem Gespräch oder vielleicht, wenn ich gerade Musik hören will
und fängt an, mich zu fragen: wie es mir gehe, trägt mir irgend
ein Anliegen vor, erzählt mir eine lange oder kurze Geschichte,
3 und sagt wohl zum Schluss: Ruf du mich einmal an! / Hier, in un-
4 serm Text ist Alles ganz anders. / Da ruft mich freilich auch
5 Einer an und unterbricht mich bei meiner Beschäftigung. / Aber
der fragt nicht lange, wie es mir geht, denn er weiss das besser
6 als ich selber es weiss. / Und er hat mir auch kein Anliegen vor-
zutragen--was könnte ich schon für ihn tun? / Und eine wichtige
Geschichte hat er mir auch nicht zu erzählen, denn die einzige
wirklich wichtige Geschichte fängt eben damit an, dass er mich
7 anruft. / Und was am Telefon das Letzte ist, das ist hier das
Erste, was dort Nebensache ist, ist hier Hauptsache, das Eine

und Einzige sogar: Rufe du mich an!

III

1/2/3/4 Wer sagt das? / Gott? / Ja, Gott! / Aber das Wort 'Gott'
wird so viel gebraucht, ist so abgegriffen wie eine alte Münze und
5 jeder versteht etwas Anderes dabei. / Und es gibt ja auch soviele
6 Götter! / Sagen wir es einmal so: Der mich da anruft und mir sagt,
dass ich ihn wieder anrufen soll, das ist der Andere: der eben ganz
7 anders ist als du und ich, als wir Alle, die ganze Welt. / Er ist der,
8 dem du gehörst. / Denn du gehörst nicht dir selber, sondern ihm,
der dich und die ganze Welt von der kleinsten Mücke bis zum Pla-
neten und Fixstern geschaffen hat, ohne den Alles nicht wäre und
9 auch du wärst ohne ihn gar nichts. / Er, der Herr aller Dinge ist
aber auch der, der es gut meint und gut macht in Allem und so auch
mit uns, mit dir und mir: gut, auch wenn wir nicht immer verstehen,
10 dass es gut ist, wie er es meint und macht mit uns. / Er ist unser
11/12 Vater. / Er ist auch unser Bruder. / Er ist freilich auch unser
Richter, vor dem wir Alle nicht bestehen konnen, vor dem wir Alle
ohne Ausnahme schuldig sind und schuldig bleiben, weil wir es nicht
gut meinen und machen: mit ihm nicht und mit unsrem Nächsten nicht
13 und mit uns selbst auch nicht. / Er ist aber der, der uns--o Wunder
aller Wunder!--dennoch lieb hat und behält, der uns also nicht
fallen lässt wie wir es wohl verdienen würden--der uns aber auch
nicht entrinnen lässt, der in grosser Geduld, aber auch in grosser

Strenge da ist und auf dich und mich wartet, den wir nicht loswerden können mit heimlichem oder offenem Trotz oder mit unsrer
Gleichgültigkeit, den wir nicht abspeisen können mit Schimpfen und
Fluchen und mit frommen Worten auch nicht! den wir nicht mei-
14 stern können, weil er immer zuerst da ist als unser Meister. / Er
ist der Andere, der uns anruft.

IV 1 Und nun ruft eben er dich an und mich auch: Adam, wo bist
2/3/4 du? / Hörst du mich? / Ja, du hörst mich wohl! / Viele Andere
und viel Anderes kannst du nicht hören und brauchst du auch nicht
5/6 zu hören. / Mich aber musst du hören. / Mich hörst du auch tat-
7 sächlich. / Du wärst ja kein Mensch und ich wäre nicht Gott, wenn
8 du mich nicht hörtest. / Was aber sagt er uns, ruft er uns zu? /
9/10 Alles in Allem tatsächlich nur dieses Eine: Rufe du mich an! / Das
11 ist die gnädige Erlaubnis, die ich dir gebe. / Das ist aber auch
der strenge Befehl, der von mir an dich ergeht: dazu mache ich
dich und dazu bist du frei, das darfst du und das sollst du tun, aber
recht tun: Rufe mich an in der Not!

V 1/2 <u>In der Not</u>: 'Not' ist ein Wort, das wir Alle verstehen. / Not
heisst Bedrängnis, Druck, Pein, die wir loswerden möchten und
3 nicht können. / Es ist überall viel Not: in den Mauern dieses
Hauses und ausserhalb, da draussen in der Stadt Basel und in der
4 ganzen Welt. / Aber, nichtwahr, du denkst jetzt zuerst an <u>deine</u>

Not, deine eigene, deine persönliche Not, die vielleicht klein ist,
vielleicht aber auch sehr gross, vielleicht leicht, vielleicht ganz
5 schwer. / Und es sind manchmal die kleinen Nöte, die die gröss-
6 ten und schwersten sein können. / Deine Not ist vielleicht eine
vorübergehende, vielleicht auch eine lange dauernde, vielleicht
einfach in der Gestalt, dass du nun eben so lange in diesem Hause
7 sein musst. / Sie mag deine selbstverschuldete, sie mag auch
eine von den Umständen oder von den Mitmenschen verursachte
Not sein--deine äussere oder deine innere Not, und es gibt keine
innere Not, die nicht auch eine äussere, und keine äussere, die
8 nicht auch eine innere ist. / Gott kennt und sieht auch diese deine
persönliche Not und sagt zu dir, dass du ihn gerade in dieser
deiner besonderen Not anrufen sollst.

VI 1 Aber vergiss nicht, dass du nicht allein bist, sondern nur
2 Einer von Vielen, die in Not sind. / Wenn man es recht bedenkt,
so ist eigentlich die ganze Menschheit eine einzige grosse Notge-
3 meinschaft. / Und das ist ihre gemeinsame und allgemeine Not,
dass wir --wie es heute immer deutlicher wird--zwar die Technik
des Lebens immer besser zu beherrschen, unser Leben und Zu-
sammenleben selbst aber immer schlechter zu gestalten wissen. /
4 Das ist eine Not, die nicht zuzudecken, geschweige denn zu heilen
ist: weder durch die Fasnacht, noch durch die Mustermesse, noch

durch ein Jubiläum, wenn wieder einmal eines fällig ist--und auch
nicht durch die schönste Olympiade, auch nicht durch moralische
Aufrüstung, wie man sie in Caux am Genfersee betreibt und auch
nicht mit noch so eindrucksvollen Evangelisationen, wie wir kürz-
5 lich in Basel eine erlebt haben. / Sie ist eine Not, die einfach da
ist und die immer wieder wie in grossen Geschwüren aufbricht:
jetzt in Algerien, jetzt im Kongo, jetzt in Kuba, jetzt in Berlin. /
6 Sie ist eine Not, die da vielleicht am Schlimmsten ist, wo man sie
nicht empfindet, wo man meint, ein bisschen den Regenschirm
aufspannen und das Unwetter kommen und vorübergehen lassen zu
können--wie wir es in der lieben Schweiz tun und die draussen in
7 der deutschen Bundesrepublik mit ihrem Wirtschaftswunder. / Und
nun musst du nicht sagen: diese Menschheitsnot gehe dich nichts
8 an. / Sie geht dich sehr wohl an: du bist auch in dieser gemeinsa-
9/10 men und allgemeinen Not. / Du gehörst auch dazu. / Und darum:
Rufe mich an--nicht nur in deiner persönlichen, sondern auch in
dieser Menschheitsnot!

2. TT: excerpt from Karl Barth, Call for God. New Sermons from Basel Prisons. London: S.C.M. Press. 1967. 30-33.

I 1 Call me in the day of trouble, I will deliver you, and you shall
praise me. Psalm 50. 15

2 Dear brothers and sisters,

II 1/2 'Call me', we read. / That reminds me at any rate of
someone 'calling' me, on the telephone that is, and interrupting
and disturbing me at my work or in the middle of a conversation
3 or perhaps when I am just about to listen to some music. / They
begin to ask me how I am keeping, or make some request, or
tell me a long or short story, and then say to finish off, 'Call
4 me sometime'. / Here in our text everything is quite different. /
5 In it someone is certainly calling me and interrupting me at what
6 I am doing. / But he does not spend a long time asking how I am,
7 for he knows that better than I do myself. / And he has no re-
8 quests to make--what indeed could I do for him? / And he has no
important story to tell me, either, for the one and only really
important story begins with the very fact that he is calling me. /
9 What is the last thing on the telephone is the first thing here;
what is a minor detail there is the main thing, indeed the one and
only thing: Call me!

III
1/2/3/4 Who says that? / God? / Yes, God! / But the word 'God' is

used so much and has become so worn, like an old coin, and
5 everybody understands something different by it. / And there
6 are really so many gods too! / Let's just put it this way: The
one who is calling me here and telling me to call him back is the
one who is different: who is indeed utterly different from you or
7 me, from us all, from the whole world. / He is the one to whom
8 you belong. / For you do not belong to yourself but to the one who
has created you and the whole world, from the smallest gnat to
the planet and fixed star, without whom nothing would have exist-
9 ed and without whom you too would have been nothing at all. / Now
he, the Lord of all things, is also the one who means well and
does good in everything, including his dealings with us, with you
and me: good, even when we do not always understand that what
10 he is planning for us and doing with us is good. / He is our
11/12 father. / He is also our brother. / He is certainly also our
judge, before whom none of us can stand, before whom all of us
without exception are guilty and remain guilty, because we do not
mean well or do good: in our dealings with him and with our neigh-
13 bours and even with ourselves! / But he is the one who--miracle
of miracles!--loves and sustains us for all that, who does not
drop us as we would richly deserve--yet who does not let us es-
cape either, who in great patience but also in great severity is
present and is waiting for you and for me, whom we cannot get

rid of with secret or open defiance or with our indifference,
whom we cannot put off with abuse or curses, or with pious
14 words either! / We cannot master him, because he is always
15 there first as our master. / The one who calls us is the one
who is different.

IV 1 And now this very one is calling you and me also: Adam,
2/3 where are you? / Do you hear me? / Yes, you can hear me per-
4 fectly well! / There are many other people and things that you
5 cannot hear and even need not hear. / But you must hear me. /
6/7 And in fact you do hear me. / You simply would not be human
and I would not be God if you could not hear me.
8/9 But what does he say to us if he calls us? / By and large, only
10 one thing: Call me! / That is the gracious permission that I
11 give you. / But it is also the strict command which comes to
12 you from me: For this I make you; for this you are free. / You
may, you shall do this--but only in the proper way: Call me in
the day of trouble.

V 1 In the day of trouble: 'Trouble' is a word that we all un-
2 understand. / Trouble means affliction, oppression, agony that
3 we would like to get rid of, but cannot. / There is great trouble
everywhere: within the walls of this building and outside them,
out there in the city of Basel and in the whole world.
4 But it is not the case that you are now thinking mainly of

your trouble, your own, your personal trouble which may be
small or may even be very great, may be slight, or may be
5 quite severe. / And it is sometimes the little troubles which
6 can be the greatest and most severe. / Your trouble may be
temporary, or it may be one that will last a long time; perhaps it simply takes the form that you must in fact spend so
7 long in this building. / It may be trouble that you have brought
upon yourself or trouble caused by circumstances or by your
fellows -your outward or inward trouble, and there is no inward
trouble which is not also an outward one, and no outward one
8 which is not also an inward one. / God too knows and sees this
personal trouble you have and tells you to call him in this particular trouble of yours.

VI 1 But do not forget that you are not alone, but only one of
2 many who are in trouble. / If you really think about it, the whole
of humanity is in fact one single great community in trouble. /
3 And this its *common* and *general* trouble--as is growing clearer
and clearer nowadays--is that whereas we admittedly know better and better how to control the technique of living, we know
worse and worse how to shape our lives as individuals and as
4 members of a community. / That is one sort of trouble which
cannot be covered up, let alone cured: either by Carnival or by
the Trade Fair or by a jubilee, if one is due once again--or by

the grandest Olympiad, or by communism or anti-communism,
or by Moral Rearmament as they practise it at Caux on Lake
Geneva, or by evangelical campaigns, however impressive, like
5 the one we recently had in Basel. / It is a sort of trouble
which simply exists, and breaks out again and again in great
ulcers; now in Algeria, now in the Congo, now in Cuba, now in
6 Berlin. / It is the sort of trouble that is perhaps worst where
one does not notice it, where one thinks one can spread out the
umbrella a little and let the storm come along and pass by--
as we do in our dear Switzerland, and as the people across in
the German Federal Republic do with their economic miracle. /
7 Now you need not say that this trouble, mankind's trouble, does
8/9 not concern you. / It concerns you very much. / You too are
10 involved in this common and general trouble. / You belong there
11 also. / And therefore: Call me--not only in your personal
trouble, but here too, in this, mankind's trouble.

VI. Political Speech

1. ST: excerpt from Winston S. Churchill, "One Great Family", in <u>The End of the Beginning.</u> London: Cassel. 1943. 245-47.

One Great Family

A Speech to the People of Bradford
From the Steps of the Town Hall
December 5, 1942.

I 1/2 Now, I come and there is no division. / All are united like one great family; all are standing together, helping each other, taking their share and doing their work, some at the front, some under the sea or on the sea in all weathers, some in the air, some in the coal mines, great numbers in the shops, some in the homes--all doing their bit, and everyone of you entitled to ask yourselves every morning or every evening: "Am I rowing my weight in the boat ?" and if you can answer that searching question "Yes, I am", then, believe me, all are bearing their part, each and every one is bearing his or her part, in one of the greatest struggles that have ever glorified, torn, and dignified the human race.

II 1 Now, we have just passed through the month of November, usually a month of fogs and gloom, but, on the whole, a month I have liked a good deal better than some other months we have seen during the course of this present unpleasantness; a month

in which our affairs have prospered, in which our soldiers and
sailors and airmen have been victorious, in which our gallant
Russian Ally has struck redoubtable blows against the common
enemy, and in which our American Allies and our kith and kin
far off in the Pacific Ocean, in Australia and New Zealand,
have also seen their efforts crowned with a considerable meas-
2 ure of success. / A great month, this last month of November.

III 1 But I must tell you, and I know you will not mind my
saying it, because I do not think it is wise to deal in smooth
words or airy promises, that you must be on your guard not to
let the good fortune that has come to us be anything else but a
2 means of striking harder. / The struggle is approaching its most
3 tense period. / The hard core of Nazi resistance and villainy is
4 not yet broken in upon. / We have to gather up all our strength.

IV 1 If by any chance unexpected good tidings come to us, that
would be a matter which we could rejoice at, but which we must
2 not count upon. / We count upon our strong right arms, upon our
honest, hard-working hearts; we count upon our courage,
which has not been found wanting either in domestic or foreign
3 stresses during the whole course of this war. / These are the
simple virtues which our island race has cultured and nurtured
during many generations, and these are the virtues which will
bear us through all struggles and in which we must put our faith.

V 1 We have broken into North Africa, with our American
Allies, and now we have, in a short time, advanced from the
Atlantic Ocean almost to the centre of the Mediterranean, a
distance of nearly 900 miles; but there are still twenty miles
to go, and very hard fighting will take place before that small
distance is overcome and the violence and military power of the
2 enemy there has been beaten down and driven into the sea. / I
do not doubt of the result, but I cannot leave you to suppose that
3 it will be easily achieved. / Away on the other side of North
Africa, our armies are advancing, taking thousands of prisoners and driving the enemy before them; but here again hard
4 fighting is to be expected. / But during this month, when so
much fighting has been carried on by the British and Americans,
there has been a feeling of gladness that we, too, are engaging
the enemy closely and not leaving the entire burden to be borne
by the Russians, who have carried this immense struggle
through the whole of this year and a large part of last year. /
5 They are defending their own country; we are defending our
own country; but we are all of us defending something which is,
I won't say dearer, but greater than a country, namely, a cause. /
6 That cause is the cause of freedom and of justice; that cause is
the cause of the weak against the strong; it is the cause of law
against violence, of mercy and tolerance against brutality and

7 iron-bound tyranny. / That is the cause that we are fighting for. /
8 That is the cause which is moving slowly, painfully but surely, inevitably and inexorably forward to victory; and when the victory is gained you will find that you are--I will not say in a new world, but a better world; you are in a world which can be made more fair, more happy, if only all the peoples will join together to do their part, and if all classes and all parties stand together to reap the fruits of victory as they are standing together to bear, and to face, and to cast back the terrors and menaces of war.

2. TT: excerpt from Winston S. Churchill, "Eine Grosse Familie", in
<u>Das Ende des Anfangs.</u> Zürich: Europa Verlag. 1948. 383-85.

Eine Grosse Familie

Rede, die von den Stufen der Town Hall von Bradford
an die Bevölkerung gehalten wurde, am 5. Dezember 1942

I 1/2 Jetzt komme ich und es gibt keine Zwietracht mehr. / Alle
3 sind einig wie eine grosse Familie. / Alle halten zusammen,
helfen einander, tragen ihren Teil und tun ihre Arbeit, einige an
der Front, einige unter Wasser, oder auf dem Wasser bei jedem
Wetter, einige in der Luft, einige in den Kohlengruben, eine grosse
Anzahl in den Läden, einige daheim--alle tun ihr kleines Stück
Arbeit und jeder von Ihnen hat das Recht, sich jeden Morgen oder
jeden Abend zu fragen: "Habe ich zumindest das getan, was ich
4 tun muss?"/ Und wenn Sie auf die forschende Frage antworten
können "Ja, das habe ich", dann, glauben Sie mir, dann hat jeder
seine Pflicht getan in einem der grössten Kämpfe, die jemals die
menschliche Rasse verherrlichten, zerrissen und geehrt haben.

II 1/2 Der Monat November liegt hinter uns. / Gewöhnlich ist er
ein nebliger, düsterer Monat; aber im Ganzen genommen gefiel
mir dieser Monat viel besser als mancher andere, den wir im Ver-
3 lauf der gegenwärtigen Unannehmlichkeiten gesehen haben. / Ein
Monat, in dem unsere Sache gedieh, in dem unsere Soldaten, See-

leute und Flieger siegten, in dem unser tapferer russischer Ver-
bündeter dem gemeinsamen Feind fürchterliche Schläge versetzte
und in dem unsere amerikanischen Verbündeten und unsere Verwandten weit draussen im Pazifischen Ozean, in Australien und
Neuseeland, ihre Anstrengungen mit einem ansehnlichen Mass Er-
4 folg gekrönt sahen. / Ein erhabener Monat war dieser vergangene
Monat November.

III 1 Ich halte es aber nicht für klug, glatte Worte zu gebrauchen
und leichtfertige Versprechungen zu machen, und darum muss ich
Ihnen sagen--ich weiss, Sie werden es mir nicht übelnehmen--Sie
müssen darauf achten, das Glück, das uns zuteil wurde, nur als
2 Mittel zu gebrauchen, um noch fester zuzuschlagen. / Der Kampf
3 nähert sich der Zeit der höchsten Spannung. / Der feste Kern des
Nazi-Widerstandes und der Schurkerei ist noch nicht gebrochen. /
4 Wir müssen alle unsere Kräfte sammeln.

IV 1 Wenn wir bei irgendeiner Gelegenheit gute Nachrichten be-
kommen, dann wollen wir uns darüber freuen, aber wir dürfen
2 nicht darauf zählen. / Wir zählen auf unsere starken, gesunden
Arme, auf unsere ehrlichen, ruhig und beständig schlagenden
Herzen; auf unseren Mut, der im Verlauf dieses Krieges weder
3 vor dem Druck innerer noch äusserer Ereignisse versagte. / Das
sind die schlichten Tugenden, welche die Rasse dieser Insel durch

viele Generationen pflegte und heranbildete, das sind die Tugenden,
die uns durch alle Kämpfe hindurchführen, in die wir unseren
Glauben setzen müssen.

V 1 Mit unserem amerikanischen Verbündeten sind wir in Nord-
afrika eingefallen und bis jetzt, innerhalb kurzer Zeit, sind wir
vom Atlantischen Ozean bis beinahe in die Mitte des Mittelmeeres
2 vorgerückt, eine Strecke von fast 900 Meilen. / Zwanzig Meilen
haben wir noch zu gehen; aber harte Kämpfe werden stattfinden,
bevor diese kleine Strecke überwunden und die Gewalt und militärische Stärke des Feindes in diesem Gebiet gebrochen ist, bis er
3 in die See getrieben wurde. / Ich zweifle nicht an dem Endergebnis,
ich darf Sie aber nicht in dem Glauben lassen, es würde einfach
4 erzielt werden. / Auf der anderen Seite Nordafrikas rücken unsere
Armeen vor, bringen Kriegsgefangene zu Tausenden ein und
5 treiben den Feind vor sich her. / Aber auch hier stehen harte
6 Kämpfe bevor. / In diesem Monat, in dem die Briten und Ameri-
kaner soviele Kämpfe führten, da war es ein Gefühl der Freude,
dass auch wir den Feind fest anpackten und nicht die gesamte Last
den Russen überliessen, die diesen ungeheuren Kampf während
dieses ganzen Jahres und während eines Teils des vergangenen
7 Jahres führten. / Sie verteidigen ihr eigenes Land; wir verteidigen
unser eigenes Land; wir alle aber verteidigen etwas, das, ich

möchte nicht sagen teurer, das aber grösser als ein Land ist,
8 nämlich eine Sache. / Es ist die Sache der Freiheit und Gerech-
tigkeit; es ist die Sache des Schwachen gegen den Starken; es ist
die Sache des Rechts gegen die Gewalt, der Barmherzigkeit und
Toleranz gegen die Brutalität und die durch Eisen herrschende
9/10 Tyrannei. / Das ist die Sache, für die wir kämpfen. / Das ist die
Sache, die langsam, beschwerlich aber sicher, unbedingt und un-
erbittlich zum Sieg gelangt; und wenn dann der Sieg errungen sein
wird, dann werden Sie sehen, dass Sie--ich will nicht sagen in
11 einer neuen, aber in einer besseren Welt leben werden. / Eine
Welt, die anständiger und glücklicher werden kann, wenn bloss
alle Leute sich gemeinsam ihrer Aufgabe zuwenden wollen, wenn
alle Klassen und Parteien zusammenhalten, um die Früchte des
Sieges zu pflücken, so wie sie zusammenhielten, um die Schrecken
und Drohungen des Krieges zu ertragen, ihnen Trotz zu bieten
und sie abzuwehren.

VII. Moral Anecdote

1. ST: Hebel, Johann Peter, "Kindesdank und Undank", in *First German Reader.* Ed. by H. Steinhauer. New York: Bantam Books. 1972. 6-10.

I 1 Man findet gar oft, wenn man ein wenig aufmerksam ist,
dass Menschen im Alter von ihren Kindern wieder ebenso behandelt werden, wie sie einst ihre alten und kraftlosen Eltern
2/3 behandelt haben. / Es geht auch begreiflich zu. / Die Kinder
lernen's von den Eltern; sie sehen und hören's nicht anders
4 und folgen dem Beispiel. / So wird es auf die natürlichsten und
sichersten Wege wahr, was gesagt wird und geschrieben ist,
dass der Eltern Segen und Fluch auf den Kindern ruhe und sie
nicht verfehle.

II 1 Man hat darüber unter anderen zwei Erzählungen, von
denen die erste Nachahmung und die zweite grosse Beherzigung
verdient.

III 1 Ein Fürst traf auf einem Spazierritt einen fleissigen und
frohen Landmann an dem Ackergeschäft an, und liess sich mit ihm
2 in ein Gespräch ein. / Nach einigen Fragen erfuhr er, dass der
Acker nicht sein Eigentum sei, sondern dass er als Taglöhner
3 täglich um 15 Kreuzer arbeite. / Der Fürst, der für sein
schweres Regierungsgeschäft freilich mehr Geld brauchte

und zu verzehren hatte, konnte es in der Geschwindigkeit
nicht ausrechnen, wie es möglich sei, täglich mit 15 Kreuzer
auszureichen, und noch so frohen Mutes dabei zu sein, und
4 verwunderte sich darüber. / Aber der brave Mann im Zwilchrock erwiderte ihm: "Es ware mir übel gefehlt, wenn ich soviel
5 brauchte. / Mir muss ein Drittel davon genügen; mit einem
Dritteil zahle ich meine Schulden ab, und den übrigen Dritteil
6 lege ich auf Kapitalien an."/ Das war dem guten Fürsten ein
7 neues Rätsel. / Aber der fröhliche Landmann fuhr fort und
sagte: "Ich teile meinen Verdienst mit meinen alten Eltern, die
nicht mehr arbeiten können, und mit meinen Kindern, die es
erst lernen müssen; jenen vergelte ich die Liebe, die sie mir
in meiner Kindheit erwiesen haben, und von diesen hoffe ich, dass
sie mich einst in meinem müden Alter auch nicht verlassen
8 werden."/ War das nicht artig gesagt, und noch edler und
9 schöner gedacht und gehandelt? / Der Fürst belohnte die Rechtschaffenheit des wackeren Mannes, sorgte für seine Söhne, und
der Segen, den ihm seine sterbenden Eltern gaben, wurde ihm im
Alter von seinen dankbaren Kindern durch Liebe und Unterstützung
redlich entrichtet.

IV 1 Aber ein anderer ging mit seinem Vater, welcher durch
Alter und Kränklichkeit freilich wunderlich geworden war, so

übel um, dass dieser wünschte, in ein Armenspital gebracht
2 zu werden, das im nämlichen Orte war. / Dort hoffte er
wenigstens bei dürftiger Pflege von den Vorwürfen frei zu
werden, die ihm daheim die letzten Tage seines Lebens ver-
3 bitterten. / Das war dem undankbaren Sohn ein willkommenes
4 Wort. / Ehe die Sonne hinter den Bergen hinabging, war dem
5 armen alten Greis sein Wunsch erfüllt. / Aber er fand im Spital
6 auch nicht alles, wie er es wünschte. / Wenigstens liess er seinen
Sohn nach einiger Zeit bitten, ihm die letzte Wohltat zu erweisen
und ihm ein paar Leintücher zu schicken, damit er nicht alle
7 Nacht auf blossem Stroh schlafen müsse. / Der Sohn suchte die
zwei schlechtesten, die er hatte, heraus, und befahl seinem zehn-
jährigen Kind, sie dem alten Murrkopf ins Spital zu bringen. /
8 Aber mit Verwunderung bemerkte er, dass der kleine Knabe vor
der Tür eines dieser Tücher in einem Winkel verbarg, und folglich
9 dem Grossvater nur eines davon brachte. / "Warum hast du das
10 getan?" fragte er den Jungen bei seiner Rückkunft. / "Zur Aus-
hilfe für die Zukunft", erwiderte dieser kalt und bösherzig, "wenn
ich Euch, Vater, auch einmal in das Spital schicken werde."

V 1/2 Was lernen wir daraus? / Ehre Vater und Mutter, auf dass
es dir wohl gehe!

2. TT: Hebel, Johann Peter, "Gratitude and Ingratitude of Children", in First German Reader. Ed. by H. Steinhauer. New York: Bantam Books. 1972. 7-11.

I 1 We find very often, if we are just a bit observant, that
people are treated by their children in old age just as they once
2 treated their old and helpless parents. / And this procedure is
3 understandable. / The children learn it from their parents; they
see and hear nothing else, and follow the example set them. /
4 So, what is said and written comes true in the most natural and
surest way; that the blessing and curse of parents descend on
their children and do not pass them by.

II 1 We have two stories, among others, on this subject;
the first deserves imitation and the second special heed.

III 1 A prince, out for a ride, met a busy and happy farmer
going about his business and entered into a conversation with
2 him. / After a few questions he learned that the farm was not
the man's property but that he worked on it as a daily laborer for
3 fifteen kreutzer per day. / The prince, who of course needed
and had more money to spend for his heavy business of government, could not figure out rapidly how it was possible to make
out with fifteen kreutzer per day and to be so cheerful in spirit
4 about it too, and expressed his astonishment. / But the good man

in his drill coat replied to him, "I would be in a bad way if I
5 needed as much as that. / I have to get along with a third of it;
with a third I pay off my debts, and the remaining third I lay
6 aside as capital."/ This was a new riddle for the good prince. /
7 But the cheerful farmer continued and said, "I share my earnings with my old parents, who can no longer work, and with my
children who must yet learn how to work; to the former I re-
quite the love they showed me in my childhood, and from the latter I hope that they too will not abandon me some day in my
8 weary old age."/ Wasn't that nicely put, and even more nobly
9 and beautifully thought and acted? / The prince rewarded the
good man's integrity, cared for his sons, and the blessing
which his dying parents gave him was honestly repaid to him
by his grateful children in his old age through love and support.

IV 1 But another man treated his father, who, to be sure,
had become cranky through age and debility, so badly that the
latter wished to be taken to a home for the poor that was located
2 in the same place. / Though the care might be scanty, there he
at least hoped to be free from the reproaches which were embit-
3 tering the last days of his life at home./ This was a welcome
4 word to his ungrateful son. / Before the sun set behind the
5 mountains the wish of the poor old man was fulfilled. / But in
the home for the poor he did not find everything as he wished

6 it. / At least, after some time he sent a request to his son to do
him a last favor and send him a few sheets, so that he would
7 not have to sleep on the bare straw every night. / The son selected the two worst sheets he had and ordered his ten-year old
8 child to take them to the old grumbler at the home. / But to
his astonishment he noticed that the little boy hid one of these
sheets in a corner outside the door and therefore brought his
9 grandfather only one of them. / "Why did you do that?" the fa-
10 ther asked the boy when he returned. / "As an emergency for
the future," the latter replied coldly and cruelly, "when I'll
send you to the home for the poor some day, father."

V 1/2 What do we learn from this? / Honor your father and
your mother so that things may go well for you.

VIII. Comedy Dialogue

1. ST: excerpt from Sean O'Casey, "The End of the Beginning", in Five One-Act Plays. London: Macmillan. 1966. 20-26.

I 1/2 Darry (hastily putting[F1] the mandolin away). I forgot/ I'll
have to get going.

II 1 Barry. Get going at what?

III 1 Darry. House-work. / (He begins to get[F2] into the overall left
2 off by Lizzie.) I dared her, an' she left me to do the work
3 of the house while she was mowing the meadow. / If it isn't
done when she comes back, then sweet good-bye to the status
4 I had in the home. / (He finds it difficult[F3] to get the overall on.)
5 Dih dih, dih, where's the back 'n where's the front, 'n which
is which is the bottom 'n which is the top?

IV 1 Barry. Take it quietly, take it quietly, Darry.

V 1/2 Darry (resentfully[F4]). Take it quietly? / An' the time gallop-
3 ing by? / I can't stand up on a chair 'n say to the sun, stand
thou still there, over the meadow th' missus is mowing, can I?

VI 1 Barry. I know damn well you can't, but you're not going to
expedite matters by rushing around in a hurry.

VII 1 Darry (he has struggled[F5] into the overall). Expedite matters!/
2 It doesn't seem to strike you that when you do things quickly,
3/4 things are quickly done. / Expedite matters! / I suppose
loitering to look at you lying on the broad of your back, jig-

gling your legs about, was one way of expediting matters; an' listening to you plucking curious sounds out of a mandolin, an' singing a questionable song, was another way of expediting matters?

VIII 1 Barry. You pioneered me into doing two of them yourself.

F6
IX 1 Darry (busy with the pot on the fire): I pioneered you into
2 doing them! / Barry Derrill, there's such a thing in the
3 world as a libel. / You came strutting in with a mandolin
under your arm, didn't you?

X 1 Barry. I did, but---

XI 1 Darry. An' you sang your song.

XII 1 Barry. Yes, but---

XIII 1 Darry. When you waltz'd in, I was doing callisthenics, wasn't I?

XIV 1 Barry. I know you were; but all the same---

XV 1 Darry. An' you flung yourself down on the floor, and got yourself into a tangle trying to do them too, didn't you?

XVI 1 Barry. Hold on a second---

XVII 1 Darry. Now, I can't carry the conversation into a debate,
2 for I have to get going. / So if you can't give a hand, go, 'n
let me do the things that have to be done, in an orderly 'n
quiet way.

XVIII 1 Barry. 'Course I'll give a hand---only waiting to be asked.

XIX 1 Darry (looking at [F7] the clock, suddenly). Is the clock stopped?

XX 1 Barry (taking up [F8] clock and putting it close to his ear). There's no ticking, 'n it's hours slow.

XXI 1/2/3 Darry. Lizzie again! / Forgot to wind it. / Give the key a few turns, Barry, an' put the hands on to half-past nine.

S1/S2 [Barry starts to [F9] wind the clock. / Darry goes over to table, gets a basin of water, begins to wash the delf, humming to himself the air of the song, 'Down where the bees are hum-
S3 ming'. / Barry winds and winds away, but no sign is given
S4 of a tightening of the spring inside. / He looks puzzled, winds again, and is about to silently put the clock back where he found it, when Darry turns and looks at him questioningly.

XXII 1 Darry. You've broken the damn thing, have you?

XXIII 1 Barry. I didn't touch it.

XXIV 1/2 Darry. Didn't touch it? / Amn't I after looking at you twisting an' tearing at it for nearly an hour? / (He [F10] comes over to
3 Barry) Show me that. / (He takes the clock [F11] from Barry and
4 opens the back, and the spring darts out.) Didn't touch it. /
5 Oh, for God's sake be more careful when you're handling
6 things in this house! / Dih dih dih. (he pushes [F12] the spring back,
7 and slaps the clock down on the dresser.) You must have the
8 hands of a gorilla, man. / Here, come over 'n wipe while I wash.

S1 [A slight pause while the [F13] two of them work at the delf. Darry

S2 anxiously watches Barry, who, being very near-sighted, holds everything he wipes close up to his spectacles.

F14
XXV 1 Darry (suddenly). Look out, look out, there--you're not leaving that jug on the table at all; you're depositing it in the air, man!

F15
XXVI 1/2 Barry (peering down at the table.) Am I? / Don't be afraid, I won't let anything drop.

F16
XXVII 1 Darry (humming the song). Dum dah de de dum da dee dee dum dah dee dee dee dah ah dum.

F17
XXVIII 1 Barry (swinging his arm to the tune). Down where the bees are hummin' an' the wild flowers gaily growing.

XXIX 1/2 Darry. Fine swing, you know. / Dum dah dee dee dum dah dee dee dum dah dee dee dee dah ah dum.

F18
XXX 1 Barry (swinging his arm). Down where the bees are hummin'--

[Barry's arm sends the jug flying off the table on to the floor.

F20
XXXI 1 Darry (yelling). You snaky-arm'd candle-power-ey'd elephant, look at what you're after doing!

F21
XXXII 1 Barry (heatedly). It's only a tiny jug, anyhow, 'n you can hardly see the pieces on the floor!

F22
XXXIII 1 Darry (just as heatedly). An' if I let you do much more,
2 they would soon be big enough to bury us!/ Sit down, sit down in the corner there; do nothing, say nothing, an', if I could
3 I'd put a safety curtain round you. / For God's sake, touch

nothing while I run out an' give the spuds to the pig.

F23 S1 [·Darry dashes over to the fire, whips the pot off, and runs
S2 out./ He leaves the door open, and again the rattling whirr
S3 of a mowing machine can be heard. / Barry sits dejectedly
S4 in a corner. / After a few moments a bump is heard outside,
followed by a yell from Darry, who, a second later, comes
rushing madly in, a bloody handkerchief pressed to his nose. /
S5 He flings himself flat on the floor on his back, elevating his
nose as much as possible.

XXXIV 1 Darry. Get me something cold to put down the back of my
neck, quick!

F24
XXXV 1 Barry (frightened). What the hell did you do to yourself?

XXXVI 1 Darry. I didn't bend low enough when I was going in, 'n I
gave myself such a--oh, such a bang on my nose on the
2 concrete. / Get something cold, man, to shove down the
back of my neck 'n stop the bleeding!

XXXVII 1 Barry. Keep the nose sticking up in the air as high as you
2 can. / I don't know where to get something cold to shove down
3 the back of your neck. / I knew this rushing round wouldn't
expedite matters.

F25
XXXVIII 1 Darry (with a moan of resentment as he hears 'expedite
matters'). Oh, pull yourself together, man, 'n remember
we're in the middle of an emergency.

XXXIX 1 Barry. A little block of ice, now, would come in handy.

XL 1/2 Darry. A little--oh, a little block of ice! / An' will you
3 tell us where you're going to get a little block of ice? / An',
even if we had one, how could you fasten it down the back of
4/5 my neck?/ Eh? / Can't you answer--where are you going to
get a block of ice?

XLI 1 Barry. How the hell do I know where I'm going to get it?

XLII 1 Darry. D'ye expect me to keep lying here till the winter
comes?

F26
[During this dialogue Barry is moving round the room aimlessly, peering into drawers, rattling the delf on the dresser with his nose as he looks along the shelves.

F27
XLIII 1 Darry (as he hears the crockery rattling). Mind, mind, or
2 you'll break something. / I must be losing a lot of blood,
Barry, an' I won't be able to keep my nose sticking up in the
3 air much longer. / Can't you find anything?

XLIV 1 Barry. I can see nothing.

XLV 1 Darry. Run upstairs 'n get the key of the big shed that's hanging on the wall, somewhere over the mantelpiece at the far
2 end of the room. / Go quick, man!

F28
[Barry runs upstairs, goes into room, comes out again, and looks down at Darry.

F29
XLVI 1 Darry (up to him). Did you get it?

XLVII 1/2 Barry. Where's the switch?/ It's as dark as pitch in there.

[Darry, with a moan of [F30] exasperation, sits up, but immediately plunges down on his back again.

XLVIII 1/2 Darry. Starts pumping out again the minute I sit up. [F31] (To

3 Barry) There's no switch in that room. / We can't have a

4 switch in every corner of the room just to suit you.! / You've only got to move down the centre of the room till you come to the fireplace; then brush your hand over the mantelpiece, along the wall, till you feel the key hanging there.

S1 [Barry goes back into [F32] the room. / After a few second's si-

S2 lence, there is a crash of falling crockery. /

S3 Darry, after a second of silent consternation, sits up with a jerk, but immediately plunges down on his back again.

XLIX 1 Darry (sinking [F33] supine on the floor). What has he done now;

2 oh, what has he done now? / (Shouting [F34] up to Barry) Eh, you up there--what have you done now?

L 1 Barry (sticking his [F35] head out of door above). Nothing much--the washhand-stand fell over.

LI 1/2 Darry [F36] (angrily). Nothing much. / It sounded a hell of a lot

3 then. / You're the kind of man if you're not chained up, 'll

4 pull everything in the house asundher! / Come down, come down, 'n stop down, or that delicate little hand of yours 'll smash everything in the house!

LII 1 Barry. My eyes are used to the darkness, now, 'n I can
2 see. / I'll get the key for you.
S1 [He goes back into the [F37] room, leaving Darry speechless. /
S2 After a few seconds, he comes out of the room in a sweat of
fright and anger, one hand tightly clasped over the other. /
S3 He rushes down the stairs, and begins to pull the things out
of the chest of drawers, every other moment leaving off to
clasp one hand over the other.

LIII 1 Barry (frantically). [F38] Get your own key, get your own key. /
2/3 Half slaughtering myself for your sake! / Why don't you keep
your razor-blades in a safe place, an' not leave them scatter-
4 ed about in heaps all over the mantelpiece? / Where is there
5 a bit of old rag till I bind up my wounds? / Get your own key
yourself, I'm tellin' you.

LIV 1 Darry. Amn't I nicely handicapped, wanting help an' having
only the help of a half-blind man?

LV 1 Barry. D'ye know I'm nearly after mowing my fingers off
with your blasted razor-blades? (Coming [F39] near to Darry,
with a handkerchief in his hand, and showing the injured
2 fingers to him) / Look at them, uh, look at them--one looks
3 as if only a thin thread of flesh was keeping it on. / How am
I going to play the mandolin now?

LVI 1 Darry. You'd play it better if all your fingers were off.

2. TT: excerpt from Sean O'Casey, "Das Ende vom Anfang", in <u>Eine Auswahl aus den Stücken, der Autobiographie und den Aufsätzen.</u> Ed. by U. Widmer. Zürich: Diogenes. 1970. 91-95.

I 1/2 Darry (tut schnell [F1] die Mandoline weg). Ach so, ja. / Ich
muss mich ranhalten.

II 1 Barry. Wieso ranhalten?

III 1 Darry. Hausarbeit. (Er beginnt [F2] den Kittel anzuziehen, den
Lizzie liegengelassen hat.) Ich hab gesagt, ob sie sich traut,
und sie hat mir die Arbeit im Haus gelassen, währenddem sie
2 die Wiese mäht. / Wenns nich fertig is und sie kommt zurück,
3 dann Gute Nacht der Stand, den ich zu Hause habe. / [F3] (Er kommt
mit dem Kittel nicht zurande.) Ti ti ti, wo ist hinten und wo ist
vorne, und was is unten und was is oben?

IV 1 Barry. Nimms ruhig, nimms ruhig, Darry.

V 1/2 Darry (ver[F4]ärgert). Nimms ruhig,? / Und die Zeit galoppiert? /
3 Ich kann mich nich aufn Stuhl stelln und zur Sonne sagen, stehe
still da, über der Wiese wo die Alte am Mähn ist, na?

VI 1 Barry. Kann ich mir verdammt vorstelln, aber du wirst die
Dinge nich befördern, indem du rumrast wie ein Irrer.

VII 1 Darry (er hat sich in [F5] den Kittel hineingekampft). Dinge beför-
2 dern! / Es scheint dir nicht einzuleuchten, machst du die
3 Sachen schnell, sind die Sachen schnell gemacht. / Dinge be-
4 fördern! / Wenn ich rumlunger und zugucke, wie du auf

deinem Buckel liegst und mit den Beinen wackelst, das ist wohl eine Art die Dinge befördern; und wenn ich zuhöre, wie du komische Töne aus ner Mandoline zupfst und ein zweideutiges Lied singst, das ist wohl auch eine Art die Dinge befördern?

VIII 1 Barry. Du hast mich selber auf zwei davon angesetzt.

F6

IX 1 Darry (beschäftigt mit dem Topf auf dem Feuer): Ich dich
2 darauf angesetzt! / Barry Derrill, hast du schon was von übler
3 Nachrede gehört? / Du bist reinstolziert mit ner Mandoline
unterm Arm, nich? ?

X 1 Barry. Das schon, aber--

XI 1 Darry. Und hast dein Lied gesungen.

XII 1 Barry. Ja, aber--

XIII 1 Darry. Als du reingewalzt bist, war ich grade bei Gymnastik, ja?

XIV 1 Barry. Das weiss ich, aber trotzdem--

XV 1 Darry. Und du hast dich aufn Boden gehaun und hast dich vollkommen verknäult, als dus probiert hast, oder nich?

XVI 1 Barry. Augenblick mal--

XVII 1 Darry. Also, ich lass die Unterhaltung nich in ne Debatte aus-
2 arten, denn ich muss mich ranhalten. / Wenn du also nicht mit
Hand anlegst, geh, und lass mich das tun, was zu tun ist, und
zwar ruhig und ordentlich.

XVIII 1 Barry. Türlich leg ich Hand an-- warte nur auf die Einladung.

XIX 1 Darry (sieht auf [F7] die Uhr, plötzlich). Ist die Uhr stehengeblieben?

XX 1 Barry (nimmt die [F8] Uhr und halt sie dicht ans Ohr). Kein Ticken
mehr, geht Stunden nach.

XXI 1/2/3 Darry. Echt Lizzie! / Vergisst sie aufzuziehen. / Dreh den
Schlüssel paarmal rum, Barry, und stell die Zeiger auf halb zehn.

S1/S2 [Barry fängt an, [F9] die Uhr aufzuziehen. / Darry geht zum Tisch,
holt eine Schüssel Wasser, beginnt abzuwaschen und summt für
sich die Melodie des Liedes 'Da wo die Bienen summen'. /
S3 Barry dreht und dreht, aber kein Anzeichen, dass die Feder
S4 innen sich spannt. / Er guckt verdutzt, dreht weiter und will
gerade die Uhr stillschweigend wieder hinstellen, als Darry
sich umdreht und ihn fragend ansieht.

XXII 1 Darry. Hast das Dreckding kaputt gekriegt, was?

XXIII 1 Barry. Habs nicht angefasst.

XXIV 1/2 Darry. Nicht angefasst? / Guck ich nich dauernd zu, wie du
bald ne Stunde dran zerrst und kurbelst? / (Er geht [F10] zu Barry.)
3 Zeig her. / (Er nimmt Barry die [F11] Uhr ab und öffnet die Rück-
4/5 wand, und die Feder schiesst heraus.) Nicht angefasst. / In
Gottes Namen, sieh dich ein bisschen vor, wenn du in diesem
6 Haus mit was hantierst! / Ti ti ti. / (Er drückt die [F12] Feder zu-
7 rück und knallt die Uhr auf die Anrichte.) Du musst Hände
8 haben wien Gorilla, Mensch. / Hier, komm her und trocken ab,
was ich wasche.

S1 [F13] [Kurze Pause, während die beiden am Geschirr arbeiten. / Darry beobachtet ängstlich Barry, der sich in seiner Kurzsichtigkeit alles, was er abtrocknet, dicht an die Brille hält.

XXV 1 [F14] Darry (plötzlich). Pass auf, pass auf da--du tust die Kanne ja gar nich aufn Tisch; du stellst die in die Luft, Mensch!

XXVI 1/2 [F15] Barry (pliert auf den Tisch). So? / Keine Sorge, ich lass nichts fallen.

XXVII 1 [F16] Darry (summt das Lied). Dum da di di dum da di di dum da di di di ahdum.

XXVIII 1 [F17] Barry (schwenkt den Arm nach der Melodie). Da wo die Bienen summen und stehn die wilden Blumen.

XXIX 1/2 Darry. Prima Schwung, verstehst du. / Dum da di di dum da di di dum da di di di ahdum.

XXX 1 [F18] Barry. (schwenkt den Arm). Da wo die Bienen summen--

[F19] [Barrys Arm fegt die Kanne in einem Bogen vom Tisch auf den Boden.

XXXI 1 [F20] Darry (brüllt). Du schlangenarmiger dreiwattäugiger Elefant, sieh doch hin, was du machst!

XXXII 1 [F21] Barry (hitzig). Is sowieso bloss ne winzige Kanne, die Stücken sind kaum zu sehn aufm Boden.

XXXIII 1 [F22] Darry (ebenso hitzig). Und würd ich dich an mehr ranlassen,
2 wärn sie bald so hoch, dass sie uns unter begraben! / Setz dich, setz dich in die Ecke da; tu nichts, sag nichts, und wenn

ich könnte, würde ich einen Sicherheitszaun um dich rumziehn. /

3 In Gottes Namen, fass nichts an, wenn ich losmach und dem

Schwein die Kartoffeln gieb.

F23

S1 [Darry rast zum Feuer, reisst den Topf herunter und läuft

S2 hinaus. / Er lässt die Tür offen, und wieder hört man das

S3 ratternde Schwirren einer Mähmaschine. / Barry sitzt depri-

S4 miert in einer Ecke. / Nach kurzer Zeit hört man einen Bums

draussen und darauf einen Schrei von Darry, der eine Sekunde

später wie toll hereinstürzt, ein blutiges Taschentuch an die

S5 Nase gedrückt. / Er wirft sich flach rücklings auf den Boden

und hält seine Nase, so gut es geht, hoch.

XXXIV 1 Darry. Hol mir etwas Kaltes und tu mirs runter ins Genick,

schnell!

F24

XXXV 1 Barry (erschreckt). Was zum Teufel hast du dir getan?

XXXVI 1 Darry. Ich hab mich nicht genug gebückt, als ich rein bin,

und ich bin da--oh, bin da derartig mit der Nase gegen den

2 Beton geknallt. / Hol mir was Kaltes, Mensch, und schieb

mirs rein ins Genick, dass das Blut aufhört!

XXXVII 1 Barry. Steck die Nase in die Luft so hoch, wie du kannst. /

2 Ich weiss nich, wo ich was Kaltes herkriege, um dirs ins Ge-

3 nick zu schieben. / Ich wusste ja, dass son Rumrasen nich die

Dinge befördert.

F25

XXXVIII 1 Darry (stöhnt gequält auf, wenn er hört 'Dinge befördert').

Ach, nimm dich zusammen, Mensch, und vergiss nicht, hier
herrscht jetzt Katastrophenzustand.
XXXIX 1 Barry. Ein kleines Stück Eis, denk ich, wär jetzt am Platz.
XL 1/2 Darry. Ein kleines--ach, ein kleines Stück Eis! / Und kannst
du mir sagen, wo du jetzt ein kleines Stück Eis herkriegen
3 willst? / Und selbst wenn wirs hätten, wie würdest dus fest-
4/5 machen das Genick runter? / He? / Na sag schon--wo willst
du ein Stück Eis herkriegen?
XLI 1 Barry. Wie zum Teufel soll ich wissen, wo ich es herkriegen
soll?
XLII 1 Darry. Erwartest du von mir, dass ich hier liegenbleibe, bis
der Winter kommt?
F26
[Während dieses Dialogs bewegt sich Barry ziellos im Raum
herum, linst in Schubladen, scheppert das Geschirr auf der
Anrichte mit der Nase, wenn er an den Regalen langguckt.
XLIII 1 Darry (da er das Geschirr klirren hört). Pass auf, oder du
2 zerbrichst was. / Ich verlier bestimmt ne Menge Blut, Barry,
und bin nicht mehr lange in der Lage, meine Nase in die Luft
3 zu strecken. / Kannst du nischt finden?
XLIV 1 Barry. Ich kann nischt sehen.
XLV 1 Darry. Lauf nach oben und hol den Schlüssel vom grossen
Schuppen, hängt an der Wand, irgendwo überm Kaminsims,
2 am andern Ende vom Zimmer. / Mach schnell, Mensch!

F28
[Barry läuft hoch, geht ins Zimmer, kommt wieder heraus und guckt zu Darry hinunter.

XLVI 1 Darry (zu ihm F29 hoch). Hast du ihn?

XLVII 1/2 Barry. Wo ist der Knipser? / Ist stockdunkel da drin.

F30
[Darry stöhnt verzweifelt auf, setzt sich, wirft sich aber sofort wieder auf den Rücken.

XLVIII 1 Darry. Rauscht gleich wieder los, den Augenblick, wo ich
2/3 sitze. / F31 (Zu Barry) Gibt kein Knipser in dem Zimmer. / Wir können nicht in jeder Zimmerecke n Knipser haben bloss dir
4 zu Gefallen! / Du brauchst dich bloss langs die Zimmermitte bewegen, bis du am Kamin bist; dann wisch mit der Hand oberm Kaminsims, die Wand lang, bis du merkst, der Schlüssel hängt da.

F32
S1/S2 [Barry geht wieder ins Zimmer. / Nach ein paar Sekunden
S3 Stille der Krach von fallendem Geschirr. / Nach einer Sekunde stummer Bestürzung setzt sich Darry mit einem Ruck, wirft sich aber sofort wieder auf den Rücken.

F33
XLIX 1 Darry (sinkt lang auf den Boden). Was hat er jetzt gemacht,
2 o, was hat er jetzt gemacht? / F34 (Schreit hoch zu Barry) He, du da oben, was hast du jetzt gemacht?

F35
L 1 Barry (steckt den Kopf oben aus der Tür). Nichts weiter --der Waschständer ist umgekippt.

F36
LI 1/2 Darry (ärgerlich). Nichts weiter. / Klang aber wie ne ver-

3 dammte Masse. / Du bist ne Sorte Mensch, wenn du nicht an-
4 gekettet bist, reisst du alles im Haus auseinander! / Komm
runter, komm runter, und bleib runter, oder dein zartes
Händchen wird alles im Haus zerschmeissen.

LII 1 Barry. Meine Augen sind an das Dunkle gewöhnt jetzt, und
2 ich seh was. / Ich hol dir den Schlüssel. /
F37
S1 [Er geht wieder ins Zimmer und lasst Darry sprachlos. /
S2 Nach ein paar Sekunden kommt er aus dem Zimmer, schwit-
zend vor Angst und Wut, eine Hand fest um die andere geklam-
S3 mert. / Er rast die Treppe herunter und fängt an, Sachen aus
der Kommode zu wühlen, wobei er alle Augenblicke anhält, um
wieder eine Hand um die andere zu klammern.

LIII 1/2 Barry. Holn dir selber, holn dir selber. / Ich schlachte mich
3 bald ab wegen dir. / Warum steckst du die Rasierklingen nich
an einen sichern Ort und lässt sie haufenweise auf dem Kamin-
4 sims rumliegen? / Wo gibts hier ein Stück alten Lappen, bis
5 ich mir die Wunde verbinde? / Hol dir den Schlüssel selber,
sag ich dir.

LIV 1 Darry. Bin ich nich hübsch lahmgelegt, brauch Hilfe und hab
nur Hilfe von nem Halbblinden?

LV 1 Barry. Weisst du, das ich nahe dran war, mir die Finger ab-
F39
zumähn mit deinen scheiss Rasierklingen? / (Kommt heran an
Darry, ein Taschentuch in der Hand, und zeigt ihm die ver-

2 letzten Finger). Guck mal da, na, guck mal da--der eine sieht

aus, als ob er bloss noch an einem dünnen Faden Fleisch

3 hängt. / Wie soll ich jetzt noch Mandoline spielen?

LVI 1 Darry. Du würdest besser spielen, wenn alle Finger abwärn.